DIVORCED FAMILIES

Meeting the Challenge of Divorce and Remarriage

DIVORCED FAMILIES

Meeting the Challenge of Divorce and Remarriage

Constance R. Ahrons, Ph.D.

University of Southern California

Roy H. Rodgers, Ph.D.

University of British Columbia

W · W · NORTON & COMPANY · NEW YORK · LONDON

Printed in the United States of America.

First published as a Norton paperback 1989

Library of Congress Cataloging-in-Publication Data

Ahrons, Constance R.
  Divorced families.

"A Norton professional book."
Bibliography: p.
  1. Divorce.   2. Divorced people—Family relationships.
3. Separation (Psychology)   I. Rodgers, Roy H.   II. Title.
HQ814.A43   1987   306.8'9   86-21686

ISBN 0-393-30622-4

W. W. Norton & Company, Inc., 500 Fifth Avenue, New York, N.Y. 10110
W. W. Norton & Company, Ltd., 37 Great Russell Street, London WC1B 3NU

2 3 4 5 6 7 8 9 0

Contents

Preface   vii

1. Is the Sky Really Falling?   3
2. The Divorce Process: A Multidisciplinary View   25
3. The Separation Transition   52
4. Family Career Implications of the
   Separation Transition   84
5. The Divorce Transition   103
6. Family Career Implications of the Divorce Transition   138
7. The Remarriage Transition   154
8. Family Career Implications of the Remarriage Transition   181
9. Strengthening Binuclear Families   201

Appendix   221
Notes   233
Bibliography   241
Index   253

Preface

IIow often have you heard the hushed whisper, "Poor child, he comes from a 'broken' home." What picture comes to your mind when you hear those words? Most of us mentally envision either a pair of ex-spouses perpetually at war or, at the other extreme, two ex's having no contact at all.

Switch gears for a minute and try to picture a Thanksgiving dinner at Sally and Jim Anderson's. It's a big group: First there's Sally's ex-husband Tim and his current partner Sandra. Then there's Billy and Julie, Tim and Sally's children. Then there's Jennifer, who is Sandra's daughter, and Bobby and Cindy, Jim's children from his first marriage. Jim's ex-wife Margot was also invited but she had plans to spend the day with her new partner's family.

These complex groupings, spurred by the realities of divorce and remarriage, are becoming increasingly common at a whole range of family celebrations — weddings, graduations, bar mitzvahs. Given the current rates of divorce, about half of all American families will need to renegotiate new ways of being a "family." And they will do this without the usual rules of kinship, planning new family landscapes without a map of the terrain.

The ideas for this book come from many years of hearing divorcing couples struggle with how to end their marriage but still keep other family relationships intact, how to uncouple without unfamilying. We ourselves have struggled with the complexities of divorce and remarriage in our own lives, in the lives of our families and friends, in the lives of our clients in psychotherapy, and in the lives of those many families who permitted us to interview them over the last decade.

The reality is that after divorce families continue to be families. While structure changes, for most people, especially those with children, the bonds of kinship remain. There are good divorces where children and adults come through the crisis with caring, nurturing family relationships and no long-term psychological damage to either adults or children, and there are bad divorces where relationships and psyches of all are irreparably damaged; in between are as many variations as we see in nuclear families. Our focus is on *how* different families cope with the many normal, complex relationship changes that result from divorce and remarriage. As we describe these changes in familial relationships, we evaluate both the positive and the negative effects on the children and adults who live in these divorced families.

THE PLAN OF THE BOOK

Our major purpose in writing this book was to present an initial model of a *normal* divorce process. It was originally written for our clinical and academic colleagues, for students in marriage and family courses, for trainees in clinical programs, for lawyers and other professionals who work with divorcing clients. Over time we heard from many people how helpful the book was to them in their personal lives. We were pleased that we were able to reach not only people who were the "helpers" of divorced families but also parents and adult children who themselves were experiencing divorce in their lives. We have tried to reach a large audience and in so doing may have compromised some aspects for each type of audience. Read what is of most interest and skip over those parts that are less pertinent to your interests.

We begin in Chapter 1 by attempting to place the divorce phenomenon in demographic, historical, and cultural context. In so doing we argue that divorce is an indication of the durability and adaptability of the American family as it adjusts to societal changes. We continue in Chapter 2 by reviewing theoretical and research literature on separation, divorce, and remarriage, as well as more general family social science theory, in order to develop a multidisciplinary theoretical approach for understanding the divorce transition. We present the view that divorce must be seen as developmental in two senses. First, the process of divorce is itself developmental. Second, the experience of divorce occurs in a family and individual developmental context. One of the reasons that divorce is so complex — so difficult to "get a handle on" — is that it happens to people and families in a variety of developmental situations. Our theory is designed to make some sense out of this complexity. In doing so it introduces a number of conceptual and theoretical ideas.

The key idea in our theoretical approach is that of the "binuclear family." This idea describes the structure of a family which has experienced marital separation. We prefer this term to such common ones as "single-parent family," "broken family," and the like. This term reflects our basic point of view that, while *marriages* may be discontinued, *families*—especially those in which there are children—continue after marital disruption. They do so with the focus on the two ex-spouse parents now located in separate households—two nuclei to which children and parents alike, as well as others, must relate.

We then move in Chapters 3 and 4 to a discussion of the initial step in divorce—marital separation. We examine this experience in both developmental ways described in Chapter 2. Several phases in the separation process are identified, and we try to see how families at different periods in their development may experience separation.

In Chapters 5 and 6 we turn to the divorce process itself. Here we identify several types of divorcing couples and some of the characteristics of divorce in each type. And, once again, we examine how these types may have variable experiences, depending upon their family developmental situation.

In Chapters 7 and 8 we analyze the experience of remarriage. While we recognize that it is possible that marital disruption will remain at the separation or divorce levels, the reality is that the great majority of divorced people remarry. Remarriage represents the expansion of the binuclear family to include new spouses for one or both former spouses, along with children and other kin. At this point the binuclear family form becomes very complex and, because of the lack of development in norms, we have no terminology to adequately label the multiplicity of relationships that result. Our analysis will deal with this complexity by analyzing the subsystems which are present in this increasingly common family structure. In addition to examining the characteristics of each of them, we once again indicate some of the variations which occur as a result of the family developmental situation.

We close in Chapter 9 with our assessment of what we believe must be accomplished by the helping professions, family social scientists, and policymakers in strengthening divorced families. This is a book with a point of view. We believe in the scientific enterprise of objectively learning as much about this phenomenon as is possible. We have a long way to go in achieving that knowledge. But we also believe that we have an obligation to use that knowledge to suggest ways in which the social structure needs to be adjusted to assist divorced families in reaching a positive personal and collective level of functioning. Divorce is a fact of our time. Instead of focusing only upon its negative and destructive impact on human beings, we believe that the potentially positive aspects need to receive the attention of scholars, professionals, students, and the lay public. Our intention is to contribute to that effort.

ACKNOWLEDGMENTS

There are, of course, many people over the years who have contributed to this project. Our students at the Universities of Wisconsin, Southern California, and British Columbia read earlier drafts of the manuscript, challenged us to clarify our thoughts, and made extremely helpful suggestions which we included in our revisions. A number of colleagues contributed, either by reading and commenting on sections of the manuscript or by talking with us about our ideas and giving us new stimulus when we had lost our momentum. Daniel Perlman of the University of British Columbia was particularly helpful. He willingly took on Rodgers' administrative responsibilities during a six-month leave when the project was started, as well as during several other periods while the manuscript was being completed. Recognition also has to be given to faculty colleagues in the School of Family and Nutritional Sciences at U.B.C., who not only put up with the inconvenience of these absences, but also suffered through more than one presentation or discussion of the contents of the book. Several of them called to our attention references which they thought might be helpful. As always, they were very supportive.

Ahrons' research on the binuclear family and the ideas that emerged from that ten-year process could not have happened without the support, assistance and input of many people. The financial support of the University of Wisconsin Graduate School and the National Institute of Mental Health made it possible to turn several small pilot studies into a major longitudinal investigation. In addition to financial support, belief in the importance of the research ideas by Anne Minahan and Eric Rude of the University of Wisconsin, and Ernie Hurst of NIMH is greatly appreciated. Especially significant were Morton

Perlmutter and Jean Goldsmith, who provided many hours of stimulating dialogue and contributed many ideas to the research. Three research teams of over 40 interviewers, research associates, dissertating students, and, of course, secretaries assisted at every level of the research and made it exciting and enriching. And most importantly— special thanks to all the families who so generously shared their feelings and personal experiences of their divorces and remarriages. Without them this book would not have been written.

We also want to thank Murray Straus, Director of the Family Research Laboratory at the University of New Hampshire, for providing us with Research Associate appointments in the Laboratory during our leaves from our home universities in the fall of 1984. Jeanne Moorman of the Marriage and Family Statistics Branch, U.S. Census Bureau, and Barbara Foley Wilson of the National Center for Health Statistics generously provided extremely useful unpublished data.

Susan Barrows, editor with W. W. Norton, has been very supportive from our first conversations with her about the project. Her knowledge of the field resulted in incisive suggestions, which have made the result considerably better than it would have been otherwise. Only writers know the indispensable contribution made by their editors.

Finally, we want to acknowledge Reuben Hill—Rodgers' teacher, colleague, and beloved friend. While he saw the original prospectus of the book (of which he was severely and appropriately critical), he did not live to see any of the manuscript. We are sure that the book is poorer because of this. Nevertheless, he often "looked over our shoulders" as we were writing. It is no secret that he found the phenomenon of divorce a very distressing one. He once likened divorce to major surgery being carried out on the cancer of a marriage when no other treatment would suffice. He cared very much, personally and professionally, about families and he found it difficult to see divorce in any positive way. Yet, he recognized the need for behavioral scientists, family therapists, and policymakers to have a better understanding of how divorced families could be helped to come through the experience with strength. We had hoped that he would have an opportunity to assess whether we had made a contribution to that need. Well, he may be reading it right now. Our regret is that we cannot benefit from his reactions!

This is a very genuine collaboration. The key concept of the book, the binuclear family, was first introduced by Ahrons. It was the stimulation of that idea in her writing that lured Rodgers into the area of divorce analysis several years ago. While Ahrons has had primary responsibility for the family therapy and much of the research data aspects and Rodgers the theoretical aspects of the writing, each made important contributions to what the other wrote. Indeed, we are no longer sure whose words are whose. Our conversations around the problems we were encountering in expressing our ideas frequently resulted in new insights that became part of the book.

Special thanks to Connie's daughters, Geri and Amy Weiseman, who over many years reminded her that the children's perspective often differs radically from the adults'. Their unfailing belief in the importance of her work and their constant insistence on replacing social science jargon with good plain language has greatly enhanced this book.

CRA
RHR
July 1986

DIVORCED FAMILIES

Meeting the Challenge
of Divorce and Remarriage

ONE

Is the Sky
Really Falling?

"The family is falling apart. Look at all the separation and divorce today. No wonder kids are so messed up — drugs, delinquency, promiscuity, premarital pregnancy, and getting married way too young. If people would only learn that you have to *work* at marriage — take the bad with the good — everything would be OK. We need to get back to the basic family values that we used to have."

Some version of the above quote can be seen in some publication, heard on a radio talk show, or overheard in conversation almost every day in almost any place in North America. Most of us, no doubt, feel some agreement with the sentiments expressed. It really does seem as if many of the troubles we see in our world would be reduced if we could return to the traditional family style. It also seems that the problem of adolescents would be ameliorated if they lived in close-knit families with two loving, caring, competent natural parents. What happened to those strong family values that we all know about?

FAMILY PROBLEMS IN SOCIAL CONTEXT

Examination of the voluminous literature on the family reveals a long history of concern about the welfare of this institution. Virtually every social problem in society has — by one author or another, at one time or another — been attributed to the breakdown of basic family values. Changes in the family have been analyzed as both cause and consequence of almost every societal ill. Some writers view the family as an institution that has merely reacted to major trends in society. From this viewpoint the family emerges as amazingly flexible and adaptable. Other writers focus on the breakdown of the family as being responsible for major problems of the period. What results from these analyses is a picture of the family in a constant state of crisis—a crisis which is threatening the basic foundation of society. The only solid conclusion that can be drawn from a review of the writings on the family is that there is no consensus.

We are strong proponents of the view that the North American family is very much alive and well and that the changes in form and purpose are evidence of the family's capacity to adjust to societal flux. In addition, we assert that the problems of children and families that are receiving so much attention today have been present in society for a long time. Incest, child abuse and neglect, alcoholism, and delinquency are not new problems, nor can we be certain that they have increased disproportionately to the increase in the population. The fact that society is addressing itself to these problems, rather than keeping them closeted in the family, is rooted in the vast societal changes of the 19th and 20th centuries.

Bureaucratic Change

There is no question that *recorded* problems have increased. This is a result of several factors. First, modern society simply keeps better records on such things. Bureaucracy is a modern fact and one of the major features of bureaucracy is the keeping of records. Thus, crime, school records, and all sorts of health information are much more widely available than in the past.

Closely related to this is the increased tendency to treat in an official way many things which were formerly handled by the family or informally in the community. In the 1920s, taking a neighbor's buggy and putting it on top of another neighbor's barn was a favorite. And the proverbial overturning of outhouses was more than proverbial! In modern times acts comparable to these might well be reported to the police and recorded as property crimes. If apprehended, the culprits might not receive severe punishment, but their crimes would be entered in the police records. And, if they had a considerable record of such behavior, they might be classified as delinquent. In "the good old days," however, these acts of vandalism were simply pranks—some more malicious than others.

Finally, we are much more aware of what is going on in the world at large than in former times. Mass communication has allowed us to know of the behavior of young people literally around the world. This is a far cry from the range of knowledge about such things in the not too distant past, when only the most dramatic events outside a very limited geographical area might come to the attention of most people. Also, since people frequently knew not only the individuals involved, but their families as well, the behavior somehow seemed less significant. It was, after all, "just the way those Carmack boys behave." What else could you expect from that family?

Similar factors make it difficult to evaluate the degree to which family problems have increased. Much of what went on in families in the first half of the century was held tightly within the family and did not come to official attention. While family doctors or religious leaders might be aware of certain situations, such as incest or child abuse, they were not likely to make them a part of their records. Most of their "files" were kept in their heads. There were no health insurance claim forms to complete in order to receive payment for fees. And the counseling carried out by ministers was of a much less formal type than mental health professionals perform today. By contrast, the modern family with its problems may come to the attention of a wide range of official and quasi-official agencies, all with records to be kept. The result is a much greater knowledge of what occurs in family life. Of course, the mass media also provide us with a wealth of information. But in many communities in the United States today, small *and* large, there are still certain families that are "protected" through the lack of public disclosure of their problems.

Our view is that in some ways there probably are more problems for youth and families today. More importantly, resources in the informal community of family and friends for the solution of these problems are less readily available. While our nostalgic yearning for the "good old days" may lead us to say that the solution to many of today's problems could be found if only people would use more discipline or work harder at their marriages, that is an oversimplification of the situation. We would suggest that there are some differences in the kind of problems, as well as in the way that they are handled. Many of today's problems arise from the kind of social structure which has developed; this makes young people and families as much the victims as the perpetrators of the difficulty.

Industrialization

   North American society *has* changed, but families have been affected
by those changes far more than they have been responsible for them.
Beginning in the late 19th century and continuing into the 20th, industrialization and urbanization changed the place of the family in the
social structure. Families became consumers of goods produced in the
expanded industrial system, rather than producers of their own requirements — often with some surplus which was used in barter or sale.
Family members became sources of labor for industry and commerce,
with the husband and father leaving the home to pursue work. (However, let us not forget that many minor children also entered industry
before the enactment of child labor laws.)
   In the agrarian family division of labor, tasks were age and gender
identified to some extent. However, it was clearly recognized that the
contributions of all family members were essential to the survival of
the family unit. The transfer of the husband/father's labor outside the
household had the effect of making a greater distinction between
women's work and men's work. The movement to a more money-based
economy had the effect of placing higher value on the wage-earning
"breadwinner" role of men, with a concomitant devaluation of the
domestic labor of women and children. Women and children became
dependents, rather than co-laborers. Along with this change came an
idealization of the home as an expressive location, in contrast to its
former identification as an instrumental place — a center of produc-
tivity. We will discuss this change in more detail shortly.
   Beginning in the 1940s women entered the labor market in increasing
numbers. Here again we must not forget that women have been in the
nondomestic labor market for many decades. The experience of many
immigrant women in the early part of this century in the garment sweat
shops and textile mills of a number of North American cities continues
today in the "cottage industry" labor of women who manufacture
products for commercial contractors, although working conditions
have been improved. In the early 20th century women entered a number
of occupations which had formerly been dominated by men — nurses,
retail clerks, secretaries, librarians, social workers, bookkeeping, and
the like — transforming them into women's occupations, with a resulting
reduction in their status in the society. Then, beginning with World

War II, women, regardless of their marital status, were needed in a wider range of work roles in the war-based industrial system. This was the era of "Rosie the Riveter."

After the war many of these women returned to their domestic roles. Some women remained in the work force temporarily while their husbands took advantage of the G.I. Bill to further their education and their career opportunities. Not all of these women returned to their homes, however, or to the traditional women's occupations. They had a "foot in the door" which they were determined not to remove. Nevertheless, the post World War II period was one dominated by a return to "normalcy," i.e., men employed in wage-earning positions and women employed as housewives and mothers. Soaring marriage rates and the "baby boom" of the late forties and the fifties made it the heyday of the American nuclear family. However, there were "clouds" on this bright horizon in the form of the highest divorce rates in history up to that time (Appendix Tables 1 and 2).

The period of the late forties and the fifties was also a time of great expansion in consumer goods production and sales. New homes for the increasing numbers of families led to an explosion in suburban developments. These modern and relatively affluent people needed all the things required to supply their new homes. Before long it became apparent that a single wage-earner could not keep up with the demands for consumer goods, extended educational opportunity for children, and the general rising expectations for material wealth. Several "recessions" in the decades of the fifties, sixties, and seventies placed economic stress on some segments of the workforce. Unemployment resulting from these and from new automated technology in many of the labor-intensive industries also began to take its toll. Women began to return in increasing numbers to wage-earning employment. Thus, women entered the workforce to supplement inadequate family incomes, replace income lost by the unemployment of the husband/father, and, in some cases, to provide for the "extras" which families wanted but could not afford. In addition, as we will see below, beginning in the sixties a revitalized women's movement had an impact by again emphasizing a broader role for women in the society. This was not a new phenomenon, as an examination of the history of feminism reveals. The sum total of all of this was that family structure changed in almost revolutionary ways.

In his wide-ranging analysis of historical changes in family structure, William Goode lists the following as the major effects of industrialization on the traditional family structure (1956, pp. 10–18):

1. It calls for physical movement from one locality to another, thus decreasing the frequency and intimacy of contact among members of a kin network — although at the stage of full industrialization this is partly counteracted by greater ease of contact at a distance (telephone, letter, etc.).
2. Industrialization creates class-differential mobility. That is, among siblings and kindred, one or more persons may move rapidly upward while others do not, thus creating discrepancies in style of life, taste, income, etc., and making contact somewhat less easy and pleasant.
3. Urban and industrial systems of agencies, facilities, procedures, and organizations have undermined large corporate kin groups since they now handle the problems that were solved within the kin network before industrialization: political protection, pooling funds to educate bright youngsters, defending a locality, lending money, etc.
4. Industrialization creates a value structure that recognizes achievement more than birth; consequently, the kin have less to offer an individual in exchange for his submission. He has to make his *own* way; at best his kin can give him an opportunity to show his talent.
5. Because of specialization, by which thousands of new jobs are created, it is statistically less likely that an individual can obtain a job for his kinsman.

Urbanization

We add to this the impact of urbanization, a concomitant of the buildup of the industrial system, which forced families to move from the more intimate and supportive communities of rural areas and small towns to cities. However, we approach generalizations about urbanization with caution for two reasons. First, cities are not new phenomena. Fans of the writing of Charles Dickens know well the character of London in his time. And it is not easy to forget the picture of Paris portrayed by Victor Hugo in *Les Misérables*. However, the *proportion* of the population living in cities has radically increased. Second, the debate in the family literature over the "isolated nuclear family" as a result of urbanization seems to have provided ample evidence that, while family ties may have become somewhat more attenuated, many nuclear families are still in close contact and communication with their kin. These kin are more frequently than not in close geographical proximity (Litwak, 1960a, 1960b; Litwak & Szelenyi, 1969; Sussman, 1953, 1959). Even for those more distant, modern transportation and communication make quick physical presence possible, if the need arises.

With these caveats in mind, let us say that there is no question that the nature of cities changed the life of the American family. First, city life did change the intimate nature of the extended family kin network. While it is now clear that our idealized image of several generations living under the same roof is not supported by the data (Goode, 1956), there was still a more continuous and supportive kin contact in the rural and small town environment. Life in cities and suburbs meant that families were much more on their own. When they could not meet their needs, they were much more dependent upon private and public agencies for help. While, especially in suburbia, there might be some close relationships with one or more other families in the neighborhood, help was not as readily available. Further, the norm of privacy made it much more difficult to know what might be happening in the house next door. This had the effect of increasing the focus on the value of the nuclear family for its members. The anonymity of urban life reduced the community and friendship networks and, to some extent, the extended family resources that provided emotional meaning in individual lives. In a very real sense the family took on a major, almost exclusive, role in the emotional support arena. Failure of the family in this area became a major inadequacy.

So, did family values change — or did the structure and values of the society change, thus having their impact on the family? We favor the latter explanation. Blaming the victim is often a way of dealing with a problem. We think that many of the ideas reflected in the quote at the beginning of the chapter have some of that quality in them. And there is a good deal of nostalgic belief, not supported by very strong evidence, that things in families were "better back then." We do not want to overemphasize the impact of industrialization and urbanization on all aspects of social life. We simply want to observe that these major developments in all of western society were not a result of changing family structure and modified family values, but, more likely, a cause of them. Indeed, in some ways, family values have continued to be quite strong in spite of this major dual revolution in societal organization.

CHANGING VIEWS
OF MARRIAGE AND THE FAMILY

In response to these vast societal changes the romanticization of the traditional nuclear family took form. In 1945 Ernest W. Burgess and Harvey J. Locke titled their pioneering work *The Family: From Institution to Companionship*. This title derived from Burgess' view that the functions served by families in society had changed dramatically. Family life had become centered on personal relationships and the emotional support which such relationships held for family members. If Burgess' idea had merit (and the literature of family sociology began to focus very much on variations of that idea), it means that views of marriage and divorce had changed as well.

Other theorists, following this same idea, have referred to the *instrumental* and *expressive* roles being played in the family (Parsons & Bales, 1955). In effect, Burgess' institutional family emphasized instrumental roles and his companionship family emphasized expressive ones. In the instrumental model of the family a good husband provided for his family and did not publicly disgrace them by his behavior. (What he did discreetly in privacy was of less concern.) If he was not particularly affectionate or loving, if he had occasional sexual dalliances or took a mistress, indeed even if he sometimes physically mistreated his wife and children in the privacy of his domain, he might still be a "good man." If a wife carried out her domestic and mothering tasks with reasonable competency, provided a sexual outlet for her husband when he required it, and confined her sexual activities to her husband, then she was a "good woman."

In the companionate model marriages became something more than the societally approved means for meeting individual sexual needs, bearing and rearing children, and providing a legitimate status in the society for family members. Marriages now became a means for individuals to meet basic human emotional needs. Certainly, meeting physical and material needs was still a part of the family expectations. These needs were usually taken care of with money earned by the husband and purchased from other systems in the society, thus elevating the wage-earner role he played. But, unless the relationships created by the marriage and birth of children satisfied the needs for love, caring, and emotional support, the marriage was not a successful one.[1] In the urban industrialized society such needs were considerably more difficult to meet outside the family. In Talcott Parsons' words (Parsons & Bales, 1955, p. 9):

> This process (of structural differentiation in society) has involved a further step in the reduction of the importance in our society of kinship units other than the nuclear family. It has also resulted in the transfer of a variety of functions from the nuclear family to other structures of the society, notably the occupationally organized sectors of it. This means that the family has become *a more specialized agency than before*, probably more specialized than it has been in any previously known society. This represents a decline of *certain* features which traditionally have been associated with families; but whether it represents a "decline of the family" in a more general sense is another matter; we think not.

Are love, companionship, and emotional support new values in marriage and the family? Most would say that they are very basic traditional values. When people suggest "returning" to traditional values, they are certainly not suggesting that these values should be abandoned. In fact, we suspect that most would assign higher priority to these expressive values than to the more instrumental ones. Indeed, a number of women make that very choice, giving up a comfortable material situation in order to be freed from an intolerable emotional one. Our argument, then, is that a central reason for the rise in the divorce rate is the high value placed on the traditional expressive values of marriage and family and a recognition that meeting the instrumental values is not enough.

This change from the instrumental to the companionate notion of marriage and family contributed to what Birdwhistell (1968) labeled the "sentimental model" of the family. Arlene Skolnick, in identifying the cultural changes that contributed to the idealization of the family, states (1979, p. 304):

> Men went out into the world and became "breadwinners"; wives and children became dependents. The home was placed in an ambiguous

position outside the realm of economic necessity. The new ideology of the family filled the void by idealizing the home and woman's role in it. Many of our traditional notions about femininity and family life were emphasized by industrialization: the idea that woman's place is in the home; the idea that the essence of femininity lies in ministering to the personal and psychological needs of husbands and children; the idea that mothers have a Pygmalion-like influence on their children.

The traditional American nuclear family—the employed father, the at-home mother, the two children, the two cars in the garage of the suburban home—gradually grew to become the ideal family form. The media idealized this family by a genre of movies such as the Andy Hardy series, followed by the TV images of "Father Knows Best." Children were taught to read by "Dick and Jane" textbooks and women struggled to be the kind of women portrayed in the "ladies magazines." Consistent with this popular portrayal of the family was the social scientists' analyses.

> Of course, as we shall see, he has other very important functions in relation both to wife and to children, but it is fundamentally by virtue of the importance of his occupational role *as a component of his familial role* that in our society we can unequivocally designate the husband-father as the "instrumental leader" of the family as a system. (Parsons & Bales, 1955, p. 13)

And again,

> We suggest that this order of differentiation is generic to the "leadership element" of small groups everywhere and that the problem with respect to the family is not *why* it appears there, given the fact that families as groups exist, but why the man takes the more instrumental role, the woman the more expressive, and why in detailed ways these roles take particular forms. In our opinion the fundamental explanation of the allocation of the roles between the biological sexes lies in the fact that the bearing and early nursing of children establish a strong presumptive primacy of the relation of mother to the small child and this in turn establishes a presumption that the man, who is exempted from these biological functions, should specialize in the alternative instrumental direction. (Parsons & Bales, 1955, p. 23)

The instrumental and the expressive functions of the family became clearly identified as men's roles and women's roles, respectively, primarily as a result of Parsons and Bales' influential analysis.[2]

SOCIAL CONTEXT OF DIVORCE

It is only in the last three decades that this idealized notion of the sanctity of the traditional American family has been seriously challenged. The contemporary feminist movement, the increase of women in the workforce, and the sexual revolution are often cited as contributing to the rapid increase in divorce rates.

In her pioneering work, *The Feminine Mystique*, Betty Friedan (1963) identified the traditional nuclear family as contributing to the oppression of women. She opened up the arena for the flood of discontent felt by many women as they struggled to meet unsuccessfully all the expressive needs of the family. She uncovered the paradox of a society that in reality undervalued "woman's work" while it simultaneously perpetuated the myth of "motherhood and apple pie." Thus began the resurgence of the current feminist movement.

The feminist writings of the past two decades have been instrumental in uncovering the myths of the ideal of the traditional American family. The inequality of worth of women's work, both in the home and in the marketplace, is a well documented characteristic of sex-role segregated societal structures. Challenging assumptions of appropriate gender behaviors has caused a reexamination of women's and men's roles in the family.

The well-documented increase of women entering the labor force has resulted in heated debates about the consequences of this social change for the stability of the family. Some argue that a move toward equality is synonymous with a move toward individualism which will essentially undermine the value of the family in society. Others argue that more gender equality in family roles will result in more satisfaction within intimate relationships. Still others argue that more equality will improve the quality of parenting and hence be beneficial to children.

While this debate has been flaming, the increase of women entering the labor force has resulted in the emergence of a new form of family, the two-worker family. This, in turn, has brought new problems for families and society. A major concern has been child-care. The family and society in general have been dependent on women to carry the major child-care functions. As middle-class women add the new role of worker to their traditional roles of wife and mother, the issue of who shall care for the children has increasingly become a major concern. The prevalence of the dual-worker family and the reduced availability of the kin network have forced other societal institutions to look at the child-care issue. Hence, there is increasing discussion of the need for family policies which will provide child-care outside the family and which will address the economic losses experienced by women as a result of childbearing.

Another factor of the dual-worker family is the changing economic position which results for women. As increasingly significant contributors to the economic condition of the family, many women have begun to expect more participation in family economic and other decisions. Several studies have identified a relationship between economic contributions and power relationships in the family.[3] From a social psychological perspective, then, this raises another important question requiring further study. How do these demands for more equality in marital power by women affect the stability of marriage?

Of importance also to the function of marriage in our society is the increased availability of birth control and abortion. Women's ability to control their reproduction has led to what has been called the sexual revolution. In the past, fear of pregnancy has served as a major control on sexual activity for women outside of marriage. With this barrier removed, women have moved more closely to men in yet another area. Women may choose to engage in sexual relations for recreation. Although some note that the double standard of sexual relations still prevails, sex as recreation — whether within or outside of marriage — has become part of contemporary American society. As women exert more control over their decisions about if and when to have children, the nature and function of marriage change as well.

Our intent here is not to enter into the current debate about what impact the current feminist movement has had on the divorce rate, but rather to emphasize that these societal changes do affect both the function of marriage and attitudes toward marriage and divorce. As women become more independent economically, their need for marriage as their source of economic support lessens. As they strive for more equality in society, their need for marriage as a source of status also lessens. Finally, when women may choose to have sexual relations without the fear of pregnancy and societal scorn, their need for marriage as their only acceptable route to sexual satisfaction is reduced as well. With the lowered pressure of these traditional "advantages" of marriage, women are freer to choose whether marriage meets their emotional needs, and if it does not, then they have the option to choose not to remain married.

THE DIVORCE REFORM MOVEMENT

In the past two decades we have witnessed major changes in divorce legislation which reflect the changes we have noted in the institutions of marriage and the family. If a major, perhaps the key, reason for marriage today is love, companionship, and emotional support, then a key justification for terminating marriage becomes the failure of the marriage to meet these objectives. Thus, the "incompatibility" grounds for divorce became more commonly cited in the increasing numbers of actions filed. In more recent years, "no fault" divorce legislation, often using such terms as "breakdown in the marital relationship" or "irreconcilable marital differences" has recognized explicitly that there is no assignable "marital offense" in such situations. Rather, two people have simply failed to achieve the goals upon which marriages are primarily based. Indeed, some of the former marital offenses, viz., adultery and desertion, are now often seen as symptoms of the breakdown in the emotional quality of the marriage. Many marriages have survived adultery because the basic emotional quality of the marriage was seen to be good and worth preserving.

Even with this shift in attitudes toward the role of marriage, the prevailing views of divorce are still steeped in the presumption of social deviance. Lynne Halem, in tracing the evolution of the ideology of divorce and its relationships to the history of divorce reform, states: "Yet because we, as a nation, operate within the context of a 2000-year-old heritage, we still regard divorce as a problem of momentous consequence, a pathological event that threatens not only the institution of the family but also social cohesiveness and order" (1980, p. 3).

It is interesting to note that even though we are in the midst of the "divorce revolution," we still cling to the long-held notion that divorce is inherently pathological.[4] In the 1970s, statutory reform in the form of no-fault legislation removed the law's punitive function in divorce. Surprisingly, however, this divorce reform movement began, not as an expression of liberalized social attitudes, but as an essentially conservative effort. The intent behind the new laws was concern for the social pathology that resulted from the breakdown of the traditional institution of marriage. Weitzman writes concerning the changes in California: "The lack of opposition to the no-fault reform from such likely foes as the Catholic Church may be explained in part by the reform rhetoric of both the Governor and his commission. No-fault was consistently portrayed as the modern prescription to 'preserve the family'" (Weitzman, 1985, p. 18). So, although no-fault legislation removes the issue of blame or fault from the legal arena, divorce is still being blamed for such social problems as delinquency, crime, alcoholism, and welfare dependency.

Child custody issues have become part of this divorce reform movement. The history of child custody decisions reveals that the custody of children has changed along with prevailing social trends. Before the 19th century women and children were the property of men. Although divorce was rare, the issue of custody was clear: children belonged to fathers. As industrialization and urbanization developed, with the associated shift from the instrumental to companionate notion of marriage and its emphasis on the importance of motherhood, maternal custody became the presumption of the courts. With the traditional nuclear family as the ideal, women were clearly accorded sole responsibility for the rearing of children. The issue of custody was clear: children belonged to mothers. It was only in rare cases, when the mother was proven to be 'unfit' due to mental illness or adultery, that custody was awarded to fathers.

Now that we are in the midst of redefining gender and family roles the issue of custody is being redefined as well. Current legislation reflects this societal shift toward equality of women's and men's roles by removing the presumptive attitude toward either parent. Custody may not be determined on the basis of sex. But, rather than clearly defining how custody should be awarded, the laws instead provide only for how custody awards should *not* be determined. This egalitarian legislative change has resulted in a more ambiguous, and hence more controversial, custody situation. Heated debates and increasing custody litigation mark the last decade. It should not be surprising, in light of changing societal attitudes toward gender roles, that joint custody should emerge as a solution. However, as we will discuss further in

Chapter 5, how parents manage to share custody and childrearing after marital dissolution is not as clear as the new mandates. As the history of custody reveals, the determination of custody based on the children's needs is more myth than reality. Child custody decisions have changed in accordance with the changes in societal attitudes toward the family.

Although we have set forth the view that the current rates of divorce are a logical response to societal trends, attitudes toward divorce are still imbued with pathology. We still cling to the long-held belief that marriage implies an "until death do us part" ideology. Any departure from that image has been labeled pathological. The clinical notion of pathology stems from the belief that divorce is the product of individual neuroses formed in childhood and played out in adult life. It follows that, if marriage is still regarded as a lifelong commitment, the decision to terminate the marriage is a result of the failure of the partners to sustain a committed relationship. This, then, implies a defect in one or both partners.

These two perspectives, individual pathology and social deviance, have guided the research and clinical writings that have emerged in the past three decades. Although it is beyond the scope of this book to analyze the results of the accumulating body of literature on divorce, it is important to note that the prevailing attitude that divorce is deviant and reflects pathology has influenced our current knowledge base about divorce. Prior to 1972, almost all of the research was formulated to look for the pathological consequences of divorce on children and adults. Hence, in psychological research almost all studies were conducted on subjects drawn from clinical settings, and in sociological research the focus was on studying the relationship between social deviance and the breakdown of the nuclear family. When the findings of these research studies are examined in a total context, they are seen to be inconclusive and often contradictory.[5]

These trends have resulted in a new appraisal of divorce. Challenges to traditional sole mother custody awards, the proliferation of joint custody legislation, and the liberalization of the divorce laws have focused our attention on the *process* of divorce, rather than on the event and its outcomes. We are in the midst of defining divorce as an enduring societal institution much in the same way as we have viewed marriage in our culture. The need for this redefinition is only underlined by the statistical trends in recent years.

THE DEMOGRAPHIC
CONTEXT OF DIVORCE

Increase in Divorce

The last decade has ushered in a significant rise in divorce rates as well as in the proportion of the population who are divorced. It is clear that the rise in the divorce rate is not a new phenomenon. The increase in both the numbers and the rates of divorce has been a long-term trend (Appendix Table 1).[6] However, this general statement must be modified by two facts. First, after the peak years of divorce during and immediately following World War II, there was a steady decline in the numbers and the rate per thousand married women, which lasted for nearly 15 years. The divorce rate again reached its peak in 1979 and has again fallen modestly beginning in 1980 (Appendix Table 2). It is too soon to tell at this writing whether this falling off is a trend in the divorce pattern.

Another factor of interest is that divorce is not confined to the young. Age group analysis shows that the proportions and the numbers divorced have risen in each birth group, continuing well into midlife (Table 1 and Appendix Table 1). Table 1 follows a given 20-year age group through four decades, i.e., from the time they were in the 25–44 age group through the time they were in the 65-and-over age group.

Table 1: Age Cohort Analysis of the Divorced Status, 1880–1980.

AGED 25–44 IN	MALE			FEMALE		
	% DIVORCED AT AGE			% DIVORCED AT AGE		
	25–44	45–64	65+	25–44	45–64	65+
1880	–	–	.8	–	–	.4
1890	–	–	1.1	–	–	.5
1900	–	1.0	1.3	–	.9	.7
1910	–	1.6	2.2	–	1.4	.7
1920	.7	1.9	1.6	1.0	2.0	1.5
1930	1.4	2.4	2.4	1.9	2.5	2.3
1940	1.5	3.1	3.7	2.4	3.7	3.4
1950	1.9	3.3	–	2.9	4.7	–
1960	1.9	5.9	–	3.2	8.0	–
1970	2.7	–	–	4.9	–	–
1980	7.1	–	–	10.2	–	–

Source: Appendix Table 3.

In each successive ten-year period, the 25–44 age group begins with a higher proportion divorced than the previous ten-year group. This proportion grows larger when they reach 45–64. The pattern in the over-65 age group differs for men and women. For men, it continues to increase for most ten-year groups. For women it consistently falls off. By examining Appendix Table 1, we see that this is a result of the high proportion of women in this group who are widowed. Women over age 65 are three to four times as likely to be in the widowed status as their male counterparts.[7] And, as Table 2 shows, men in this age group are twice as likely as women to be married. This latter figure is due, of course, to the greater opportunities that men in the older age groups, whether divorced or widowed, have for remarriage.[8] These marriages generally involve a bride younger than the groom.[9] While the proportion of divorced in the over-65 group is relatively low, we can, on the basis of trends in the younger cohorts, expect a change in this in future decades. This increase is explained by the social context already discussed in detail.

Increase in Marriage

Marriage remains very popular. Appendix Table 1 shows increasing proportions of both sexes married in each successive census decade up to 1970. While it appeared for a time beginning in the 1960s that there

Table 2: Age Cohort Analysis of the Married Status, 1880–1980.

AGED 25–44 IN	MALE			FEMALE		
	% MARRIED AT AGE			% MARRIED AT AGE		
	25–44	45–64	65+	25–44	45–64	65+
1880	–	–	64.7	–	–	33.9
1890	–	–	63.7	–	–	34.7
1900	–	79.8	63.8	–	69.1	34.3
1910	–	80.2	66.2	–	70.0	36.0
1920	72.1	81.0	72.5	78.2	70.7	37.1
1930	74.8	83.2	71.8	79.5	71.9	35.5
1940	75.6	84.7	77.6	78.9	73.3	39.7
1950	83.5	86.5	–	84.5	75.5	–
1960	84.5	85.3	–	87.7	74.6	–
1970	84.6	–	–	86.6	–	–
1980	75.3	–	–	77.2	–	–

Source: Appendix Table 3.

was a reduction in interest in marrying, it now appears clear that this was a change to delaying marriage, rather than foregoing it. A similar delay in childbearing made it appear for a time that childless couples were on the increase.[10]

Again, the age group analysis displayed in Table 2 is of interest. It is clear that the proportion of women married in the older age groups falls off dramatically, rather than modestly, as in the case of men. We have already noted that this is due to an increasing proportion of women falling into the widowed category, as well as to the greater remarriage probability for men in these age groups.

Remarriage Rates

There is little evidence that the rise in divorce indicates a disillusionment with marriage. The remarriage statistics indicate that a more accurate interpretation would be that divorce represents dissatisfaction with a specific marriage, not marriage in general. In 1981 the following figures of marital status at the time of marriage of brides and grooms are of interest: brides — 66.4 percent single, 3.2 percent widowed, 27.1 percent divorced; grooms — 64.8 percent single, 3.0 percent widowed, 29 percent divorced. Looking at it another way, of the marriages registered in 1981, 54.7 percent involved both parties being single, 11.8 percent involved a remarriage for the groom and a first marriage for the bride, 10.1 percent involved a remarriage for the bride and a first marriage for the groom, and 23.4 percent involved remarriages for both parties (National Center for Health Statistics, 1985b).

As we have seen, there are cohort differences that put older women at a disadvantage for remarriage. The combination of the longer life expectancy of women and the cultural value placed on physical attractiveness in women is reflected in the pattern of older men marrying younger women. Thus, older women have a dual demographic deficit — fewer living men in their age cohort and these men tending to marry younger women.

Surprisingly, the rate of remarriage has fallen considerably over the past 15 years or so. A comparison of the figures for 1965 and those for 1981 in Appendix Table 3 shows that in all age groups the rate of remarriage per thousand divorced women has dropped steadily and significantly. This is especially so for the under-25 age group — a reflection, perhaps, of the marriage delay that has also been observed in first marriages. Despite this drop, remarriage among the divorced continues to be a substantial contributor to the overall marriage statistics of the United States.

New Family Forms

The high incidence of divorce, along with high remarriage rates, provides evidence for a well-established pattern of "serial monogamy" or, as one set of analysts has termed it, "conjugal succession" (Furstenberg & Nord, 1985, p. 903). This pattern gives rise to one of several new family forms that have resulted from the changing characteristics of marriage, divorce, and remarriage — the "blended family" composed of at least one formerly married spouse, the children of the previous marriage or marriages, and any offspring of the new union. Cherlin and McCarthy (1985) report that in 1980 20 percent of the married couple households contained at least one spouse who had been divorced and that one-sixth of all children under 18 lived in such a household. In some cases, of course, such a blended family could include children from more than one previous marriage of one or both spouses.

Cherlin and McCarthy (1985, Table 2) present some interesting details about the variety possible in blended families. They identified two basic types: (a) no children younger than 18 from the current marriage (66.8 percent) and (b) one or more children 18 or younger from the current marriage (33.2 percent). Each of these could occur in three variations: neither spouse had children under 18 from previous marriages (a = 40.7 percent; b = 15.9 percent), one spouse had children under 18 from previous marriages (a = 17.7 percent; b = 14.0 percent), and both spouses had children younger than 18 from previous marriages (a = 8.4 percent; b = 3.3 percent). It must be remembered that these individuals could have had children in one or more of these categories in previous marriages who were over 18 years of age.

Another pattern is remarriage involving one or two noncustodial parents or childless divorced individuals. Such couples may or may not produce children of their own. Still another new family form is the nonremarried divorced couple who continue to relate at some level as parents to their children. Finally, there is the genuine "single-parent family" in which a custodial parent — usually the mother — has not remarried and no longer has any meaningful contact with the former spouse. As we will see, each of these family forms has its own distinctive characteristics. We prefer to apply the general term *binuclear family* to these new family structures, which contrast so dramatically with the traditional American nuclear family structure. Table 3 summarizes all of the possible types of individuals who in combination form various binuclear families. These various family forms will be discussed in more detail in later chapters.

The emergence of these new family forms has had a profound impact on contemporary North American society. Whether that impact is

Table 3: Characteristics of Individuals Constituting Binuclear Families

---

I. Remarried.
  A. Children this marriage.
    1. Under 18.
      a. No children previous marriage.
      b. Children previous marriage all over 18.
      c. Children previous marriage under 18.
        (i) Custody.
        (ii) Non-custody.
    2. All over 18.
      a. No children previous marriage.
      b. Children previous marriage all over 18.
  B. No Children this marriage.
    1. No children previous marriage.
    2. Children previous marriage.
      a. All over 18.
      b. Under 18.
        (i) Custody.
        (ii) Non-custody.
II. Not remarried.
  A. No children.
  B. Children.
    1. All over 18.
    2. Under 18.
      a. Custody.
      b. Non-custody.
III. Not previously married.
  A. No children.*
  B. Children.
    1. All over 18.
    2. Under 18.
      a. Custody.
      b. Non-custody.

---

*Only a marriage between two persons of type IIIA constitutes a non-binuclear family. Even remarriages between two previously married childless individuals involves them in binuclear family relationships with extended family.

positive or negative is a matter of considerable controversy. As Bert Adams notes: " . . . whether we see today's changes as problems or solutions to traditional problems depends to a great extent on what we value most" (1985, p. 525).

A NEW ASSESSMENT OF DIVORCE

The gradual shift in ideology — from viewing divorce as pathology to viewing divorce as an institution — is clearly having an impact on the study of divorce. The study of divorce is no longer narrowly defined within a deviance perspective. Instead, we are able to begin to identify which of the many complex factors associated with divorce result in negative consequences for the participants. As a necessary concomitant, we are beginning to identify which of these factors result in healthy functioning. But even now, as we are moving in our attitudes toward normalizing divorce in our society, we still have difficulty ridding ourselves of the pathological model. We still tend to think in terms of pathology, looking for the absence of pathology rather than focusing on the normal family patterns that result from divorce.

This book looks at the divorce transition in a radically different way. We believe that divorce is both normative and, for many couples, nonpathological in character. Each of these ideas requires some elaboration.

Norms, in sociological language, are expectations for behavior. Divorce is based on the belief that marriage should meet very important needs of the spouses. If this does not occur, the expectation is that the marriage should be terminated — a basic norm related to marriage and divorce in our society. However, we do not have well-developed norms about how divorced couples ought to deal with each other and with their children, their kin, their friends, and the community — or how these people should relate to the divorced couple. There is a very definite lack of clarity in the norms surrounding postmarital behavior — a condition labeled *anomie* in sociology. If spouses should not continue a marriage which is unsatisfactory, how should former spouses behave toward one another and how should others behave toward them once they have severed their marital ties? Much of what we have to say in the following pages is directed to this situation.

Furthermore, if these norms concerning marriage prevail, severing an unsatisfactory marriage should not be seen as pathological. Many marriages have conflict and serious differences. Marriage partners fight, argue, discuss, and negotiate over these differences. They often reach mutually agreeable solutions. On the other hand, others find it impossible to come to such agreements. Viewing them as "sick" or "bad" or labeling them in other pathological ways lacks basic validity. It is true that some spouses are emotionally disturbed and incapable of meeting basic expectations for behavior both in and out of marriage. However, many more marital partners simply find it impossible to develop the kind of marriage which meets their expectations. While in former times they would have been expected to "grin and bear it," they are no longer under such pressure. Therefore, we do not see divorce as a symptom of pathology in marriage and the family. At the most it may involve individuals with pathological characteristics acting out their sickness in the marital setting. Most divorces, however, involve persons well within the range of normality acting on norms that reject remaining in an unsatisfactory marriage.

None of this is to say that divorce is not painful, stressful, crisis-producing, and often infused with conflict. Nor is it to say that divorced couples and their families necessarily find themselves better off than they were before the divorce. We are not "in favor" of divorce as compared to marriage. Obviously, most of us would prefer to have happy and successful marriages. But, failing that, we believe that divorce can be successful and that it can lead to better life situations for all concerned. Our purpose in writing this book is to identify some of the conditions which lead to such success, as well as those which lead to failure.

In authoring this book, we too are caught in this transitional struggle. Our training has rooted us in the deviance model. Having no guideposts, we are still tentative in our attempts to describe a conceptual framework for a normal process of separation, divorce, and remarriage. The model of divorce as a normal developmental process presented here is taking shape within a society that still views these families as deviant. As society makes the shift to accepting divorce as a normal pattern within the broader definition "family," we expect that families themselves will incorporate new ways to master the transition. As family therapists and sociologists, we will ultimately follow these families into this new territory.

TWO

The Divorce Process:
A Multidisciplinary View

Why is divorce such a stressful experience for those involved? Is it possible to identify the characteristics of individuals and families at various points in the course of the ending of a marriage, in order to understand that process better, to intervene effectively in the process, to reduce crisis, and to develop policies and programs to prevent serious disruption in these families' lives?

From a legal and social status perspective, divorce is an event; it moves individuals from the condition of being legally married to that of being legally divorced. At the point the divorce decree is final, and not before, the former partners are eligible to remarry. In many legal jurisdictions, property acquired during the marriage is jointly owned until the day of divorce. Socially, the former partners, although they may have been separated for a considerable time, are viewed differently once the divorce has taken place.

However, looked at from a family dynamics and not a legal standpoint, divorce can best be regarded as a process. It has roots somewhere in the past, before the divorce event, and carries with it effects that extend into the future. Each family member will be profoundly affected by it; as members of a new kind of family, individuals will be forced to learn new ways of coping and of relating to the society at large, as well as to each other.

Viewing divorce as a process requires an adequate theoretical model. In this chapter the interweaving of several theoretical sources forms the basis for a multidisciplinary developmental approach to the process of divorce. This will enable us to suggest ways to effectively intervene in the process, to identify policies and programs the society might develop to prevent serious disruption in individual lives and family dynamics, and to enhance our general understanding of family systems.

THE FAMILY SYSTEM

Across sociological, social psychological,[1] individual, and family therapy literature there is agreement that the family is a system. Each of these approaches tends to emphasize one of the "facets" of family life — the societal-institutional, the group-interactional, or the individual-psychological (Rodgers, 1973, Chapter 3). While each approach contributes to our understanding, the family systems literature has in recent years done the most to bring together all three facets.

The Sociological Approach

Social systems theory focuses primarily on the institutional characteristics of the system. Robert Bierstedt (1963, p. 341) has pointed out that, in the strictest sense, institutions are organized sets of *ideas* about how something ought to be done in the society. As such, institutions do not have members and cannot be located in space. Groups and the behavior of members of these groups reveal the existence of the institution. Therefore, the structural characteristics of social systems are *institutionalized*; i.e., there is an organized set of ideas about how systems should be formed and carried on. These ideas are generally understood by the members of the society or of a particular social system and are translated into behavior by the individual members.

Institutions (such as government, business, religion, education, medicine, or the family) require structure in order to carry out necessary functions; ideas about how these functions are to be performed shape the structure. Social systems theorists, such as Bennett and Tumin (1948, p. 49), posit necessary functions (and associated structural arrangements) which the various systems of the society must perform for the survival of the society, as well as of the system.[2] These prerequisites can be used to identify systems whose primary role is to carry out one of the major institutional functions of society, or they may be used to analyze a single system's structure as it organizes to meet each of the functions for its own survival. Although they were intended to be applicable to any structure of a given society, we discuss them here as they relate specifically to the family system, since they have a direct bearing on the processes of disorganization and reorganization in separation, divorce, and remarriage.

Bennett and Tumin first identify the maintenance of biological functioning of group members, which includes those structures designed to deal with the health, safety, and nutrition of individuals. It is clear that families expend a major amount of effort to feed and clothe their members, as well as to maintain their health and care for ill members. Second is the reproduction or recruitment of new group members. As applied to the family, this encompasses the structures established for the control of biological reproduction, the adoption of members into the family, as well as the practices associated with courtship and marriage. Third is the socialization of new members — the teaching of beliefs, values, skills, and roles associated with being a member of that group. As the primary agents of socialization for the society (along with the educational system), families are very much involved in this socialization function. A fourth function is that of the production and distribution of goods and services by and for group members. This is generally termed the "division of labor" in family analysis. A fifth function, the maintenance of order, focuses chiefly on the power, authority, and decision-making structures of the family. (While the fourth function involves who *does* certain things and who *receives* certain things, the fifth identifies who *decides* who does what or receives what goods and services.)

Finally, Bennett and Tumin postulate the function of the maintenance of meaning and motivation for group activity. Here the emphasis is on those structures which deal with the values, goals, beliefs, and ideals which make group membership significant. In families this might be a particular set of religious beliefs, ideas about the significance of marriage and the family as central to life, the importance of emotional nurturance given by the family, or an idea that families insure one's immortality. Without such value structures members of a group soon lose any particular attachment to the group and abandon it as unworthy of their presence. Indeed, some acts — children running away, spousal desertion, suicide, and, of course, divorce — can often be traced to the loss of meaning in group membership.

As will become apparent later, members of families encountering stress and crisis find that the system must focus its struggle on the maintenance of functioning in one or more of these areas if it is to survive. Depending upon the makeup of a given family and the period of the family history in which the stress arises, some functions may be more subject to disruption than others.

The sociological treatment of the family system tends to be macroscopic and abstract in nature, focusing as it does on general aspects of the system. Social psychologists and psychologists have carried out more microscopic study in order to discover the ways the concrete behaviors of groups and individuals affect or are affected by the system.

The Social Psychological Approach

With Ernest W. Burgess' classic conception, in 1926, of the family as " . . . a unity of interacting personalities," we move away from the abstract institutional level of families as systems of ideas to a view of families as individuals behaving towards one another in both institutional and non-institutional ways. The institutional ideas are, in a sense, the themes of family life. Such ideas as "families are the foundation of the society," "the family is always there when you need help," or "your first loyalty is to your family" are common family themes. "The man is the head of the house," "children should learn to take responsibility in the family," or "a wife's first responsibility is to her husband and children" are examples of others. The dynamic behavior of individuals and unique family groups reveals many *variations* on these and other themes.

As a member of the "Chicago School" of symbolic interactionists, Burgess' analytical interests focused on understanding how people played out the everyday drama of institutionally defined roles and positions. To the symbolic interactionists personality was a consequence of the communication processes — verbal and nonverbal — developed in social interaction, and the family was one of the first and focal arenas for that interaction. While symbolic interactionists did not use modern systems terminology, many of those ideas were present in their analyses.

The systems idea of "feedback" is a good example. Feedback is the idea that, when an actor in the system behaves in a certain manner, there is a response from one or more other actors in the system which serves to indicate some approval, disapproval, or disinterest in that action. Feedback serves to maintain, modify, or even radically change the nature of the system. Feedback is certainly at the heart of Cooley's

(1902) idea of "the looking-glass self," which postulated that individuals gained a sense of themselves by imagining some action, imagining the reaction that the other person would have to that action, and then revising it to fit more closely with the reaction they wished to obtain.

G. H. Mead's (1936) complex portrayal of the development of self is another early example of the feedback idea. Mead, however, differentiated between behavior with those one knew intimately — "significant others" — and that in the more public and less specific interactive settings — with "generalized others." Thus, an individual walking down the street alone behaves in a predictable manner (walking forward, tending to keep to the right, etc.), which reflects his or her sense of self in response to the generalized other. When she or he meets a friend, the behavior shifts to the self responding to this specific significant other.

Twenty-five years later Reuben Hill (Waller & Hill, 1951) revised the Burgess definition of the family to that of a " . . . semi-closed system of interacting personalities." By this is meant that the family system is neither totally closed nor unconditionally open to the intrusion of other systems of the society. This modification in definition reflected the interest of social psychologists in analyzing the positional and role structure of the family — not only within its immediate boundaries, but also in relation to other systems of the society. This redefinition reflected the "generalized other" and "significant other" perspective set forth by Mead. The study of family members as workers, students, extended family members, members of religious groups, consumers, or citizens provided a more complete understanding of the internal dynamics of the family.

Using the terminology of role theory (Bates, 1956) — norms, roles, role behavior, position, group, and the like — extensive literature has been built up around examination of the interactions and transactions of the family system. This literature, which has reached a rather high level of sophistication, is best represented by the work of Burr, Hill, Nye, and Reiss (Burr, 1973; Burr et al., 1979). The analysis of behavior of *individuals* in the family system, however, is not a primary focus of this approach. It remained for those who were interested in therapeutic intervention with families and who worked from a more psychological frame of reference to deal with the individual in the family system.

The Family Systems Therapy Approach

The systems approach as it has been addressed by family systems therapy theorists places major emphasis on the subsystems of the family. This approach becomes particularly significant in the analysis of the reorganization of the divorced family system.[3]

David Kantor and William Lehr. In their pioneering research begun in 1965, David Kantor and William Lehr (1975) pursued an intensive investigation of 19 urban and suburban Boston area families, some of whom were categorized as "disturbed" and some as "normal."[4] At the outset of their report of this research, Kantor and Lehr put their readers on notice that their interest is in *all* families, not just the pathological — a view which we enthusiastically endorse.

> To date, family therapists and researchers have concentrated on extraordinary family phenomena, such as the generation of psycho-somatia, social deviance, and schizophrenia. As a result, many of them have overlooked an obvious truth: families, even those families which suffer from serious schism and disablement, devote most of their time to everyday affairs. . . . Although we do not wish to deny their importance, we believe that disabling processes occupy a considerably smaller subclass in the universe of family events than the literature of family pathology might lead us to believe. . . . It seems to us that if a theory or model of family behavior is to be viable, it must be applicable to "healthy" or "normal" family processes as well as pathological ones. Consequently, our primary concern . . . is to focus on the intrinsic nature of family process itself rather than on its pathological aspects. (Kantor & Lehr, 1975, pp. ix–x)

The dynamics of families coping with the stress and crisis of post-marital reorganization can be captured in the analytical system set out by these researchers. They use a spatial metaphor which is expressed in the key concept of their theory — *distance regulation*. Distance regulation is a means of identifying the processes by which family members maintain and control the boundaries of the systems in which they live. The concern for boundary maintenance is one which has been especially significant in the family therapy literature — and it is one which we find of great importance in our understanding of family reorganization after separation and divorce. Two key questions emerge: How does the family set up and maintain its territory? How does it regulate distance among its own members?

Kantor and Lehr concentrate on three family subsystems — the family unit subsystem, the interpersonal subsystem, and the personal subsystem. They focus on the way subsystems "interface":

> An interface is a meeting ground of two or more systems or subsystems, each with its own boundary, each with its own set of interrelated parts, and each with its own rules and metarules for governing how its parts are to work in various contexts. Interface experience becomes meaningful only when at least one system or subsystem recognizes that it is in a meeting ground with another system or subsystem. (pp. 24–25)

Interfaces provide the setting in which feedback takes place between the members of the subsystems. There are two basic types of feedback loops: *constancy* and *variety*. The former are those messages which are designed to maintain a steady state in the system and to correct any errors which may arise.[5] Variety feedback is intended to "amplify variety and deviation and either maintain or increase system disequilibrium." This kind of feedback serves to introduce system "mutations" which can respond to change in the system. The significance of feedback lies in the behavior to which the feedback is directed and the intent of the actors involved in the interface. Thus, new behavior on the part of a family member may receive feedback which denotes approval and has the effect of introducing a new role definition into the system (variety). However, if disapproval is indicated, the new role will not be established (constancy).

In essence, Kantor and Lehr's approach sees family relationships as a highly complex set of interactions designed to capture or allocate the resources of *space*, *time*, and *energy*, employing techniques which utilize *affect, power*, and *meaning*. Over time typical *family strategies* develop which define territories of access to these valued resources. A strategy is " . . . a purposive pattern of moves toward a target or goal made by two or more people who are systematically bound in a social-biological arrangement" (p. 18).

Strategies have five characteristics: *purposiveness, members' awareness, collaboration, shared responsibility for outcome*, and *allowance for contingencies* in the playing of parts. Thus, a family may have as a general goal that education is important for the children to get ahead.

Family members may develop a complex strategy that involves saving for college educations and mapping out curricular routes in high school that are designed to prepare children for particular universities and programs within that university. Pursuing this strategy means that certain members will hold the power to allocate space and to control time in such a way that energy is available to attain the goal. One or both parents may be employed in order to earn funds for college (time and energy are required). Children will be provided rooms of their own, desks, and books, and they may have their extracurricular activity regulated so that they will have the space, time, and energy to study effectively. Affect and meaning will be used, along with power, in various kinds of feedback designed to ensure that all involved meet their obligations. Such a strategy requires a very purposive effort on the part of parents and children, of which they must be aware, in which they collaborate, and in which they share considerable responsibility for the outcome. It also requires some contingency planning about what they will do if there is insufficient money, or if children do not do well in a particular course of study or are not admitted to their first choice of university or program.

Strategies are of three types: *maintenance, stress,* and *repair.* Reorganization of the family in separation, divorce, and remarriage may involve family strategies aimed at reaching a goal of fulfilling child-rearing obligations. Specific examples might include divorce settlements which designate specific funds for college educations. There may be specified custody arrangements allowing both former spouses contact with their children, so that both parents can continue to motivate the children to pursue the educational goals established during the marriage. Modifications in these strategies might occur under the stress of a child's academic failure or rejection of an application to a particular university or program. Further, the reorganization process of the family postdivorce might require either stress or repair types of strategies to be developed. For instance, parental divorce may mean less money, as income is distributed to two households, and this may affect the children's educational plans.

Kantor and Lehr (Chapter 9) identify three family system styles of relating — *closed,* which uses stable structures as reference points for order and change; *open,* in which change is expected to result from evolving family structures; and *random,* in which unstable structures are experimented with as reference points for order and change. They are able to identify characteristic aspects of family system organization for each of these types. However, noting that families do not always attain their ideals, they describe "flawed versions" of each type which they assert support a "crisis chain" (pp. 151–56). An analysis of how families of each of these types deal with reorganization postdivorce might well reveal which is most vulnerable to becoming "flawed."

Finally, Kantor and Lehr (Chapter 11) place the individual family member in the dynamic system — the actions of the individual as a "player" in the system, i.e., his/her experience of *self in relation to others*, and the *relation of others to self*. *Psychopolitics* is the term applied to this thematic area of family process, in which individuals try to cope with the demands of the institutional requirements of the family unit and its interpersonal subsystems, while at the same time attempting to protect their own rights. They identify four individual player types in family dynamics: (1) the *mover* — one who initially tries to gain access to the target, thus establishing the context for others' behavior; (2) the *opposer* — one who reacts to the mover, creating a challenge by blocking the mover's direction or intended destination; (3) the *follower* — one who supports either the mover or the opposer, thus giving others power through support; and (4) the *bystander* — one who stays out of the direct action, making no alliances with any of the three other players except, perhaps, private ones to secure his noninvolved position. As the postdivorce family members deal with their positions in the newly developing structure, these individual styles are often revealed.

What Kantor and Lehr have developed from their research is a complex means for examining the family system and its associated subsystems at a microscopic level. We turn to Salvador Minuchin for further development of family systems analysis.

Salvador Minuchin. In setting forth his schema for family therapy, Minuchin (1974, Chapter 3) conceptualizes "boundaries" as the "rules defining who participates, and how." He sees the function of boundaries to be the protection of differentiation in the system. Central to his point of view is the idea that each subsystem must be free from interference of the others. In other words, the *clarity of boundaries* becomes essential for effective family functioning.

Boundary clarity falls along a continuum from very rigid (*disengaged*) to very diffuse (*enmeshed*). Minuchin sees enmeshment and disengagement as transactional styles — preferences for a type of interaction. That is, in the disengaged pattern, the subsystem boundaries are so clearly defined that there is relatively little allowance for relating across the boundaries. On the other hand, the boundaries in the enmeshed pattern are so unclear as to allow for involvement of the members of any subsystem in the business of another. While Minuchin does not identify these extremes in style as inevitably dysfunctional, he does see them as areas for potential pathology.

Enmeshment requires surrendering autonomy, while disengagement creates lack of loyalty, belonging, and interdependence. Thus, children in the enmeshed style may find parents involving themselves in every detail of their sibling relationships and, consequently, children may never learn to handle these relationships on their own. In the disengaged style, by comparison, children may receive so little attention that they may conclude that parents don't really care about them. The impact of any stress in a subsystem in the enmeshed family reverberates in other subsystems, while in the disengaged family system only the most severe stress creates any effect across subsystem boundaries. As Minuchin illustrates it, "The parents in an enmeshed family may become tremendously upset because a child does not eat his dessert. The parents in a disengaged family may feel unconcerned about a child's hatred of school." Clear — but neither too rigid nor too diffuse — boundaries provide the most effective family system and subsystem functioning.

Three subsystems are particularly important to Minuchin — the spousal subsystem, the parental subsystem, and the sibling subsystem. The spousal subsystem, to be effective, requires complementarity and mutual accommodation. If these are present, this subsystem can foster growth in the marital partners, providing both a shelter from and a base for contact with external systems. Once again Minuchin stresses that a too protective subsystem may result in overdependency of one spouse on the other. Permeable, but clearly defined, boundaries are necessary within and between subsystems during each of the stages of separation, divorce, and remarriage.

Minuchin emphasizes the importance of husband and wife keeping the spousal subsystem boundaries clearly separated from the parental subsystem boundaries. Although children require access to parents, parents need to maintain the emotional support provided by the spousal system. The parental subsystem must remain reasonably open and flexible, enabling the children to relate within the sibling subsystem and to extrafamilial systems. Too rigid boundaries in the parental subsystem limit the development of autonomy in the offspring. Intrusion of parents into the sibling subsystem, while at times appropriate in their parental roles, may retard the development of children in dealing with peers and other nonfamily individuals.

Pauline Boss. As one of the investigators in an intensive study of the stress experienced by families who had husbands and fathers classified as "missing in action" during the Vietnam War, Pauline Boss (1975a) developed the idea of *boundary ambiguity*. This concept is important for the study of boundary maintenance in families who experience "loss and separation." She defines the term as "a state in which family members are *uncertain in their perception about who is in or out of the family and who is performing what roles and tasks within the family system.*" It is clear, then, that boundary ambiguity is related to the way families define the situation of member absence.

"Definition of the situation," one of the basic ideas in social psychological theory, is central to understanding the process of coping with stress and crisis. Boss operationalized it by measuring the degree of *psychological presence* in families where the father was physically absent. She discovered two important relationships in her empirical analysis of families of this kind: (1) high psychological father presence impaired family functioning, and (2) high psychological father presence blocked the regenerative power of the family system (Boss & Greenberg, 1984, p. 536).

In theoretical extensions of her work, Boss has applied the idea to families who experience adolescents leaving home, chronically ill members, widowhood, and divorce. She has identified two sources of boundary ambiguity. Outside the system the family may be unable to obtain the facts about the status of the missing member. For example, the family simply may have no information on the whereabouts of a runaway child or may not be able to find out the prognosis of a chronically ill member. These families might continue to focus on a missing child or cut themselves off from a terminally ill member. Inside the system the family may deny or ignore the facts. Families may cut themselves off from an alcoholic member or continue to behave as if a dead member were still present. Each of these ways of dealing with psychological presence has an impact on family functioning and on the family's reorganization process. Clearly, both are significant in postdivorce family functioning. Boundary ambiguity, therefore, is an important variable in understanding family reorganization after divorce.

Murray Bowen. Bowen's theoretical ideas focus on the emotional relationships of individuals in the family system (1976; Hall, 1981). In a genuine sense Bowen centers on the establishment and maintenance of boundaries between the individual's emotional and intellectual life and that of other individuals and subsystems in the family. Of particular interest for our purposes is his concern with the relationship between the family and the integration and differentiation of the self. Bowen concentrates on the tension between the emotional and the intellectual aspects of self development and ties this to the way the individual deals with family system.

The degree to which the individual is able to separate the emotional and the intellectual determines the *differentiation of self*. Individuals with high levels of emotional-intellectual fusion cannot separate themselves from their families of origin. The degree of differentiation has pervasive implications for the way individuals relate in their families and in the broader society. For Bowen much of this is determined in childhood by *triangulation* — the process of a third person being drawn into dyadic relationships experiencing high tension. Much of this dyadic tension, of course, is between the spouses and it is the child who is drawn into the triangle. Thus, an important boundary between the spousal and parent-child subsystem is breached. This results in the child being unable to develop the differentiation which is required for his or her own emotional and intellectual autonomy.

One of the important processes which may occur in the differentiation process is *emotional cutoff*. Individuals who cannot develop adequate differentiation may withdraw emotionally, establishing a firm, often impermeable, boundary between themselves and the other subsystems of the family. Bowen sees this process as profoundly influential in the individual's lifelong style of handling emotional relationships. While there are other aspects to Bowen's theory, we will see the relevance of these three ideas in the ways divorced spouses cope with the postdivorce family reorganization process.

Four of the theorists we have discussed — Kantor and Lehr, Minuchin, and Bowen — are identified as "structural theorists" by Okun and Rappaport (1980, Chapter 5). We have not included therapeutic theorists they label "communication theorists," such as Jackson, Satir, and Haley, since our theory addresses itself primarily to the changing structural characteristics of the family system in postdivorce reorganization.

THE FAMILY CAREER

In describing the family system we have used the term "dynamics" to refer to the specific set of interactions and transactions that might take place in the family system at any one time. However, there is another dynamic in the family system — a developmental one. Family patterns change over time as a result of a complex interplay between changing membership composition, changing life courses of family members, expectations for change originating in social norms, and changing circumstances of the physical and social environment. Both social psychologists and, more recently, family therapists have looked at this developmental change in the family, which we refer to as the "family career."

Developmental Theory

Among social psychologists, concentration on the developmental character of the family system originated in the 1940s. Our purpose here is not to trace that history, but rather to identify the key ideas which contribute to our understanding of the divorce process.[6] When social psychologists use role theory terms to illuminate the interactions and transactions of the family system, they are analyzing the family system at one point in time. Bernard Farber (1961), in attempting to capture something of the time dimension of the family, defines a family as "a set of mutually contingent careers." In effect, Farber is pointing to the fact that families bring together individuals who occupy positions, play roles, and are subject to social and group norms that continue *over time*.

To capture this dynamic change in role content of the positions over time, several new concepts have been introduced or borrowed from other theorists: *role sequence* (Deutscher, 1959) to capture the changing character of a particular role as it alters through the life course of an individual; *role cluster* (Deutscher, 1959) to identify the set of roles that a person may play at any one point in the life course; *role complex*

(Rodgers, 1962) to identify the set of reciprocal role clusters in the family system existing at any one point in the history of the system; *positional career* (Farber, 1961) to label the sequence of role clusters held by an individual in the family over time; and *family career* (Rodgers, 1962) to indicate the sequence of role complexes which make up the family history.

While the family career and all of the contingent individual positional careers are usually played out in a more or less continuous fashion, major changes occur within the family which are more disjunctive in nature. Developmental theorists have used various terms to attempt to capture these changes and their effects. Perhaps the most familiar is the term "family life cycle stage." There are problems associated with using this concept to identify significant categories of the family career. The idea of a "cycle" implies a determined and irreversible path through which all families must move, and "stage" implies a homogeneity of characteristics. Both of these are difficult to validate empirically.

Furthermore, stage identification is determined to a large extent by arbitrarily chosen criteria. If, for example, one uses the birth and development of children as a primary criterion, the changing characteristics of the adults in the family get lost in the analysis. And, of course, once the children leave home, this criterion is difficult to use to capture the long period of family life yet remaining to the spouses — to say nothing of the extended family dynamics that are a continuing aspect of family careers.

In addition, it is clear that some families skip a stage or several; the childless couple and the family in which a parent has died "prematurely" are good examples. Other families appear to repeat some of the stages, as in the case of parents who have one or more children late in their married life after having already reared a set of offspring. Such "deviations" are, in fact, quite normal and frequently observed. Suffice it to say that many different patterns can be observed in ordinary family life, and many changes occur in the role structure of families. The determination of which family cycle stages are "significant" and "typical" and the development of a categorical system to effectively analyze them have thus far escaped developmental theorists and researchers.

It is primarily for these reasons that the concept of the *family career* seems more useful. A career may take many different paths, all of which are quite normal—that is, governed by clearly understood societal norms. There is nothing predetermined in a career. Some directions may be more probable, given the previous history of individuals and of the group, but other less probable patterns are also observed. Indeed, what makes the family career concept so potentially rich in analytic insight is the recognition that the directions taken by families are very much related to their past history and to anticipated and desired goals for the future, as well as to the current family situation.

Combrinck-Graham (1985) has identified similar problems in her attempt to set out a developmental model for family systems therapists. She notes that the linear and unidirectional nature of individual developmental theories is not a very effective way of dealing with family system development. She cites the Carter and McGoldrick (1980) six-stage model of the family life cycle as having contributed importantly to the recognition that family systems developmental models require taking into account the reciprocity which takes place between subsystems in the family.

Combrinck-Graham (1985) builds on analyses by Carter and McGoldrick, Terkelson (1980) and Hoffman (1980) which analyze the "second-order change" in family system development precipitated by the individual developmental experiences of family members. She proposes a "family life spiral" model which "is a representation of the cycles of individuals in the family in relationship to the cycles of individuals in other generations. The individual life cycles may be conceptualized as the threads from which the family context is woven" (pp. 142–143). (Though stated differently, this is remarkably similar to Farber's idea of the family as a set of mutually contingent careers.)

Combrinck-Graham sees the family life spiral as oscillating between periods of strong centripetal forces and periods with strong centrifugal ones (p. 143). Thus, times in family life such as childbirth and marriage tend to pull family systems together. Adolescence, midlife, and retirement are seen as times in which individual identity and personal issues take precedence, thus pulling the family system apart. Combrinck-Graham views these oscillations as periods "for experiencing intimacy and self-actualization and for reexperiencing these at different levels of maturity and through different tasks as the individual develops in the family" (p. 144). Another way of labeling these oscillations would be to identify them as periods of stability and periods of transition.

Some theorists have felt that the best way to understand the family career is to center analysis on the characteristics of particular family career categories (stages), when families are in periods of relative stability. Others contend that more information would be provided by focusing on the periods of family change—the transitions from one set of roles to another. Because this book is concerned with the changes brought about by separation, divorce, and remarriage, it should be no surprise that the authors tend to focus more on transitions than on stable states. At the same time, however, we recognize the importance of a family's previous way of organizing for the way of it reorganizes after divorce. Two pieces of research which take this sort of developmental perspective on divorce are useful in pointing up its value.

Family Lineages

Gunhild Hagestad and her colleagues (Hagestad, 1981; Hagestad & Smyer, 1982; Hagestad, Smyer, & Stierman, 1984) have focused on the intergenerational consequences of life events. They have been exploring a methodology which attempts to trace their impact on family lineages. Hagestad explains the concept in this way:

> Neither traditional life course analysis nor a family development perspective can capture the intimate interconnections of life matrices in the family. . . . We now need to . . . recognize that people's coping abilities and available supports are influenced not only by a constellation of events but also by a *family* [emphasis added] constellation of events, affecting individuals and their significant others. For example, an older woman might become widowed at a time when her son has had a heart attack and another child is going through a divorce. . . . An experience of overload among the middle-aged is likely to be produced by factors in three or four generations: the needs of one or two generations of elderly, the needs and resources of the young, and the number of available siblings in the middle generations as well as their tangible and intangible resources. (1981, pp. 34–35)

In her study of midlife divorce Hagestad refers to the midlife group as the "bridge generation" and emphasizes the family lineage consequences of divorce within this group. She emphasizes that in the past research on the impact of divorce on dependent children has been plentiful, but has neglected to deal with the effect on grown children of their parents' divorce or with the effect on parents whose grown children divorce.

Because divorce is a "culturally unscheduled event" and thus an unstructured transition, Hagestad and Smyer see controlling it as problematic. They identify two types of "orderly" divorces and seven types of "disorderly" divorces in middle age; these exhibit varying levels of control of the process. Those who experienced orderly divorces, about two-thirds of the study sample, had either total or partial control of the process.

Those in total control divorces tended to report lengthy dissatisfaction and problems in the marriage, with an extended struggle to maintain it. "There was a final resolution that 'enough is enough!'" (Hagestad & Smyer, 1982, p. 179). These researchers also recorded frequent reports of delaying the final dissolution of the marriage because of factors such as the children. Some spouses delayed longer than others and, as a result, felt in control of the process and were most often the initiators of the break when it finally did come.

In contrast, partial control respondents usually found the spouse making the first indication of a break. Nevertheless, they reported that "if that's the way it's going to be" they would take some control of the situation. Some were "holdouts" who refused to grant divorces to spouses in order to reach terms that satisfied them. Others delayed the divorce until the spouse became involved with another individual; as a consequence, the holdouts were in a stronger bargaining position in the divorce settlement. Thus, while they had not initiated the break, they did take considerable control of the process of dissolution (Hagestad & Smyer, 1982, pp. 181–182).

The one-third of the study sample identified as having disorderly divorces exhibited a wide range of characteristics. Using three criteria — (1) sharing of daily life, (2) attachment to the spouse role, and (3) emotional investment in the spouse — a seven-category logical typology was developed. According to Hagestad and Smyer (1982, pp. 183–186), the types were:

(A) Divorced in name only — all three characteristics present.
(B) I wish it hadn't happened — all except sharing daily life present.
(C) I've got you under my skin — only emotional attachment present.

(D) The common-law arrangement — no attachment to spouse role present.
(E) Why not be roommates? — no emotional attachment present.
(F) Married status has its advantages — only attachment to the spouse role present.
(G) Business as usual — only shared daily life present.

All but types D, E, and G appeared in the study sample, chiefly, the investigators believed, because the study sample was a midlife cohort. The values about marriage and family for midlife people prevented them from engaging in these kinds of relationships. Disorderly divorcées had in common the fact that, while the divorce had occurred, one or both partners were still relating emotionally or behaviorally to the other in some fashion and, thus, had not completed the divorce process. These data provide additional insight into the *family* consequences of divorce.

Transitional Processes and the Binuclear Family

Constance Ahrons' longitudinal research on divorce in Dane County, Wisconsin, examines the consequences of divorce and remarriage for the family unit by focusing on the transitional processes.[7] Central for this research is the concept of the *binuclear family* system undergoing a process of reorganization. Ahrons notes:

> The reorganization of the nuclear family through divorce frequently results in the establishment of two households, maternal and paternal. These two interrelated households, or nuclei of the child's family of orientation, form one family system — a BINUCLEAR FAMILY SYSTEM. The centrality of each of these households will vary among postdivorce families. Some families make very distinct divisions between the child's primary and secondary homes, whereas in other families these distinctions may be blurred and both homes have primary importance. Hence, the term BINUCLEAR FAMILY indicates a family system with two nuclear households, whether or not the households have equal importance in the child's life experience. (1979, p. 500)

A transition is "a turning point, a crucial period of increased vulnerability and heightened potential within the life cycle" (Erikson, 1968,

p. 96). Ahrons sees five transitional processes occurring during marital separation: (1) individual cognition, (2) family metacognition, (3) systemic separation, (4) systemic reorganization, and (5) family redefinition (1980, p. 535). As interpersonal conflict and personal dissatisfaction increase, at least one of the marital partners begins to recognize that the source of these problems is the marital relationship itself (transition 1). The individual will then attempt a range of coping strategies. If these fail, the unsatisfactory state of the marriage becomes more generally recognized by the whole family. The family system as a whole begins to change. It is likely that there will be open discussion of the situation, thus explicitly bringing the problem into the family interactional arena (transition 2). Various sorts of solutions and the consequences of these — or the consequences of not taking any action — may be discussed. Eventually, physical separation takes place (transition 3). The system is divided into two subsystems. Even though the physical presence of one spouse is lost, the family still must take that spouse into account in various ways and he/she must take the family into account. The reorganization of the family into a *binuclear family* system begins (transition 4). Finally, as this reorganization takes place, a new definition of the family emerges (transition 5). Individuals take on new roles, and they present themselves as a family in their social structure in a new way. Ahrons sees each transition as encompassing a complex interaction of overlapping experiences.

Ahrons also identifies the issue of system boundary maintenance as central in the binuclear family. Following Minuchin's lead, she observes:

> To separate their spousal from their parental roles, divorcing spouses need to establish new rules that will redefine their continuing relationship. . . . Each parent needs to establish an independent relationship with the child: the process of continuing parent-child relationships, however, also requires that former spouses continue to be interdependent. Within this continued interdependency, new rules and behavior developed by former spouses toward one another can be expected to have repercussions for all family members. (1980, pp. 437–438)

Thus, clear boundaries between the former spousal relationship and the parental relationship must be firmly established. We will return to this issue again and again in the chapters which follow.

Stress and Crisis Theory

Developing her conceptualization of binuclear family reorganization further, Ahrons discusses the role of family stress theory.

> The process of divorce results in changes in the family system's characteristics (i.e., the rules by which family members relate), but it does not necessarily obliterate the parent-child unit. Systems theory helps describe this process of family change. Family stress theory (Burr, 1973) provides constructs for identifying and explaining the relationships between major stressors in the divorce process and their impact on the family and allows the further clarification of a model for clarifying normative family transitions that result from the divorce process. (1980a, pp. 533–534)

There has been a great deal of development in family stress theory in the few short years since Ahrons made that observation.

McCubbin and Patterson. These two theorists have extended the pioneering work of Hill (1949) on family stress, which they label the "double ABCX" model of family adjustment and adaptation (McCubbin & Patterson, 1983). They make an important distinction between a stressor and a crisis. There are many stressors in the lives of all families. A stressor is a life event or transition "which produces, or has the potential of producing, change in the family social system." A crisis "is characterized by the family's inability to restore stability and by the continuous pressure to make changes in the family structure and patterns of interaction. In other words, stress may never reach crisis proportions if the family is able to use existing resources and define the situation so as to resist systemic change and maintain family stability" (pp. 8–10).

A particular stressor (e.g., separation, divorce, and remarriage) becomes a crisis through a highly complex process. This process involves both the particular stressor and the possible pileup of other stressors, existing and new resources of both the family group and individuals, and familial perceptions of the stressors, resources, coping styles, and the crisis itself. This conceptualization deals specifically with the family's response to a particular stressor or set of stressors as a process *which takes place over time*. It fits well with the family development approach, the Hagestad family lineages idea, and with Ahrons' binuclear family notion.

Rodgers (1986) had applied the McCubbin and Patterson theory to the separation, divorce, and remarriage process, as follows. McCubbin and Patterson identify three phases to the process of coping with stress and crisis in families: *adjustment, restructuring,* and *consolidation.*[8] In the *adjustment phase*, families try to handle the stressor by avoidance, elimination, or assimilation. In the case of separation, divorce, or remarriage the strategy of avoidance does not appear to be available. These are stressors of such a magnitude that they cannot be ignored. Elimination of the stressor in the case of separation would result in reconciliation. In the case of divorce and remarriage, however, elimination also appears to be a strategy not available. The strategy of assimilation involves incorporating the stressor into the existing structure in a way that reduces the stress. While some families may be able to accomplish this, the major restructuring requirements of separation, divorce, and remarriage make this an unlikely strategy as well. Nevertheless, if the impact of prior strains and the hardships which the stressor may produce are not too great — and the existing resources and the definition and appraisal of the situation are satisfactory — the family may resist a crisis. (Hagestad's "divorced in name only" type would be this kind of family.) Their adjustment may lie somewhere between *maladjustment* and *bonadjustment* — with maladjustment, of course, leading to crisis.

When *restructuring* the family must establish new patterns of interaction which take account of the fact that the marital relationship no longer is present in the system. Here, a new element appears — *pileup* — which calls attention to the fact that other stressors and events may combine to make the crisis even deeper or to precipitate additional crises. (Pileup is equivalent to Hagestad's idea of overload.) The way these factors operate explains whether or not the family can reach a level of adaptation adequate to allow it to move on to the *consolidation* phase. If family members cannot handle the load added by pileup, if the resources are inadequate, if they cannot reach and implement mutually acceptable solutions to their situation, and/or if the maintenance of the system fails, they remain in crisis. They must continue their attempts to restructure. Or, having consumed their energy in coping, they may enter an organizational state of *exhaustion*. In this state we could expect to find the family members essentially helpless in their struggle to establish new role patterns. Outside intervention would probably be required to assist them in resuming their efforts at restructuring.

Where the restructuring process leads to an adequate level of adaptation, the family enters the phase of *consolidation*. Here the new patterns are firmly incorporated into a new structural arrangement. Refinement in the use of available resources and the further development of shared definitions and problem solutions allow them to reach a new level of maladaptation/bonadaptation which may be more or less effective than the one which existed prior to the onset of the stressor. McCubbin and Patterson use *member to family fit* and *family to community fit* to test the level of adaptation reached by the family. While they have not specified the characteristics of these criteria, we could expect to find family members again relating at an acceptable level both within the family and in their transactions in the community. If the consolidation process is not successful, the family may reenter the restructuring level or enter once more into crisis—and, quite possibly, into exhaustion.

Separation, divorce, and remarriage each may be an example of a stressor. Thus, they are not theoretically distinct. That is, the adaptation and restructuring dynamics in each stage involve the same process described by McCubbin and Patterson even though the family is experiencing a different aspect of the marital dissolution process. While we can analyze the distinctive aspects of each, we can also look at the general process of family reorganization which results from any one of them. Families that are often called "intact" must cope with stressors such as marital or family conflict. They usually do so in a reasonably effective manner. However, separation may be the response to marital stress and the family may consolidate in the separated state. When the partners divorce, the new situation will create new stress and possibly precipitate a new crisis. Successful adaptation to divorce does not mean that the family will avoid the stress resulting from the remarriage of one or both of the former spouses. Remarriage may start a new round of crisis.

Furthermore, it is possible to use this analytical approach starting with any period of the family career. Families experiencing marital disruption in the childbearing years are certainly going to face different restructuring issues than those in the midlife period. Thus, we see the dual developmental nature of dealing with stress and crisis in the process.

Figure 1, reprinted from Rodgers (1986), is a minor redrawing of McCubbin and Patterson's original paradigm (1983, Figure 2).

David Reiss. As a result of an extensive empirical study of families with schizophrenic members, David Reiss (1981) developed the idea that families who encounter stress develop their own *construction of reality* about their experience in crisis and reorganization. A *family paradigm* is created " . . . as the family's active response to extreme stress and the origins of the stressor event as well as its own efforts to restore integrity in the wake of disorganization" (p. 175). These ideas are quite similar to McCubbin and Patterson's shared definition of the situation. The concepts also carry much of the flavor of Kantor and Lehr's family themes and strategies (Reiss gives credit to Kantor and Lehr for some of his thinking). In his theory the family's construction of reality is the central element in the degree to which members are effective in developing a family paradigm to deal successfully with the process of coping with crisis and reorganization.

For Reiss the process of family disorganization develops in three stages (pp. 177–185). The *emergence of rules* represents the first family response to stress. These rules are usually verbal regulations which are set forth to handle the lack of clarity which results from the stressor, to coordinate planning of family members, and to monitor the family's response to the stressor. Sometimes this is enough for the family to regain control and return to a satisfactory level of functioning. However, if it is not, then a new stage of the *explicit family* emerges. Here there is a coalescence of the rules into more rigid controls. "All family members now become aware of their family as a working, struggling, combative, or defeated group." Finally, there is *rebellion and action*, when either the entire family or one member is perceived as the source of the problem, while the rest of the family members no longer see their contribution to it.

These stages have much in common with Ahrons' individual cognition, family metacognition, and systemic separation transitional phases. For Reiss the stages provide a means to describe how the family moves from implicit constructions of reality to increasingly explicit ones designed to explain the stressor event they are encountering. He sees the family becoming preoccupied with family process and, as the

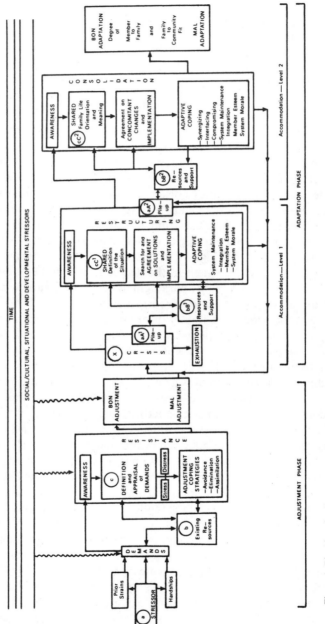

Figure 1. Binuclear family reorganization following separation/divorce/remarriage. (Modified from McCubbin and Patterson, 1983, Figure 2.)

disorganization continues, becoming process oriented. At its deepest level disorganization results in a more significant role for "outsiders." One kind of outsider, of course, may be a person who becomes involved because the crisis has affected a family member's performance at school, at work, in the extended family, or in some other social area. But another kind is actually one of the family members. Reiss suggests that during family disorganization a given family member may begin to perform in a new way in the family process. In this new role performance he or she demonstrates characteristics which in a very real sense make him or her an outsider to the other family members. It is clear that new behavior of this sort could have either positive or negative effects on the family process.

Family reorganization has three polar dimensions in Reiss' schema (p. 200). The *template for reorganization*, that is, the vehicle for a new construction of reality that enables the family to surmount the crisis, may range from one which emphasizes *recognition through experience* to one focusing on *revelation through meaning*. The first extreme emphasizes the family's reorganization through " . . . its growing experience, knowledge and understanding of the external stresses, its capacity to deal with them, the resources it can draw on from others, and the experience of other families." At the other extreme the "family's reorganization is shaped by the symbolic significance of the immediate stressor and its context." There is a strong element of the instrumental approach in the first extreme, while the second is much more expressive in nature. Templates which stress experience involve gathering facts and acquiring new skills to deal with the crisis. Revelation templates emphasize the symbolic meaning of the crisis as a way of arriving at a common understanding of it.

In the *enactment of reorganization* families may emphasize *collective action* or *individual action*. As the terms imply, members in the first see their efforts as part of the group effort, while in the second each member concentrates on his own accomplishments and understandings. Either extreme may occur in either the experience or revelation templates. Of course, the first leads to a stronger group cohesion, while the latter leads to increased isolation of members from each other.

Finally, the *resources of reorganization* may be drawn primarily from the family or from the environment. Again, either source may occur in either template. Where the family resources are emphasized " . . . the *recognizing family* learns about its own inner resources, whereas the *revelation family* becomes symbolically tied to its own past." When emphasis is on environmental reosurces " . . . the *recognizing family* experiences its enlarging grasp of critical people and events in its experiential world while the *revelation family* derives a central strength from a venerated person or meaningful event."

This elaboration of the development of common definitions of the situation during the family crisis and reorganization process provides further basis for understanding the variety of responses which may be observed in divorced families. While the theoretical approach we have set forth emphasizes the significance of shared meanings in the reorganization process, it is clear from Reiss' empirically based theory that these can be highly divergent. It is also clear that some shared definitions of the situation may be more functional than others in attaining a satisfactory level of reorganization. Indeed, some of the templates which families develop could result in further crisis and exhaustion in their efforts to recover.

THEORETICAL INTEGRATION

The key theoretical foundations for an analysis of separation, divorce, and remarriage begin with the view of these processes as normative processes involving major role transitions in the family system and its subsystems. These processes carry a kind of "nested" developmental character. That is, they have their own developmental characteristics which take place over time within the context of the individual life courses and family career period of the people involved. These multiple developmental processes are all influenced by a complex set of societal, group, and individual developmental expectations. Transitions involving stress may lead to crisis, depending upon a complex set of dynamic influences arising from these expectations, the manner in which the family and its individual members respond using the resources available, and the type of interaction patterns they adopt. The stress/crisis coping mechanisms employed by the family revolve around key functional areas in the family system. Redefinition of system and subsystem boundaries is needed to adapt to the new binuclear family structure resulting from the severing of the marital bonds. Finally, in this dynamic adjustment and adaptation process, the family and its members pursue strategies designed to regain or maintain specific themes which they value in family life.

Our interest in this highly abstract theory lies in its power to illuminate the very concrete reality of families experiencing separation, divorce, and remarriage. Understanding those realities could assist those who deal with these families to develop more effective intervention strategies. Better understanding of the process might also lead to public policies intended to make these transitions less stressful and crisis-prone. In the next chapters we turn to the reality behind the theory during the transition of marital separation.

THREE

The Separation Transition

"Nancy and Jim have separated." This drastic change in the lives of Nancy and Jim indicates that they no longer live together in one unit, as part of a couple or family. Unless we are intimate friends or family members of Nancy or Jim, however, we are not likely to know what separating means to them.

"Being separated" can connote many things. It can be seen as temporary respite — "time-out" from a highly stressed marital situation — or it can be viewed as a "trial separation" — a chance to see what living apart feels like. A "structured separation," often achieved with the help of a marriage counselor or family therapist, is a "time-out" that has specific goals and rules for the way the separated period is structured. Finally, separation can be a temporary stage prior to receiving a legal divorce, as required by law in most states, or it can be viewed as a permanent status when legal divorce is not sanctioned by religion.

Of course, Nancy and Jim may attach different meanings to the separation — he seeing it as a time-out, she seeing it as a step toward divorce. Because of the semi-closed nature of the nuclear family unit and the norms regarding privacy about personal matters, we frequently do not know the meaning of the separation for the people involved. However, what the separation means to them is critical to understanding their behavior.

PATTERNS OF COPING

McCubbin and Patterson (1983) have identified the family crisis coping process as involving two distinct phases — *adjustment* and *adaptation*. They further divide the adaptation phase into two accommodation levels. In each of these phases specific processes take place which determine the level of reorganization following a crisis. Families and individuals encounter many stressors in their individual lives and in the family career. It is only when the family is unable to adjust to a stressor that the family is seen as being in crisis. The context of the rest of their lives — other strains and hardships — and the resources that they can bring to bear to deal with the entire situation explain the way a family defines the event. On the basis of this complex appraisal process, the family brings one or more coping strategies to bear. Thus, in the McCubbin and Patterson framework the event of marital separation would be labeled a *stressor*. How the family defines and copes with the separation would determine whether it becomes a *crisis*.

One common coping strategy is *avoidance*. Acting as if "nothing has happened" may delay the necessary realignment of roles and relationships, but it is not likely to provide a stable adjustment. Denial is another common mechanism. In the case we will follow throughout this chapter, Jim has used denial of Nancy's expressions of marital dissatisfaction as a way of coping. Denial is used most frequently in the early stages of separation or during the preseparation times. As a common unconscious defense mechanism, denial permits the individual to pretend that all is well with his or her world, even in the wake of disaster.

A second strategy for dealing with stressors is to *eliminate* them. Elimination of marital separation would require reconciliation of the couple. For some couples (it is estimated that over 50 percent of separations end in reconciliation), this coping strategy reduces the stress and prevents crisis from occurring at this particular time. However, we will see that this strategy is frequently unsuccessful. While it may eliminate one set of stressors — the stressors of the separation itself — it does not eliminate the stressors of the marriage that led to the decision to separate.

Yet a third strategy described by McCubbin and Patterson is *assimilation*. Essentially this strategy implies that the family and marital systems have the resources to move relatively quickly to a stable reorganization, incorporating their new situation into the existing structure. The intense and pervasive character of the separation experience is unlikely to be handled with such ease. Although there are some couples who *appear* to move very quickly through the separation transition into legal divorce and even remarriage, it is likely that we are just not aware of the stress, conflict, and negotiation in which they have been engaging. In most cases, assimilation is a protracted process that takes place over several months, or even years, while the family adjusts to being a divorced family.

Individuals and couples may have attempted more than one of these strategies — often all of them — before finally recognizing that they face a genuine crisis. Marital separation is such a radical experience that it is unlikely that any of these initial strategies will effectively bring the family system to the level of reorganization required to meet the demands of its members. In Chapter 5 we will focus more precisely on this reorganization and consolidation process.

Building on her earlier work (1978) on methods of crisis intervention, Naomi Golan (1983) has focused on the idea of transitions as a way of understanding family and individual crisis. Golan sees two sets of tasks which must be accomplished in order to pass through transitions: material-arrangemental (instrumental) tasks and psychosocial (affective) tasks. She cites ten basic characteristics of crises:

1. They may occur episodically throughout the normal life-span, as a result either of some hazardous event (stressor) or series of such events.
2. The hazardous event places the individual (family) in a vulnerable state.
3. If the problem continues and is not resolved, a precipitating factor, during which normal adjustment processes cease to work, plunges the family into disequilibrium and active crisis.
4. The individual (family) during the development of the crisis may perceive the stressful events as *threats* to needs, autonomy, or well-being; as *losses* of a person, ability, or capacity; or as *challenges* to survival, growth, or mastery.
5. Each perception carries its own characteristic emotional reaction — threat elicits anxiety; loss brings depression, deprivation, or mourning; and challenge brings anxiety coupled with hope and expectation.
6. Crises are neither illnesses nor pathologies, but a realistic struggle with a current life situation.
7. Crises follow a series of predictable stages which can be plotted.
8. While the time may vary from a particular crisis, it is usually limited to four to six weeks.

9. During the resolution of a crisis the individual is particularly amenable to help.
10. Depending upon the availability of help and its use, the individual may emerge as more effective or as less capable of functioning adequately.

While we find Golan's list useful, we tend to see crisis as continuing for longer than four to six weeks. And we prefer Ahrons' (1980a, p. 535) five transitional processes of marital separation:

1. individual cognition,
2. family metacognition,
3. systemic separation,
4. systemic reorganization, and
5. family redefinition.

Specific types of stress accompany each of these transitions, posing a precondition for crisis in the family.

The Limits of Patterns

Separation is a multidimensional process. It is one set of transitions in the total process of moving from family organization in marriage to family reorganization in divorce and remarriage. While we will present it in an essentially linear form, with certain events occurring at each of the phases of separation which we posit, it must be emphasized that it is, in fact, somewhat more disorderly than this. Families may retreat to earlier patterns of behavior which seemed more satisfactory. Or they may seem at times to be in a circular pattern, moving from one coping style to another but making little progress. At other times overlapping or multiple styles of coping appear, perhaps because a given approach only deals with a part of the problem or because there is a desperate attempt to try anything that appears to give some promise of getting out of the current crisis. Then, too, some events occur at more than one point in the process or at different points in different families.

In addition, the separation process must be examined within the context of the social structure, family structure, personal life space, and individual life course of each family member. We will focus our attention in this chapter on the psychological and social elements of marital separation as they interact in a series of transitions that precede a legal divorce. The emotional responses of each of the spouses interact with the societal context to provide the foundation of the separation process. This process provides the basis for patterns that define future interactions and transactions of the family system. As a major shift in the career of the family involved, the separation process requires that individual family members cope with the attendant anxieties and stresses at each phase of the transition. Based on each individual's life course history, different coping strategies will be employed, which will in turn result in different patterns of divorced family functioning. The particular set of coping strategies used during the separating process will have profound effects on how the family continues to function after divorce.

THE PHASES OF SEPARATION

Preseparation

The act of physical separation is preceded by a gradual emotional separation. This movement toward separation is rarely a mutual effort. More likely it begins when one of the spouses decides that the marital distress or dissatisfaction is not likely to disappear or change. However, this recognition does not usually follow a linear course.

The idea of separation as a resolution to marital distress is a thought that crosses most married persons' minds during the course of their marriages. When that occasional thought of separation as a way of coping with marital distress becomes a more concrete, acceptable form of coping, energies become more directed toward separating than toward coping with the distress within the context of the marriage. Because, for the majority of us, separation is a drastic solution to a marital crisis, we usually exhaust our customary repertoire of coping strategies before settling on separation as the resolution.

The example that follows explores the feelings of Nancy and Jim as they experience the preseparation transition.

> *Nancy*: When Jim and I were first married I thought I could get him to communicate with me if I was very patient and understanding and asked him lots of questions. I tried doing that for a year or so, but when he wouldn't talk to me I began to get very angry. I then began to scream

and yell at him to talk to me about what he was feeling, but he just seemed to sit there and watch TV or go out and work on his car. One day I just told him that I didn't want to live with him any longer. I didn't really mean it but I didn't know what else to do. I was feeling desperate and angry. He got very upset, told me he loved me and said he would try to talk with me more. So we set up some times when we could talk, but it never seemed to go anywhere. This happened a number of times.

After David was born things seemed to be a little better but I wonder now if that was just because I was so busy taking care of him. And then, when David was about a year old, I decided to go back to work. We needed the money and, besides, I missed the outside world. Then Ellen came along. After a while—I don't know, maybe a year or two—I stopped trying to get Jim to talk to me. When I needed to talk I would call up one of my friends. Sometimes, I spent the better part of the evening on the phone.

Then I decided I needed to get out a couple of evenings a week and joined the church bowling club. From there things just happened. I met Dan and he was so easy to talk to. I started to imagine what it would be like not to be married to Jim. It was scary, mostly because of the kids, but I began to think it would be better than the way Jim and I were now living. That was about a year or so ago. I started going out more in the evenings because I dreaded staying home. One night after I came home from bowling I told Jim that I thought it would be good for both of us if we separated for a while. I hadn't planned to say it that night but I had been thinking about it for a while. Jim was surprised and upset. He said he couldn't live without me. We both cried and decided we would try to improve things. We planned some activities together, turned off the TV during dinner, and made some attempts at talking.

Although Jim really tried, I knew after a couple of weeks it wouldn't be any different. I told him that. He didn't say anything. He just went out into the garage and worked on his car. A week later I asked him to move out. I just couldn't stand it anymore. It's not that it was easy for me. I felt so guilty. Jim is a nice guy. It would be so much easier if he weren't—if he drank or something.

Jim: I didn't expect a whole lot from marriage. Nancy was a good cook, took good care of the house and then was a good mother when David was born. Things seemed to go along pretty well. Every now and then Nancy would get angry with me for not being more talkative with her but that seemed to blow over and then things were pretty much the same. I'm not a very talkative person and I don't know how to talk about

the things Nancy wants me to talk about. When she first talked about
separation I really got scared. I thought things were fine. I don't know
what I would do without Nancy. I thought if I could just calm her down
and we could do things her way for a while it would be okay. When
Nancy started going out in the evenings I was glad. I could watch TV
or work on my car and not feel like she was angry with me. That's why
it was such a shock when she told me she wanted to separate. I really
don't understand it but I hope that maybe after she lives alone for a
little while she'll change her mind.

Nancy's decision to separate from Jim was very much a one-sided
decision. She spent several years emotionally separating from Jim and
had tried several coping strategies before actually deciding on separation. Early in their marriage patience and understanding as ways of
coping with Jim's inexpressiveness were tried but had no effect. Feeling
thwarted, she became frustrated and reacted with anger. When her
anger did not bring the desired results, she withdrew from Jim emotionally as a way of coping; she was able to avoid experiencing the pain
of failing to communicate. She then tried to escape the problem by
attempting to fill her needs for companionship by going back to work
and by calling up friends. When these more traditional methods of
coping, i.e., of investing more energy in extrafamilial interests, failed
to relieve her dissatisfaction with the marriage, she considered more
drastic measures. She actually went through these patterns a number
of times before she decided that separation was the immediate solution.
Of course, Nancy could have tried other types of coping strategies.
She could have sought counseling, which might have resulted in some
change within the marriage and provided both her and Jim some
insights into their communication patterns. She could have used drugs
or alcohol as a way of escaping the problem—a common dysfunctional
approach to reducing stress. Or she could have "fallen in love" with
someone else, exposed the relationship to Jim, and thus produced an
immediate crisis. (Meeting Dan provided some fantasies about this,
but it appears that she did not permit herself to move into a full-blown
"affair.") Rather, she chose coping strategies that were familiar to
her—safer and less potentially destructive ones similar to those she had
used to face other life crises. When these strategies failed to ameliorate
the distress she sought a more extreme solution.
The preseparation period has its social structural aspects, as well

as its personal emotional characteristics. To begin with, it is clear from Nancy's account that she began in a very private way. Her early coping attempts were chiefly attempts to deal only with Jim and their relationship. Characterizing preseparation as being more private in character does not negate the very real social norms which influence both Nancy's and Jim's behavior. A lifetime of socialization about how to behave in marital and parental roles is present.

Nancy reveals the way that one social role can affect another. She mentions that, after they had a child, things went better for a while. Perhaps the decision to have the child was itself a coping device for Nancy and Jim. Many couples, in their desire to improve an ailing marital relationship, seek to bring a new, promising experience into their lives. As we shall explore in more depth later in the chapter, the developmental stage of the family and their financial resources may dictate their choice.

Certainly the fact that things went better after David's birth was partly a result of Nancy's attention being diverted to his care. David also provided daily chores and events for Jim and Nancy to share. And, of course, a new set of roles as parents provided an additional bond in their relationship. Finally, it must be recognized that Nancy needed to maintain as much as possible her self-image — and the image she presented publicly — of a good wife and mother. When she says she was "scared" especially after they had children, she is probably responding — at least in part — to the threat that separation poses to that image.

Even though there are personal dissatisfactions, public roles tend to be played as if there is nothing wrong. Relationships with kin, friends, and the several social organizations with which they carry on social transactions allow only for minimal indications of problems in marital relationships. Couples who are experiencing marital distress — even contemplating separation — continue to assume their usual relationship roles when they appear in public. It is not unusual for the separating to hear, upon announcement to acquaintances of the separation, "You looked like such a happy couple last month at the picnic!" Rituals, like holding hands when walking in public, may continue right up until actual separation. At one level, these rituals permit the couple to cope with their anxieties by appearing "normal" in public. Revelation that there is something more than the "normal" marital difficulty is a serious act which changes the character of their social relationships.

For some couples, when they are no longer able to keep up the pretense and the marital distress becomes too difficult to keep private, they withdraw from social situations rather than permit the state of their relationship to be viewed in public.

Nancy might confide to her mother or a sister something of her more than usual dissatisfaction with her relationship. But she is likely to do so in a context, at least at first, which tends to characterize it as something that is temporary. She is not likely to make it general knowledge or discuss it openly in family gatherings. Similarly, if she has a very close woman friend, she may talk to her about it as a confidence not to be shared generally in the friendship network. Meanwhile, she will continue to behave in all probability in very "normal" ways in all her spousal and maternal roles when in the presence of these people. And she is not likely to talk with them about her dissatisfactions in Jim's presence. To do any differently would put the difficulties in a much more public domain.

Moving to the other coping methods, Nancy began to make the marital difficulty potentially more public. While bowling several nights a week in a women's league can be a normal activity, it is less likely to be an activity carried on without one's spouse in a mixed sex setting. Explanations that "Jim doesn't really like to bowl" can deal with his initial absence, but consistent solitary social activity is not normative in North American marriages and raises questions in the minds of acquaintances about the marriage. She moved even more closely to making the situation public by her development of a relationship with Dan, with whom she compared Jim. While her statement does not specify the settings in which their meetings took place, it is probable that they occurred privately, in public places not usually frequented by friends and family, or in socially ambiguous circumstances, such as the local pub after an evening of bowling. It is doubtful that she brought Dan into her conversations with family and friends with any frequency, if at all. To have done so would have run the risk of making her dissatisfactions with her marriage even more clear. To have allowed her relationship with Dan to become a love affair would have almost certainly moved her marital dissatisfaction into the public domain. Thus, Nancy's choice of coping strategies are closely related to the social structural situation and the degree to which she wishes to introduce her marital problems into that social structure.

Neither Nancy nor Jim have faced the many issues that being separated will entail, but Nancy has begun the process of emotional separation. On the other hand Jim, because he did not experience the marital relationship as unsatisfactory, has not really thought much about it. For Nancy, the separation has been preceded by several years of questioning and inner turmoil — for Jim those same years were relatively stable and satisfactory.

Again we can see some social and structural reasons for Jim's relative satisfaction. From the male normative point of view of what a marriage, a husband, and a father should be, Jim was not particularly deviant. He was following the rules quite well. He was apparently responsible in his economic role, he appears to have spent most of his non-work time at home, and he apparently did not abuse either Nancy or his child. In sum, he was a "good" husband. Nancy, in fact, reveals that she feels "guilty" because of her dissatisfactions, implying that she should have nothing to complain about. Gilligan (1982) provides an interesting treatment of the differing views of women and men in moral decisions. Men, says Gilligan, tend to formulate issues in terms of justice as defined by clearly rational rules. Women, on the other hand, focus on the implications for relationships. Jim was following the norms, but Nancy was not finding the relationship very satisfactory.

Furthermore, we can be pretty sure that in this preseparation period Jim's social network was essentially unaware of any problems. Clearly, this is not because Nancy did not confront Jim with the problems of their marriage. To some extent it is because of the way that he interpreted those confrontations personally. It is also because, as Nancy controlled the public revelation of her problems, so Jim controlled his. It is less likely, for example, that he shared these problems with his father, a brother, or a close friend. To have done so would have violated masculine norms of privacy with respect to serious personal relationships. Men are expected to handle their problems by themselves. If he did mention marital problems, it is likely that he did so with a comment such as, "I don't understand her. Women! You can't live with 'em — and you can't live without 'em." In this way, he could characterize the situation as normal in the male perspective. Such comments do not detract from the general presentation of himself as a good husband and father. On the other hand, had Nancy moved to more public means of coping, Jim would have been forced to acknowledge personally and publicly the serious nature of the situation. As it was, his social structure and the way he played his social role kept a sense of "normality" associated with Nancy's complaints.

This pattern, of an asymmetrical preseparation transition based on differing perceptions of the marriage, is a common phenomenon. Marriage and family therapists accept these differential perceptions as normative and use their expertise to help a couple understand each other's perceptions. Sociologist Jesse Bernard (1972) has written extensively on "his" and "her" marriages. Because so much of social science research has utilized women as spokespersons for the family, she has astutely noted that the speciality called "Sociology of the Family" should be titled more accurately "Wives' Sociology."

As Nancy and Jim move beyond the preseparation phase into the other transitions of separation, their individual reactions during this early phase will form the basis for their later reaction. Since Nancy has experienced the emotional impact of a failing marriage relationship for several years, this preseparation transition has been more distressful for her than Jim. Jim, on the other hand, is ill-prepared and will most likely experience his greatest emotional distress during the first few months of separation. What emerges quite clearly here is the pattern of the "leaver" and the "left." Initiators, or leavers, identify their predominant emotion as guilt. They feel responsible for the breakup and for inflicting pain on the other. The assenters, or left, most usually feel anger and often want to punish the spouse. The seeds of these emotions are planted in the preseparation transition but are more likely to flower later, infusing the further transitions of separation and divorce with many conflicts originating from them.

Early Separation

Nancy: For the first week after Jim moved out I didn't feel much of anything except relief. I cleaned the house, rearranged some of the furniture, and enjoyed just being alone. When Jim came over on Saturday to pick up David and Ellen for the day it felt good to see him. We had a cup of coffee and talked about the week. As I was waving goodbye to the kids I started crying without even knowing why. And then the next few hours were awful. I didn't know what to do with myself. I kept wondering what Jim and David and Ellen were doing. I felt jealous, wishing I were with them. Finally, I called one of my friends and spent the afternoon over at her place. I just didn't want to be alone.

When Jim returned that evening to bring the kids home, they both cried when they said good-bye. It tore me apart to see them. I spent the night tossing and turning, asking myself how I could do this to my children and Jim. I wasn't even sure anymore why I was separating. I began to think again that maybe it was something about me. Maybe I just wasn't able to have a committed relationship. Jim was a good father and provider.

The next evening after work I called a divorced woman I had met bowling and spent some time talking with her. That helped a lot. She said she had some of the same feelings early on in her divorce. Jim and I got together a couple of times in the next few weeks. He wanted to know how long I thought we needed to be apart. I found myself getting really angry with him for not understanding what the problem was. Each time after he left I felt that I knew why I didn't want to live with him anymore. It just wouldn't work. But yet there were times when I felt very lonely. I missed doing some of the things we did as a couple. The weekends especially felt kind of empty.

Jim: Living back home with my mother again was terrible. She kept asking me questions about Nancy and our marriage. I just didn't know the answers. The first time I went back to the house to pick up David and Ellen I felt like crying. Nancy had moved my favorite chair into the garage! It felt like she couldn't wait to get rid of me. The place looked different and so did she. I didn't want to upset anything because she seemed pleased to see me so I didn't say anything about it. I took David and Ellen over to my parents for the day and watched the football game on TV. The kids didn't seem to know anything was any different but when I brought them back to the house Ellen wanted me to stay. I just broke down. I don't understand Nancy. I don't know what she wants. I don't know how much longer I can take this.

Here, in this early phase of separating, Nancy is experiencing the range of feelings and self-questioning that is characteristic of the leaver. Jim, on the other hand, still views the separation as Nancy's, and he is experiencing the sense of loss with no picture of life beyond. Jim has not told any of his friends at work about moving out and has not really had to encounter much of his social world, living in the protection of his parental home. Nancy has told her family and some of the people at work that she and Jim have separated "temporarily." However, to her close friends and the new friends met through bowling, she has left off the time dimension and just told them she was separated. It was much easier for her to tell friends who were not friends of the "couple."

This early state of separation plunges the individual into an intense state of emotional and social *anomie* — literally, normlessness. Old roles have disappeared, but new ones have not yet developed. Anomie comes in several forms. There may be no definition of a particular situation available. "How am I supposed to act or feel about this?" Or there may be competing or conflicting definitions of the situation which require the individual to make a choice. "Should I do (or feel) this or should I do (or feel) that?" Finally, the definition of the situation may be unclear. "What's happening? What is this all about?"

There are no clear-cut rules for the separating. Who moves out? How often should the partners continue to see each other? When should you tell family and friends? Should you tell your child's teacher? Who should attend the school conference scheduled for next week? What about the season's tickets for the concert series? These types of questions, seemingly trivial in our everyday life, plague the newly separated.

Most frequently the situation poses itself before the individuals have had the opportunity to figure out their individual or collaborative answers. A mother may decide unilaterally to attend the school conference meeting alone; father may not even find out about the meeting until several days later. He may feel left out of his child's life and react with anger at his wife for excluding him. This sequence of events could begin a long angry battle between spouses, as each tries to assert parental rights; or more positively, it could open up a discussion in which the parents could make some mutual decisions about how they will handle this type of event in the future.

In addition to the lack of rules for behaving, this period is also characterized by highly ambivalent feelings. Much of the emotional distress found in the early phases of separation is caused by the continuing bonds of attachment between former spouses. Robert Weiss (1975) explains that the persistence of these attachment bonds between spouses is responsible for the lingering feelings of loneliness and depression that characterize the separation process for most people. The fact that one may choose to leave one's mate does not negate the longing for the comfort of the other's presence or their daily interactions. This comes as quite a surprise to many who fantasized only relief and positive feelings when their mate was finally gone. They are confused and upset when their feelings vacillate between love and hate, anger and sadness, euphoria and depression. In spite of strong negative emotions, the old habitual attachment persists. Absent spouses are "missed." Partners feel "lonely."

Interpersonal situations and physical settings activate these feelings of attachment. Seeing the favorite chair or a gift received for an anniversary will evoke sad feelings. In the space of a few hours, or even less, anger may erupt over having to deal with a long neglected repair which the absent spouse should have made. A telephone call from a mutual friend may cause one to be depressed about the past social history as a "couple" that will no longer be available. Sometimes there is a feeling of emotional malaise for which there seems to be no cause. This can be followed by a feeling of euphoria arising out of a sense of autonomy because of a new accomplishment. Fixing the leaky faucet — or even negotiating with the plumber to do it at a reasonable cost — can leave a woman feeling as though she has achieved a true sense of independence.

Added to the lack of behavioral guidelines and ambivalent feelings is the ambiguity of the separation itself. Like Nancy and Jim, most spouses separate without deciding whether the separation is a temporary or permanent one. Sometimes they decide together what they will tell family and friends, but frequently there is too much anger and anxiety surrounding the separation to make joint decisions. When physical separation occurs without some discussion of the tasks of separating (family metacognition), the early separation phase is more likely to be a time of potential crisis for the family.

It is not only that there are few clear role definitions for separated people, but also that separated individuals must decide whether to continue to treat the separated situation as temporary or to begin to act as if the relationship has ended. Norms about fidelity in marriage are still quite powerful, despite the prevalence of extramarital affairs. Establishing any kind of relationship with a new partner, no matter how "platonic," invokes those norms. From role theory we know that the less familiar we are with the expectations of a new role, the more difficult the transition to that role will be (Burr, 1973). The role of the newly separated person, although experienced currently by large numbers of people in our society, is still uncharted. When we add the lack of adequate role expectations to the ambiguity of the family status (i.e., a temporary "time-out" or a movement toward divorce), what results is a living situation lacking in structure or definition. Very few of us have the tolerance necessary to be comfortable with that level of disorganization.

This combination of emotional ambivalence and social ambiguity poses a real condition of *crisis* for both the individual and the family system. In this early stage of the separation transition roles are unclear, the status of the family is undefined, and the relationship between family and community is tentative. This places the family in a highly vulnerable state. Whenever old ways of feeling or doing things no longer work, new patterns are called for. But until these new patterns are established, events, rather than individuals, are in control. There is a sense of powerlessness — of inability to manage even the most routine activities. It is quite common for both the adults and children in families during this transition to report that they are unable to concentrate at work or school, unable to get the simplest daily chores completed, and unable to manage many of their social interactions. But such daily requirements for living cannot be avoided.

From the demanding newborn to the seemingly insatiable adolescent, children have to be fed. In most families the time-consuming tasks of shopping, cooking, cleaning-up, etc., become routinized to a high degree. Change in family structure precipitated by separation shatters this routine, with the habitual ways of handling daily requirements suddenly requiring conscious attention. Perhaps one of the basic reasons for the crisis-prone nature of marital separation is the pervasiveness of the fact that even the most routine activities suddenly require thinking and decision-making. What was effortless requires effort.

In separation, the responsibility for caring for the children becomes transformed into issues of custody and visitation. This is a topic which we will be examining in depth in the Chapter 7. Some aspects of these issues, however, need to be recognized here. Since the primary obligation for child-care is almost always the mother's, and since custody arrangements take time to work out, she is likely to feel the early stress. She must now reallocate her time and energy over a broader range — or she must engage in decisions around the reallocation of these tasks, which itself takes time and energy. Visits to the pediatrician or the dentist with children take valuable time. Illnesses, even common childhood ailments, become complex organizational problems and can precipitate a crisis. Even when joint or shared custody arrangements are developed informally early in separation, fathers usually have less responsibility for health and nutritional needs.

As illustrated in the case of Nancy and Jim, both partners find themselves having to develop new patterns. The rituals around dinnertime are important in most families; in families with young children the disruption in eating schedules and patterns is often very disturbing. With older children, reallocation of family responsibilities carries all the attendant difficulties that turning such duties over to novices entails. Older children usually are called upon to assume more responsibility, both for household tasks and for care of younger siblings. It is not infrequent for the oldest child — particularly if that child is male — to be assigned many of the tasks that were handled by father, especially during the early phases of separation. Children may be left home alone for the first time or for longer periods of time than they were accustomed to in the married family.

The departure of any family member, as when an older child moves out of the family home, always requires reorganization of the division of labor in the family. In this developmental period the process of reorganization involves greater complexity. Working out these responsibilities by two parents living in separate households involves much more coordination and explicit contracting than families are accustomed to. When the possibility of reconciliation is present, reorganization of responsibilities takes on a tentative character. Under any circumstance, separated families approach the restructuring of the division of labor in a tentative, trial and error fashion.

There are immediate tasks which demand attention. These range from the mundane to the highly complex. Trash must be disposed of, houses must be cleaned, clothing laundered, dishes washed, meals prepared, pets cared for — the list goes on and on. Handling this myriad of tasks in the separated family requires conscious decision-making. The realization that the gutters need cleaning or that the furnace needs new filters before being turned on in the fall precipitates the recognition that this was something "your father always did." *How* it was done may be a mystery to the other members of the family.

The need for economic resources continues. Who provides those resources and at what level cannot wait for the slow process of legal arrangements. Groceries must be bought, clothing purchased, and bills paid. The father, usually the chief "breadwinner," encounters the reality of a dual set of expenses — his personal ones, which are considerably expanded, and those related to his wife and children. Sole breadwinner or not, societal norms and expectations of the family place continued responsibility upon him. The gainfully employed mother who has the capability of assuming the sole support of herself and her children is the exception in North American society. Except in unusual circumstances she will be faced with a lower standard of living (Weitzman, 1985).

The development of a mutually satisfactory arrangement in the area of money will take some period of time. These arrangements are closely bound up with the beginning stages of the division of property. The out-of-home parent will need to furnish and equip new quarters with a place for children. Some items of property are clearly "his" or "hers," but more of them are "theirs." "Theirs" in this developmental stage is not merely a combination of his and hers but also includes property being used by the children. The question of the division of the economic goods will also be confounded with the issue of custody. While a childless or midlife couple may argue over who keeps the television or the washing machine, when there are children these household goods are used by the children as well.

Not all families will experience crisis at this stage. Some will move quickly toward defining the situation by deciding the separation is permanent and will start to reorganize. Some will have adequate support systems to handle some of the everyday overload. Family and friends may help out, but the strongest support may come from a new relationship (Hetherington et al., 1979; McLanahan et al., 1981). However, for families without adequate means of coping, crisis does occur. In these families, an individual parent or child may develop serious physical or emotional problems. A parent may start drinking heavily, an adolescent may abuse drugs or get pregnant, or an overtaxed parent may lose control and resort to child abuse. Unfortunately, these dysfunctional coping strategies are common in American society as a reaction to stress.

Mid-Separation

Nancy: I just couldn't seem to manage it all — the marketing, the car, the cleaning, getting the kids up and dressed and off to school before work, having to pick them up on the way home. That was the worst part — after work. Ellen always seemed to be cranky, wanting me to play with her as soon as we got home. I didn't realize how much Jim really did. It wasn't like he did *all* these things, but he used to pick Ellen up from the sitter's and play with the kids while I got dinner and often he would clean up after dinner, while I helped the kids get ready for bed. And, of course, he was there on the evenings I went out.

When I realized I didn't have the money to hire a babysitter to go out in the evenings, I asked Jim to give me more money. He really got angry, said he didn't want to live with his mother anymore and would need more money himself. We then made a new schedule and Jim came over a couple of evenings each week to take care of the kids while I went out. I didn't like coming home with Jim there. It was uncomfortable for both of us. So Jim started picking Ellen and David up two days a week from school, but he still had to come home to put them to bed and stay until I got home.

Then Jim called me one morning when I had already made plans to have a drink with a friend after work and told me he couldn't pick up the kids. No reason, except something came up. I really blew. It wasn't fair that he could just decide on a whim not to pick Ellen and David up! What would happen if I did the same thing?

In the middle of all that my sister found out that she had a tumor that might be malignant. It was all just too much. Jim said he wanted some of the furniture to set up his own place, couldn't give me any more money, and wanted to have the kids stay overnight with him some nights. We got together to divide up some of the furniture but we ended up being too upset to do it. I found myself crying and telling Jim how hard it was to manage everything and I don't exactly know how it happened but we decided to get back together.

The first couple of weeks were really nice. We went out to dinner a couple of times and Jim did a lot of stuff around the house but then it just all went sour again. Jim seemed to go back to his old ways and the times together seemed pretty much the same. We didn't have anything to say to each other; Jim didn't initiate anything. I realized I was the one who made all the decisions and he just went along with everything. One night I just exploded and Jim walked out, saying he was sick and tired of me not liking anything he did.

Jim: I hated living at my mother's. And Nancy seemed to expect me to do more and more. Babysitting with the kids when she went out. She didn't even tell me where or when she'd be back. I was just supposed to be there. The place felt strange too. One night Nancy even got angry because I had fallen asleep on the bed. And she expects me to give her all the money, too.

My God, she has the house, the furniture and David and Ellen. What do I have? She says I have my freedom to do whatever I want without any responsibilities. That's not really true. I went to the old bar I used to go to with the guys on Friday nights but it felt strange. I've always been quiet and have trouble being able to make small talk in that type of situation.

About the third time I was there, though, I met a woman and we just started talking. Her brother had been separated recently and she really understood what I was going through. I met her again there the following week and she asked me if I wanted to go to a movie the next night. I was supposed to pick up the kids but decided Nancy always had her way and I could change nights if I wanted to. Boy, did she get angry about that. But I had a nice night with Peggy. It felt strange to be with someone else but it was nice to have someone who seemed to like being with me.

That's when I decided to get my own place. Trying to decide on who gets what piece of furniture was terrible. I felt like I should get some things but it was so awful to think about tearing up the house. And it was the first time I really saw Nancy upset about the way things were. She was the one who suggested we get back together. I felt tremendous relief and tried to do whatever it was she wanted me to do. But it all fell apart again. Only this time I was really angry. She wants everything to be her way.

Characteristic of this mid-separation period is the impact of the hard realities of separation. As in early separation the emotional distress is still felt. In this period, however, it is compounded by the daily management tasks of living in two separate households. The beginning attempts at reorganization often reveal the importance of the absent spouse. The system is now faced with a deficit in structure. An individual who has occupied a position in the system with attendant role responsibilities has left the system. Most role performance is habitual in nature, with little thought required by the actors occupying the position. When these habitual ways of interacting are disrupted by the absence of an actor, thought is required to realign the relationships. This process of realignment passes through a series of transitional periods in which there is much testing and experimentation. As we have seen in both Nancy and Jim's account of this period, their attempts to work out child-care arrangements produce anger and conflict. Nancy is feeling the stress of trying to reorganize her life in a one-parent household and finds the tasks too many for her to handle. She then revises her expectations of Jim, only to find out that he is not going to meet her needs. Their competing needs as they try to reorganize their lives is a persistent theme in this period of adjustment.

Given the amount of role overload experienced today by two-parent families in which both parents are employed outside the home, it is no surprise that in separation the tasks are overwhelming for one parent. Research on the effects of marital disruption on children has indicated that role overload for separated mothers is a major stress which frequently results in temporary emotional distress in children (Hetherington et al., 1978, 1979). During this time of adjustment it is often difficult, if not impossible, for parents to divert their attention from their own immediate needs to the emotional needs of the children. It consumes almost total energy to "survive" the day — to deal with the immediate tasks of daily living — and little energy is available for meeting the emotional needs of children.

Nancy's account of this period provides a picture of the overload she feels. Tasks handled by two parents now have to be handled by each separately. Often in this period the sharing of child-care has not been fully worked out, primarily because the needs have not been thoroughly identified until this mid-separation period. As Nancy notes: "I didn't know how much Jim really did." This admission is often difficult for a spouse to make; there is often too much at stake in needing to see the other as "all bad." Blaming the other spouse for the marital failures, painting a picture of the other spouse as inadequate, immature, or selfish, is a common defense against feeling ambivalent. It provides a mechanism with which they can convert their anxieties into "other directed" anger. They can avoid questioning their own feelings and behavior, thereby protecting their own rather precarious level of self-esteem.

Out-of-home fathers find it very difficult to share in the child-care responsibilities when they have neither the facilities nor the skills necessary to handle them appropriately. If they have not shared in the cooking responsibilities in the married family it becomes very difficult to know how to care for the children during their visits. And even if they have had some responsibility for meal preparation they are likely to be living in very small quarters without adequate kitchen supplies to prepare meals. It is not uncommon on the weekend to see tables of fathers and children at local fast-food establishments. But the Saturday lunch at Burger King during the weekend visitation is hardly comparable to the daily requirements for breakfast, lunch and dinner. Mothers also can be resentful of fathers "who get to take the children out for good times" while they bear the burden of the daily responsibilities.

If the child becomes ill during the visitation, Dad is likely to take the child home for Mom to care for. During longer visitations, fathers find themselves facing their children's nutritional and health needs, perhaps for the first time, as a basic responsibility. It is one thing to handle the meals and medical needs for oneself; it is quite another to develop patterns for meeting the needs of one or more children for several days.

Dealing with the health and nutritional needs of the children during separation requires a total restructuring of tasks; this often requires additional support outside of the parents. These needs are so omnipresent that, while an occasional call to a grandparent, other relative, or neighbors may provide relief of an episodic nature, it is difficult to incorporate such assistance into a regular organizational pattern. Some child-care arrangements may routinely involve one or more meals and care during minor bouts of illness. The fact remains that this is not easily delegated outside the family structure. Although dual-worker married families require these supportive services, a separated family usually needs to increase its dependency on them, even while its financial resources are shrinking.

In our earlier discussion of coping and crisis, we said that there were two phases in coping strategies for families in crisis. In the first level of accommodation, members of the family must begin the process of defining the situation in the context of the other stresses they are experiencing and in terms of the resources and sources of support upon which they may draw. Having failed to avoid, eliminate, or assimilate the stressor of separation, they must now develop a shared definition of their situation which will enable them to address many issues. In this first phase of accommodation this definition is likely to be focused rather narrowly on the means for immediate survival. "Things aren't going to change right away so we have to decide how to deal with today." Immediate ways of dealing with the most urgent pressures of economic requirements, daily schedules, emotional needs, social contacts, and the like become the focus of this early activity. Although there must eventually be some agreement on handling these demands, many spouses go through prolonged periods of conflict while attempting to resolve these issues. Cooperating in the midst of separating emotionally is a confusing and overwhelming task. As we shall see in Chapter 5, forming a coparenting relationship is one of the most difficult tasks divorced spouses face.

Agreements in mid-separation are for the most part tentative and experimental. Frequently, relatives, friends, and community support services are sought out for assistance with immediate problems. The degree to which such resources are available, of course, has much to do with how effective such initial solutions are. Much effort will be expended during this time in trying to achieve some level of integration into the system. Additional energy is invested in supporting individuals as they struggle with their own self-esteem and in the more general aspect of system morale.

In addition, the presence of other stressors, or the introduction of new ones, will have an impact. It is clear from Nancy's account that she is feeling overwhelmed. Her sister's illness pushes her to the point of crisis — a point where she no longer feels able to cope. In their studies of other kinds of family stress, McCubbin and Patterson (1983) point to the phenomenon of "pileup" as critical in the family system's coping with crisis. If there is illness, unexpected expense, a dependent parent, difficulty at school or work — any of these draw on the limited coping resources of the system. The overall character of the period might be compared to fighting a series of brush fires. Just when things seem to be under control, a new problem arises. Already stretched resources are called upon to deal with this new issue. The depletion of these resources may launch the system into a new cycle of crisis. On the other hand, if resources are adequate, the system may reach a level of reasonable restructuring and be able to move forward to the second phase of coping.

For Nancy, reconciling with Jim was her way of coping with the pileup of stress in her life. For many individuals in the early and mid-separation transitions, the most available resource — and sometimes the only known resource — is the spouse. They have not yet reorganized their lives sufficiently to develop other resources. For some, parents and siblings are available when the stress is too great to handle; but, as in Nancy's case, there may be other family needs which have priority in the system at that time. If extended family is not available, or a new partner is not part of the picture, then the separated spouse becomes the most reasonable source of support (Hetherington et al., 1979).

As we noted in the earlier transition, people use a great variety of coping strategies to deal with crisis or impending crisis. Nancy chose a relatively common one, and also one that was not dysfunctional. She could have collapsed either emotionally or physically, could have lost her job, or resorted to alcohol, drugs, or promiscuity to escape the feelings of stress. All of these strategies of coping could have eventually created additional stress and produced a more severe, debilitating crisis in the family. So her choice of reconciling was a way of reducing the stress temporarily while she regained her equilibrium. For Nancy and Jim, the reconciliation was brief, with a couple of weeks of a "honeymoon" stage, followed by the return of the marital distress. It is important to note that Nancy and Jim had not done anything to deal constructively with the issues underlying their communication patterns. It was inevitable that these patterns of relating would persist once the immediate distress of the crisis was averted.

But the reconciliation did move them further along in their transition toward divorce. For many spouses there is a need to "try once again" after being apart for a while. As we noted in the early part of the chapter, attachment for the separated spouse — regardless of the quality of the relationship — persists over time. The daily stresses of adjusting to living separately only compound the situation, thus highlighting the positive aspects of the marriage and making it appear more acceptable. For many couples children's pleas for "daddy to come home" may be more guilt-producing or painful than a spouse can cope with, and an attempt to put the family back together again will be tried.

Although most spouses consider reconciliation when the stresses of separation become too difficult, many will not reach the point of actually reuniting. Reconciliation may seem even more disorganizing to one of them than continuing to deal with the process of separation. But, as in the case of Nancy and Jim, a brief reconciliation which occurs when coping capacities are drained may actually make the next step in the reorganization process somewhat easier. It can be a way of resolving the ambivalence by convincing themselves that the marriage is indeed worse than the separation.

For many couples reconciliation is not a mutual decision; rather, it is a decision made by one spouse out of guilt at seeing the other spouse not coping very effectively. Or, as in the case of Nancy, the leaving spouse may doubt his or her decision and ability to handle living alone. In some instances, reconciliation initiated by a guilty spouse can increase the stress of the other and retard their reorganizing into a separate household. False hope is then generated around the meaning of the reconciliation, and they may cease trying to cope with a separation not of their choosing.

For other couples, separation and reconciliation form a circular repetitive pattern that may continue for years. The stress in families during these intermittent periods of separation and reconciliation resembles the stress experienced by wives of military personnel missing in action and by corporate wives (Boss, 1977, 1980a). Like these families, the family in separation is in a state of flux, and family members may be in doubt about new family roles and boundaries. In the most common divorced family form, mother and children remain as one unit, while father moves out and functions as a separate unit. The mother-headed household faces a dilemma: Should it reorganize and fill roles enacted by father, or should it maintain his psychological presence in the system by not reorganizing?

When there are a series of reconciliations followed by separations it is difficult to decide what to do. If the mother/child(ren) unit tries to reassign roles, the father's return will be met with resistance. If, on the other hand, they deal with father as psychologically present, they perpetuate family disequilibrium and stress. This cycle produces the state of "family boundary ambiguity" identified by Boss, which we discussed in Chapter 2. This keeps the family in a highly vulnerable state for crisis. The children face a difficult and very stressful transition if the family remains in this state of disequilibrium created by the father's intermittent exit and return. We have very little available information on the frequency and duration of reconciliations, although we do know that it is a common pattern between separating spouses. We also do not know how many of these reconciliations are permanent and do not lead eventually to divorce.

Late Separation

> *Nancy*: It was my friend Sally's suggestion that I go to see a lawyer. She said I had better find out what my rights were and get some things straightened out. It was such a final feeling. The lawyer asked me about lots of things that I hadn't even thought about. I had to make a budget and decide on what things I wanted. I wasn't quite ready to do all that yet but I needed to have more money. And Jim had his own place and

wanted David and Ellen to spend a night or two there during the week but not every weekend. I don't know. Ellen is only eight and I'm not sure she can handle not sleeping in her own bed every night. She has been having bad dreams and wetting her bed sometimes, and she seems to be crying more easily now too. Jim doesn't have a separate room for the kids but he has a few pieces of furniture from the house and then a couple of things his mother gave him. And then there's this woman he's seeing. I don't think the kids can handle that yet. But Jim is really demanding it and my lawyer says I should do it.

I have a new job too. Although it pays more money and I like it, it takes more of my time. Other things are happening too. My mom took care of the kids last weekend while I went camping with Sally and some of her friends. It was really a strange experience. They were all single. I didn't seem to fit very well. Everyone seemed so relaxed but I found myself not knowing what to say. I'm usually pretty relaxed in social situations but I just felt out of place there. Sally said it would get more comfortable after I got used to going out again. And Dan, the guy I met at the bowling club, has come over for dinner a couple of times. It's been nice but I'm not ready to get involved with anyone right now. It's nice for David too, though, to have a man around.

Jim: I really don't like living in such a small apartment with no place to work on my car. But I don't stay home much. Most of the time I eat at my mother's and I have been eating at Peggy's some too. It's hard when the kids come over. We play together but Ellen has trouble going to sleep and cries a lot. My lawyer has asked me a lot of questions about how often I want to see the kids and how much money I need to live on. I'm not really sure about it all but I know I need more money than Nancy says I do. Nancy seems really unreasonable about David and Ellen coming over when Peggy is here. She's really helpful to me around the kids and I don't like being alone. But a divorce seems so final.

As the case of Nancy and Jim illustrates, this late separation period is a time when the family begins to reorganize after some of their needs as a separated family become more known. Gradually old patterns give way to new ones. In terms of the five major transitions of moving from a nuclear to a binuclear family presented in the introduction, *systemic separation* actually begins to occur at this time. While in the earlier phases there may have been confusion about how to feel or what to do, this begins to happen less frequently in the late separation period. Invoking the memory of the absent spouse or frequently getting in touch with the spouse for help or advice is replaced by addressing the situation with a new approach. All of these new approaches are not satisfactory, of course. Again, this is a time of much trial and error, but also of identifying equally or even more satisfactory ways of meeting a particular need.

Individuals who have been used to meals with a spouse as being a time for discussing the day's events and for making major or minor decisions may find these times especially lonely. If meals were a social event, as well as a nutritional one — as they usually are — then stress around preparing and eating alone is highly likely. "Appetites" in North American culture are highly infused with social meanings. Redefining the meaning of meals is a significant reorganizational task for nutritional reasons, but also for emotional ones. Jim found mealtimes to be lonely, and he coped with that by going to his mother's or Peggy's, rather than attempting to develop some mealtime rituals for himself. Nancy has the children to prepare meals for most of the time, which provides her with some structure during the evening meal hours. For employed women with children, the evening meal may not change significantly after separation. It is usually an important social time when mother and children exchange the events of the day. But for noncustodial fathers, who have been accustomed to a family dinnertime, the evening meal can be very lonely and signal that the family is really gone.

The power struggles of the marriage are likely to become even more exaggerated in separation and divorce. Especially around matters dealing with children, the decisions are often so loaded with conflict that the power struggle will continue with little or no resolution. All families have rules related to children's social activities and general behavior. They are not always clear; nor are families always aware of who is primarily responsible for a particular standard. In separation children are quick to sense those areas in which parents do not agree or are indifferent about a previously enforced standard. The statement, "Dad doesn't make us do that when we're at his place," may precipitate a major conflict. Again, more than the specific issue is involved. The more significant issue to separated parents may be the apparent undermining of their authority with the children.

The conflict, fueled by the normal anger which attends separation, is likely to extend into areas of the relationship where other resentments reside. Once again, however, such events may lead to clarification of the authority structure of the separated family. While families have power struggles in all periods of their careers, the interdependency of parents and their parental rights make decision-making, power, and authority issues much more complex during childrearing than during any other family career period.

Meanwhile, reassessment of the economic condition of the family proceeds. Goods, services, and activities which were assumed to be required or desirable are reexamined. Priorities are established and, inevitably, some economies are introduced. Nancy begins to feel economic pressures when she needs to hire babysitters to spend an evening out. Jim feels the financial stress when he makes plans to leave his mother's and establish his own home. Supporting two households with the same income that previously supported one brings the economic realities into sharp focus.

For most separating families, separation does require a change in lifestyle: children's music lessons may have to be suspended, a weekly trip to the hair stylist relinquished, and/or new carpeting for the living room postponed in the light of the new circumstances. Any unanticipated expense represents a potential crisis in the financial structure. Knowledge about the economic behavior of either spouse can be the focus of feelings of "extravagance" or "lack of concern" on the part of that individual. The seeds of conflict about money are already present in the soil, awaiting only the proper conditions for germination. In a highly consumer-oriented society, these seeds will not lie dormant for long.

At the same time, the absent family member is facing his or her own set of challenges. In some ways, this can be even more stress-producing. Without the luxury of several family members upon whom to call for assistance, the services heretofore taken for granted may be overwhelming. A missing button on a favorite jacket, discovered while dressing for an important appointment, can represent a genuine crisis.

One of the authors has had occasion to meet with a group of separated and divorced men around the topic of "surviving singleness." Most of the issues discussed were not oriented towards major matters of emotional well-being or the development of new relationships with friends or potential new partners. Rather, these men related episode upon episode of difficulties with meeting the basic needs of day-to-day living. Their deficit in these skills was powerful evidence of the dependence that family members have upon one another — much of it gender related. Expressions of confusion, indecision, frustration, and anger seasoned each anecdote told. Fervent emotions of genuine triumph accompanied stories of conquering the process of ironing a shirt or preparing a favorite dish. Chagrin at failures to master apparently elementary skills was frequently heard. Empathic comments often were interjected as a participant told of having to call his spouse to ask for assistance. Occasional applause followed the narration of an accomplishment achieved "in spite of" a former partner's unavailability.

If the relationships are somewhat amicable in the earlier phases, it is not uncommon for the "out of home" father to return periodically to continue doing some of the tasks he has always done. In exchange for these services his wife might offer him a meal, let him use the washing machine, or even continue to do his weekly wash. But in this later phase this sharing of tasks is more difficult to continue. Each has started the process of reorganizing into a separate lifestyle, and the "togetherness" that the sharing of tasks represents does not fit. One or the other of the two may have a new partner who objects; the sharing may begin to feel too inequitable or too intrusive; the beginning of the adversarial process of legal divorce may result in too much conflict.

As each individual takes on new tasks not performed before, new skills must be developed. It does not take long to learn that all of this cannot be done by one single family member assuming all of the vacated responsibilities. The established fabric of interdependency must be unraveled, at least partially, and rewoven. Once more the process is to some extent one of trial and error—and, frequently, of success! Individuals discover unknown abilities and new satisfactions in accomplishments at activities never before attempted. Family members' repertoires may be substantially expanded during the process of family reorganization of the division of labor.

Finally, transactional relationships with other social groups in the community require reordering upon separation. This begins in the earlier phases but does not really root until this later phase of separation. The changes required range from such simple things as filing change of address cards with the post office and businesses to dealing with school and governmental officials, establishing independent credit records with businesses, and so on.

These kinds of reorganizational tasks are stressful for most separating couples. They signal the reality and finality of the separation. It is not unusual for individuals to make lists of all the tasks that need to be done — only to postpone most of them until an immediate situation arises requiring that a task be tackled. A woman may go to her usual department store and want to charge a purchase only to find out that the charge account has been closed by her husband. Or a man may put off giving the post office his change of address as a way of continuing to "stop by the house" every couple of days. His wife may then open a piece of mail that he did not want her to know about, which will then precipitate an argument, followed by his issuing a change of address. But there are always those pieces of mail addressed to "Mr. and Mrs. X." Who receives them after a change of address may be up to the mail carrier and show little consistency, often leading to arguments about who has the rights to the "family" mail.

We have said that divorce is a reorganization not only of the nuclear family but also of the extended family and friendships. The networks of family and friends are affected by the separation but they also have an effect on the separating family. Given the "couple" orientation of our society, old friendship networks are usually focused around the marital pair. Some of these friends may attempt to continue to involve the separated persons in their social network. The issue of which one of the separated spouses to invite is a frequently expressed concern. The decision involves an interesting interplay of individual feelings and societal norms. Friends are concerned about hurting one of the spouses' feelings by excluding them, yet it is not socially appropriate to invite them both. Occasionally friends will try to alternate invitations or will invite both, hoping the spouses themselves will decide which one will attend. After the initial early invitations, the separated person is likely to be included less frequently or may begin to decline the invitations — probably to the mutual relief of all.

Including a recently separated person in a "coupled" dinner party of old friends may feel awkward for all. Inevitably conversations invoking some of the separated couple's history result in embarrassing situations. One often hears estranged spouses expressing the sentiment that it is in such times that you learn "who your *real* friends are." Of course, one partner's "real friend" in such cases is the other's "traitor." This is one more situation in which the competing needs of the spouses result in loss for one or the other.

This is a time when the separating need the support of friends, yet it is also the time that such situations may simply be too difficult for everyone. The "breakdown" of a friend's marriage can threaten one's perception of one's own marriage. It is a clear statement that marriages may not last forever. Although most of us know intellectually that our marriage has a 50-50 chance of surviving until the death of one partner, we tend not to accept that fact on an affective level. It is similar to learning about the death of a friend or even a public figure in our age range. The possibility of our own premature death, while real enough, tends to be emotionally rejected.

A second factor making it difficult to support separated friends is similar to "guilt by association." Some mates feel very threatened when their spouse maintains a friendship with a separated person. It is as if the spouse will learn some things that the other does not want him or her to, i.e., that surviving independently is possible. Indeed, it has been reported that "divorce runs in some friendship networks." Without adequate data we do not know whether there is some foundation to this perceived threat. It is possible, of course, that the married learn from the separating that it is possible to survive separation, which may give them the courage necessary to leave a bad marriage. While the threat may be one more imagined than real, the presence of such an idea supports the fact that friends do have difficulty in maintaining relationships with separating partners.

On the other hand, friends of one or the other of the separated spouses may make an effort to include them in new sets of acquaintances where the old history is less powerful and a new one can be created. Invitations to dinner or to a party may be extended. Another single guest may be invited to "balance" the guest list. Or the individual may be invited without such a provision. To the degree that the separated can begin to take some initiative on their own, they may start building new friendship networks which have no history at all with the marriage relationship. The longer the marriage the more difficult this process appears to be, simply because stable established networks have difficulty incorporating new members — especially unattached ones.

It is out of this loss of friends, however, that the impetus for making new friends and developing new friendship networks may arise. A wife whose friendship structure focused chiefly on the business associates of her husband may find a new world of close relationships available. She may feel freed from the burden that comes with friendships tied to the success of her husband's career. She may also find much greater satisfaction in the friendships founded on her own than those established through her husband. Husbands experience similar new relationships developed in a context not involving their spouse as a necessary ingredient. The development of such friendship networks, of course, may not come easily. Many social situations are based on assumptions of having a spouse or partner.

Relationships with extended family also undergo change during this time. Not only are the separated unsure about how they should relate to in-laws, but the in-law family network is also confused. Except in the case of the most amicable separation there tends to be side-taking. No-fault divorce legislation makes accusation of fault unnecessary in the legal process. However, it does not negate the psychological need to find fault or place blame somewhere for the failed marriage.

It is also quite common and understandable that, during the course of the failing marriage and the separation, many individuals turn to their families to share their feelings. If "secrets" or "stories" about the bad deeds of the other spouse are shared with family, it is then difficult for those family members not to take sides. Usually they only know one person's account of the episode or story which biases them. In addition, for many families, loyality is an important value. As with friends, it is then difficult to continue to relate to both spouses once separation has occurred. Most of the relationships tend to continue along blood lines, and the relationships with in-laws are less likely to continue. This severing of relationships with in-laws can be very traumatic for all concerned.

A note needs to be made here about the impact of the legal system on the separation process. The separating spouses may interact with the legal system any time from preseparation through late separation. But when they do, it can alter the separation process considerably. Much will depend, however, on which attorney and which method of dispute resolution the separating spouses choose. Although nearly all states now have no-fault legislation, the process of reaching an agreement on financial and custody issues is still usually resolved in an adversarial process. When the adversarial process interacts with the other processes of separating, it can increase the distress by adding an additional stressor to an already burdened system. It can cause the separating partners to cease communicating with each other and to continue their negotiations through their lawyers. In high conflict relationships this may be beneficial and even speed up the separation process. In other cases it can be detrimental, creating even more anger and conflict than was already present in the system. In Chapter 5 we will explore in more depth the legal aspects of divorce and custody.

A major theme for families with young or adolescent children experiencing marital separation might well be characterized as the need to create a sense of family for all members in a society which continues to define the nuclear family as the norm. Much effort will undoubtedly go towards reviewing the family values and the values that each individual holds, which are equally valid in a binuclear family. Marital disruption may place in question a number of central values which were tied to the continuation of the marriage. The task, of course, becomes to reinterpret those values so that they may continue to exist in the value framework of individuals and the family as a whole even though the marriage is ending. Children, as well as spouses, need considerable time to redefine their understanding of the place of marriage, as well as other central life values, in the face of a disrupted marital relationship. Achieving this redefinition of meaning in the face of the society's widespread nuclear family value structure is no small task.

FOUR

Family Career Implications of the Separation Transition

Family development theory has been effective in developing a framework for understanding the dynamics of family life. However, the developmental theoretical approach has not paid a great deal of attention to the impact of marital disruption in separation and divorce. Rodgers has observed, "Like cohabitation, divorce is an embarrassment to a conceptual approach which emphasizes the centrality of the nuclear family unit progressing from formation at marriage to dissolution in death of one of the partners. Remarriage, of course, only further complicates matters, especially if one or both partners bring dependent children to the new union" (1986, p. 242). Important insights into the separation process are gained by taking a family developmental perspective, however. By concentrating on a particular period of the family career, it is possible to highlight those aspects of the family which are most likely to require reorganization. The following discussion looks at the key aspects of the separation experience in selected family career periods.

CHILDLESS COUPLES IN EARLY MARRIAGE

Perhaps this period of the family career is the least structurally complex of any. Whether a couple is in the "establishment" phase of marriage or has been married for several years, the internal organization of the family involves only the marital dyad. Transactional relationships with extended family, friends, the work place, the economic

84

structure, and the political structure comprise other chief organizational aspects. It would be a mistake, however, to assume that separation in this period is emotionally or organizationally simple. While it is true that childless couples may not have built up the complexity of family structure encountered in the later periods, there are factors associated with this developmental period which, for many couples, make the breakup of their marriage no less traumatic.

At the outset we must recognize that a high proportion of childless couples are relatively young.[1] Many are in late adolescence or early adulthood. This has a number of implications for the way they experience marital separation. For one thing, this is often the first experience many individuals have had in living out of the parental home. Others, of course, have lived away from home at college, have lived in other types of group living situations, or have cohabited. While each of these experiences provides opportunity for developing individual styles of living without parental presence, the married state is one which carries special cultural significance. The pressures to "succeed" are great. One can change roommates or rooming houses without experiencing the kind of cultural impact which is attached to separating from a spouse.

In addition, marriage often represents a means to alleviate the loneliness individuals may have felt in their away-from-home life, or it may have been a secure, socially sanctioned means of "leaving home." This does not diminish the deep affection with which spouses usually enter marriage. It does explain, perhaps, why they are reluctant to separate when the marriage begins to deteriorate. Beyond this, childless married couples are often in the early stages of an occupational career in which they hope to find personal achievement and economic reward. The pressures to succeed in this new role responsibility and in the new expectations of marriage can interact to make each more stressful than either would be alone.

Thus, a young woman in the first or second year of a position with an advertising agency may find it quite manageable to work the long hours and take the occasional business trips required if she is to advance, while carrying on the courtship with her future husband. Courtship is often demanding in time and energy, but it remains less demanding than marriage — especially in the early months of marriage when, judging from the statistics, many of them begin to deteriorate. And, were she not employed, she might be better able to cope with the demands of the new marriage. Combining the demands of the two new roles becomes more than she can handle. Young men may encounter similar kinds of stresses in attempting to combine marriage with their early occupational careers. Perhaps this accounts for some of the rise both in unmarried cohabitation in this age group and in delayed marriage. Cohabitation may be less demanding than formal marriage in the minds of individuals in this age group. We have only impressionistic data on any of this, of course.

Concern with health and nutrition is always a major focal area of the family. However, in the childless family, where spouses are presumably healthy, functioning adults, separation provides little difficulty for each individual in meeting his or her own requirements. If one of the partners is disabled or has some particular health problem, separation could pose some difficulty.

Several of the reorganization requirements for childless separated couples are closely tied to sex-role specialization. Perhaps the most frequently mentioned problem for healthy adults is that experienced by some men who have developed minimal skills in the preparation of food. The popularity of aprons with such inscriptions as "Look out, McDonald's!" as gifts to single men is indicative of the incompetence which is assumed because of the sex-role relatedness of meal planning and food preparation. To the extent that the couple has developed a gender specialized style in which the wife is responsible for grocery shopping and making appointments with the family doctor, separated men may encounter some stress in meeting these new requirements. They may account for the stereotype of "going home to mother" sometimes associated with separated men. It may also account for the tendency of some men to develop rather rapidly a new relationship in which such care-taking requirements may be met by the new partner.

There are several issues which arise for separating childless couples around the functional area of reproduction. Whether or not to have a child may have been a major issue for the couple. At least with respect to the spouse, this issue is handled by default in separation, assuming that the partners cease to have sexual relations with one another. Should the wife be pregnant at the time of separation, this becomes a significant focus for potential crisis. Certainly, both separating partners will find knowing that a pregnancy exists a source of stress. We can see also that, if there are strong desires on the part of either individual to have children, separation represents a frustration of that desire. It is also true that in the 1980s the freedom to choose whether or not to have children may create conflictual desires resulting in new reasons for divorce.

All marriages have to deal with the matter of decision-making patterns. When separation occurs, the focus shifts from issues about who will make decisions in particular areas within the marriage to issues of how the couple will relate as separate individuals. Such issues are undoubtedly less complex in the dyadic situation. Separated childless couples are more likely to have minimal interaction with each other after some of the basic issues of the separation have been settled. *Not* relating to one another is one kind of reorganization. Each will be faced, nevertheless, with areas in their individual lives which formerly involved taking the other into account and must now be reassessed.

If the husband has been the financial support for the couple, the issue of his continued support can represent a focal area of conflict between the couple. Indeed, it is in this area that the highest degree of reorganization in the relationship between separated childless partners will be found. Much of the early focus of legal negotiations between estranged couples centers here. Women who have entered marriage with little training or employment experience face important tasks of developing satisfactory financial arrangements. Establishment of credit ratings on the part of women who have not had independent incomes is often a major problem. Husbands may discover that the financial demands placed upon them are considerably more stressful than they may have anticipated. We have already noted that, to the degree that roles were organized along gender lines, the absence of the spouse may introduce considerable stress. Such matters as routine household tasks, automobile maintenance, and financial management come to mind. Spouses who have become dependent on each other in these matters may find that the separation introduces genuine crisis in their life.

In transactions with extended kin — especially parents — and with the friendship network, concern is likely to arise over the separated individuals' finding new partners. Separated wives may find parents expressing concern over their "need" for a spouse to "support" them, while separated husbands may hear similar concerns over the "need" for someone to "take care" of them. And, of course, the individuals themselves may begin to reorganize their role relationships with their estranged spouses in order to allow for the development of such new relationships. The potential for remarriage is high in this group, with approximately 90 percent remarrying within three years after divorce.[2] We would also be naive if we failed to note that, in some cases, one of the precipitating factors in the separation decision may have been the desire to enter into a new relationship with an already existing, or potential, partner.

The late separation period for the childless tends to find the former spouses attempting to stabilize their lives in their return to single living. They have been here before. Unlike those in later family career periods, they have not become so enmeshed in family networks as the result of having children, with all of the organizational and emotional complexity which this involves. While they may express some fear of "starting over," they are more unfettered as they do so. It is somewhat easier to return to the uncoupled friendship networks, since most childless couples have a mixture of coupled and uncoupled friends.

Perhaps one of the most significant areas which we will discuss with respect to each family career group is how separating couples deal with the sense of meaning in their lives during the separation process. Few individuals enter a marital relationship without a high sense of commitment to that relationship. It may be that the degree of crisis associated with separation may be underestimated in this group because of their youth and the relatively short duration of many childless marriages.[3] Even in short-term marriages the partners may have assumed a "couple mentality," deriving their sense of identity from the spousal role. Many individuals in this developmental period have not developed autonomy. Thus, the emotional distress of separation in interaction with the individual's developmental level can potentially produce high levels of stress.

Much of the reason for being may be tied to the marriage. Individual self-esteem is closely tied to marital roles. but individuals in the childless period may be even more dependent upon the mate, since they have relatively limited life experiences in other areas which validate them as adults. When the marriage is disrupted, new purpose for the individual is required. Joint goals, in which much investment may have been made, are no longer viable. Much of the emotional turmoil associated with separation resides in identifying new goals around which one may organize one's life. This task becomes essential to a continued sense of emotional well-being. Affectional needs, a significant aspect of meaning in life, must be sought in other ways. Individuals who have placed their primary investment in the marriage may find themselves in major crisis. The support of family and friends, as well as professional therapeutic assistance, may be required in the reestablishment of new meaning in life. Of course, some may find separating not very stressful at all. If they have maintained independence, both financially and emotionally, and if they have friends that predate the marriage, return to singleness may be relatively easy—at least in comparison to separation in other family career periods.

The study of separation and divorce in childless couples has not been a high research priority. Systematic data are almost nonexistent. This is due in part to the high mobility of the childless separated. Another reason, however, is that they *are* childless and thus not defined as a "complete" family. Perhaps it is a more difficult process than we imagine. Only systematic investigation can help us identify the unique concerns in this period.

THE CHILDBEARING
AND CHILDREARING PERIOD

Because we have extensively discussed the childbearing and rearing family career period in the previous chapter, the discussion here will be less detailed. Our intent is to give an overall perspective on separation during childbearing and childrearing.

The structure of families during this period is so diverse that it is impossible to deal with all of the variations. Developmental theorists often assume some homogeneity in structure through the use of the labels "preschool," "school age," "adolescent," and "young adult" or "launching" families. All that we can hope to do is identify some of the types of tasks which face separating families with children.

The key themes of this family career period, of course, will relate to the organizational complexity precipitated by the presence of one or more children, each with individual developmental needs. Parenting, whether in married, separated, or divorced families, is the primary concern to both the family itself and the society. When a family is reorganizing from a nuclear to a binuclear structure, continuation of parenting roles is perhaps the most difficult task—one which has long-range implications for both parents and children. In no other developmental period is it more important for the family to continue its functions in spite of its structural changes.

Having a child may stress the marital relationship structurally and emotionally, preparing an especially fertile ground for crisis. When the role of parent is added to that of spouse, the character of the spousal relationship changes. Not only is there less time to devote to those activities which the couple has come to value as significant to their lives, but there is also a whole set of new activities in which differences between the spouses may appear. Each new parent comes from a background in which implicit socialization took place about parental roles. As children, they gained ideas about parenting from their own parents, by observing the parental behavior of other adults, and perhaps by explicit teaching. These ideas may result from seeing their parents handle certain matters in a particularly satisfying way which they wish to emulate. They also come from negative reactions to their own childhood experiences, which they do not wish to repeat as parents.

Thus, as in other aspects of marriage, each partner brings a unique culture to the role of parenting. Now that they *are* parents, this socialization is put into action. Before the advent of the first child, the spouses have probably discussed in the abstract how they would behave as parents. They may be surprised, nevertheless, with their actual behavior! Coupled with this factor is the appearance of a child to whom affection is directed. The ideal for mature parents, of course, is that this should not threaten the marital relationship. The reality, however, is that it frequently does.

It is not surprising, therefore, that research findings consistently show a reduction in the marital satisfaction of spouses during the childrearing years (see Spanier & Lewis, 1980, pp. 828–829 for a review of this literature). This is more pronounced for men than it is for women. Approximately 60 percent of all divorces are granted to couples with children under 18, although only about 52 percent of married couples have children under 18 (U.S. Bureau of the Census, 1984a, Table 267; National Center for Health Statistics, 1985b, Table 2–28). This over representation of divorce in this family career period is evidence of the considerable stress encountered, not only as a result of the interpersonal situation it represents, but also because of the major emphasis which society places upon its importance. No parent is unaware of the significance placed upon the role of parent. The cultural rewards — and the negative sanctions — associated with parenting make this quite clear.

Most of the current research, as well as the societal concern, is focused on this family developmental period. In fact, the concept of family itself is almost synonymous with the presence of dependent children, a fact brought home by the recent reappraisal of definitions of "the family" (see for example, Tufte & Myerhoff, 1979; Pogrebin, 1983). Although lip service is given to variations to the typical nuclear family, these variations are labeled as "alternatives," which relegates them to a separate category. Social policy aimed at ameliorating problems resulting from marital disruption has been concerned almost solely with the socialization and well-being of children. Since the major role of the family is to provide for the socialization of children, any disruption in the traditional living structure results in immediate concern for their welfare.

SEPARATION IN MIDLIFE

Family research has paid much more attention to mate selection, early marital adjustment, childbearing, and childrearing than to the postparental periods. Throughout our discussions, "midlife separation" refers to spouses who are experiencing marital disruption after their children have grown to maturity. Though somewhat arbitrary, we define this as the age group 45–65.[4] We think this is a reasonable division, though the delay in marriage and in childbearing for those marrying in the sixties and seventies may move the lower boundary of this division upwards in the years ahead.

The very term "postparental" reveals a kind of blind spot concerning one of our central theses — that parental positions and the roles attached to them cannot be given up. They continue even after children leave home and, of course, even when the marital relationship is dissolved. It is this central fact that gives the *binuclear family* concept its significance. The statistics on divorce reveal dramatically that a major increase in the number and proportion of divorces has occurred in these later segments of the family career (Appendix Table 1).[5] There is no reason to believe that this is a short-term trend. Given the current proportion of mid-life divorces, increased attention appears merited, since it seems reasonable to expect that many families and individuals will be involved with midlife marital disruption, either as principals or as children, grandchildren, parents, or siblings. While we have relatively little empirical information on separations in childbearing and childrearing families, we have even less on these processes in midlife.

Perhaps what is most distinctive about separations during this period of the marital and family careers is that the patterns of organization are likely to be much more stable and to have been in place for a longer period of time. We might suggest as a major theme for the separated midlife family the disruption of what had been anticipated as a time of recovery from childbearing and rearing. It is often looked forward to as a time for financial recovery and consolidation of financial and social status, as well as a time of stability in marital and parent-child relationships. This is the period when material resources and physical condition allow for many anticipated pleasures for the married couple. It is also the time when the dream of extending the family through the marriages and childbearing of their children may come true. In short, it is often anticipated as the time when the couple will be able to "enjoy life." On the other hand, it may also be anticipated by one spouse, at least, as the time when he or she will no longer be needed to take care of the children's needs and can escape from an untenable relationship. Regardless of the nature of these anticipations, when separation requires establishing new ways of relating, the long-term marriages of midlife may have more potential for crisis than in either of the earlier periods we have reviewed.

On the positive side, spouses in midlife may have available a greater range of resources to cope with the stress brought on by separation and so be less vulnerable to crisis. They are likely to be in reasonably good financial condition, in good health, and without major responsibilities for dependents. Both will be experienced in having met a number of stresses in their lives over the years and will be knowledgeable about the general range of resources available to them. Men will be firmly established in their occupational careers, though many may be experiencing the plateau in earnings and promotions typical of this age group. As we will note later, however, they are less likely to have the kind of social network supports that women seem to develop. Nevertheless, they will have some resources in kin and friendships. Women may have developed a much more effective social network, of both kin and friends (Gilligan, 1982; Rubin, 1983). They have had to be resourceful in their married lives as those chiefly responsible for coping with the range of stressors which arise in families with children. So, men and women in midlife seem to have both some positives and some negatives on their side. We know of little empirical data which would shed light on the net effect these have on the midlife separation process.[6]

Separation in this period represents a major disruption in a long-established division of labor. Many of the issues already examined in the previous family career periods remain issues for this period. However, there is probably a considerably greater dependency inherent in the division of labor on the part of both spouses by the time they reach midlife. Also, they have established a certain level of living, which is in large measure a consequence of the pattern of providing goods and services for one another over a period of many years. Because of the history of this age cohort, these couples are likely to be supported by one income earned by the husband. These are the women who were married from immediately after World War II until into the sixties, when marriage and family still held first priority, perhaps combined with part-time work after the children were a bit older.[7] The wife's not inconsiderable contribution in this system has been in managing a household and much of the non-income-producing efforts of the family. She is less likely to have gained extensive experience in an income-producing occupation either prior to or during marriage. She is much more dependent financially, therefore, just as the husband is extremely dependent on her for a wide range of management activities which have supported their lives together. It is precisely this group of women who make up the category of such societal concern—the displaced homemaker (Shields, 1981; Vinick & Sheldrick, 1979; Vinick, n.d.).

The midlife couple has a highly habituated relationship, about which neither thinks a great deal. (Of course, it is clear that, if separation has occurred, one of them has been paying more attention to it recently!) Marital separation plunges both into a highly stressful situation. The issues which present themselves immediately are not merely matters of individual survival. They involve a much higher order phenomenon encompassing an entire style of life—a style to which both have become accustomed. This is true not only for the wealthy and middle-income couples, but also for those less prosperous. Perhaps only among those below the poverty line are the issues narrowly associated with basic survival. The reorganization in division of labor, then, is highly vulnerable to crisis for midlife separated couples in every walk of life.

Not only is this system much more habituated, but it also is much more encompassing. Individuals in midlife are usually enmeshed in a large network of friends and kin. Help patterns to aging parents and to married or single adult offspring are a central part of the division of labor of most midlife couples. Hill (1971) found the parent generation to be the generation "in the middle" in providing goods and services to the older and younger generations, giving more than they received in both directions. In addition, sibling relationships of both husband and wife often involve mutual or unidirectional provision of goods and services.

In the early stages of midlife separation this imbalance may be reversed, as extended kin come to the support of separated individuals during this traumatic time. Kin and family networks represent not only "problems," but also resources. Women who have depended upon their husbands have available to them sons, daughters, siblings, parents, and the spouses of these relatives. Some of those in the friendship network also represent resources. Dealing with the income tax return for the first time may be made less stressful when an accountant friend offers assistance. The balky furnace or the recalcitrant washing machine may be dealt with by her father, a son, son-in-law, or brother. Men may draw in a similar way on mothers, daughters, sisters, or women in-laws to assist in domestic problems which arise. Because this age cohort is one which was particularly subject to gender specialization in the division of labor, it is quite likely that they are going to experience more stress in reorganizing their lives in these areas. Gender stereotyping is more than an abstract sociological concept — it is likely to be an auto-biographical fact for this age group.

In seeing kin and friends as resources, it is interesting to contemplate the role which adult children may play in assisting separated parents to reorganize their lives. If these offspring have been less subject to a sexual division of labor, they may provide a socialization function for their parents in developing new competencies. Some of these separating couples will have offspring who have already experienced marital disruption. While much literature has explored in depth the effect of divorce on children, we are not aware of any research data which report the effect on parents of an adult child's divorce. In midlife it is possible that the already existing divorce of an adult offspring could prove a positive force in the role reorganization of the less experienced separating parents. Finally, it is interesting to speculate how the divorce experience of an adult child may contribute to the willingness of their parents to contemplate dissolving an unsatisfactory marriage. This is an intriguing twist to the traditional question, "Does divorce run in families?"

The other traditional question, "What is the effect of divorce on children?" also seems not to have been answered with respect to midlife couples and their grown offspring. Several aspects of the relationships between the separated couple and their kin and family networks appear to be important. Whereas these networks have been used to dealing with the married couple as a unit, they must now establish relationships which treat each partner individually. Children of the separated couple — and grandchildren — are faced with issues of loyalty. If the birthday of an adult child or grandchild has been a traditional family affair with well-established rituals, who will be included? In families where celebrations and holidays have been highly ritualized, these times are difficult for all. Adult children are torn between which parent to invite — or which parent's invitation to accept. As a result, many families attempt to develop new rituals. These, however, take time to become adopted. While they may attempt to avoid such issues, it is unlikely that they will be successful in the early stages of separation. As the spouses settle many of their own issues, they may have less need for the assurance of the continued love and concern of these relatives. Geographical distance, of course, can make this a less stressful situation. If children and grandchildren are close by, the probability of greater frequency of contact precipitates more stressful events, as well as more support.

The parents of the midlife separated also find themselves in a difficult position. The extensive structural ties and the family history with the estranged spouses introduce additional stress. Since the marriage has been of considerable duration, the patterns of interaction with in-laws have been well established. If these have been generally conflict-free, the separation may introduce problems which the aged parents of the couple are reluctant to handle. If there has been a pattern of in-law conflict, the separation may only magnify that pattern. Again, geographical distance may serve as a major factor in determining the degree to which stress and crisis are introduced into these relationships.

In-law relationships are often very close — losing much of their early strangeness in genuine affection. A daughter-in-law may have represented the always wished-for daughter in a family who only had sons — or the reverse may be true. A son-in-law or daughter-in-law may have become an important source of help to an aging parent. The separation requires reorganizing these relationships. One of the authors is familiar with a case which may be typical. After a couple's reconciliation ended a separation, the wife's mother confided to her daughter that, had the separation continued, she did not think she could have stopped *her* relationship with the son-in-law, since he had "become like a son" to her. Nevertheless, when the couple finally separated permanently, the mother-in-law found the divided loyalties too much to handle and, after only a brief and tenuous period of maintaining contact, she finally stopped relating to the former son-in-law. She was no doubt sincere in her earlier feelings, but they were only expressed after the temporary reconciliation. When the reality of the break in the marriage presented itself, she found it more difficult than she had imagined to maintain her relationships with both her daughter and her son-in-law.

The friendship network also faces major stress. Of course, since friendships do not carry the obligatory quality of kin relationships, there may be less likelihood of crisis. To the degree that any set of friendships was a consequence of an initial relationship with one or the other partner — a consequence of work or of activities in the community by one spouse — we can anticipate that the initiating individual will maintain those relationships with some changes. In the case of those friendships which are genuinely mutual in nature, the friends are presented with similar issues of loyalty to those facing kin. One partner's moving from the area may reduce this to some extent. Nevertheless, we can anticipate witnessing a process of gradual attrition in the friendship system. To the degree that friendships and kin have represented major resources to the couple, this process can precipitate grave crisis for either partner.

In this period many marriages have been in existence for 20 years or longer. Given the birth cohort of these couples, we are dealing to a great extent with people who were socialized to find one of the central meanings in life to be marriage and family living. Wife/mother/caretaker and husband/father/provider are roles which have been the source of a primary identification. So enmeshed are the spousal and parental roles that even at this developmental period the termination of the former affects the latter. This role symbiosis is illustrated by a 50-year-old woman who was experiencing separation after 28 years of marriage. In the course of a therapy session with one of the authors the woman was lamenting what the separation meant to her life. She said, amidst her tears and devastation: "I was so looking forward to becoming a grandmother." She had no model for being a grandmother without being part of a marriage. The role symbiosis was even more pronounced in her case, since her physician husband had not been a very active participant in the family. She was not experiencing the loss of his relationship or presence as much as she was feeling the loss of her role, and hence, her identity as wife, mother, and potential grandmother.

Beyond this, such long-term marriages have built up a considerable set of meanings around the goals and aspirations which the spouses have developed together. Material things, such as a home, a vacation cottage, a boat, a motor home, and the like, represent evidence of their "success" as a couple. Plans for retirement or travel "now that the children are grown" have similar significance. Grandchildren may carry meaning as evidence of their accomplishment as a successful family. The common sight of the bumper sticker "Happiness is being a grandparent" on a recreational vehicle combines two central life interests for more than a few couples in their middle years. (Another — "We're spending our children's inheritance" — expresses a somewhat different sentiment, but with the same theme!) Marital separation represents a major blow to such vital values.

While men may tend to focus on their occupational careers as a way of redefining meaning in their lives, it must not be forgotten that these occupations frequently have been a *means* to an end, rather than an end in themselves. For women, the loss of the position of wife is less easily transformed. Separated women in this generation are less likely to have careers to which they can turn for meaning. If they turn to work, it is more likely in response to financial need than as a way of providing meaning in their lives, and the work may not be of the type which gives much ego enhancement.

Both men and women may develop new recreational pursuits, hobbies, or volunteer activities. They may center on their children and grandchildren or on aging parents as appropriate ways of filling the void. Some may return to abandoned religious or philosophical orientations, or pursue an intensified interest in such matters. And, of course, there is always the possibility of new relationships with potential partners, although, as we have observed, the cultural and demographic circumstances do not make this an easy option, especially for women. Concentrating on new and old friendships, while presenting some difficulties, provides one of the most fertile possibilities for new life meaning. When all is said and done, the loss of meaning related to the marriage probably holds the highest vulnerability for stress becoming crisis for the separated midlife individual. This results both from the major investment which marriage represents to them and from the scarcity of resources available.

AGING AND SEPARATION

In turning to the aging period of the family career we are left with little beyond demographic analyses to inform us. We have drawn heavily on social scientific and therapeutic theory, as well as on case material from our own research and experience, to develop this analysis.

Once again demographic and cultural characteristics help us set the scene. If we set the very arbitrary boundary for "aging" as being above the age of 65, the demographic picture is quite dramatic (Appendix Table 1). As we discussed in Chapter 1, most in this group are either married, usually to their first spouse, or widowed. The demographic disadvantage for women is great, since the death of a spouse strikes more of them than their male counterparts and widowed men are more likely to remarry. We will have more to say about the implications of this in the chapters on divorce and remarriage. While separation in the aging cohort is not as numerically imposing as in the earlier family career categories, we can anticipate that it will increase in the future. Therefore, it is important to examine it, not only for its current implications, but also because of those we can anticipate.

Culturally, older marriages are viewed as "permanent." This fact in itself serves to reduce the likelihood that those in marriages which are unsatisfactory to one or both partners will move to separation. And, of course, this cohort is even more steeped in the view of marriage as continuing "until death do us part." Perhaps more than any other cohort, the aged are least likely to adopt values of individual happiness and adjustment as criteria for marital quality. The theme, then, for separated aging couples focuses centrally on the abandonment of a lifetime relationship which probably carried expectations of continuing until death.

One of the factors especially distinctive for the aged who have separated is the special nutritional and health needs which arise in this period of life. Being subject to the increased possibility of illness and without a spouse to provide basic care, the separated aged may have special adjustment problems. Aging individuals are quite used to being dependent upon their spouses during illness. Without this resource, they must identify alternative means for handling their daily needs during periods of temporary disability.

Proper nutrition is particularly important for the elderly. Appetite is a highly social phenomenon in North America. Aged persons experience a normal decrease in appetite under any circumstances. The absence of the partner may only add to this. Men in this cohort, of course, are especially vulnerable, since they are not likely to have developed the skills related to proper meal planning and preparation. Thus, their nutritional intake may be quite inadequate unless they develop these skills. Separated women, however, may also fall into poor nutritional habits, finding that they simply are not motivated to prepare meals in the same way they did before.

Relating to kin and friendship networks presents some potential crises for the aging separated couple. Typically, aging is a time of some reduction in these network structures. With retirement from employment, it is likely that only those friendships that were based on more than the common interests of the work place will be maintained. If the retirement involved a move to a new locality, it is even more likely that most of this network has been lost. New friendships may be developed in the retirement community or as a result of a changed pattern of activity in the old community. However, friends—old and new—are most likely to also be in the aging years, and the network is constantly subject to reduction as a result of death. Siblings, and even adult children, are lost also in this way. Marital separation compounds this shrinkage of the social network by the loss of some of those friends and relatives with whom the couple has consistently interacted over the years.

Those friends shared by the separated couple may experience considerable difficulty in developing a pattern of relationship. It is likely that in the past, at an earlier age, they have experienced divorce in the family and friendship networks. However, it is not as likely that they have experienced it in their advanced age cohort. As noted, they have undoubtedly experienced the loss of friends through death. However, the patterns of interactions with widowers and widows are not likely to be directly transferable to the relationships with separated friends. An anomic state is likely to prevail for some period of time.

While aging individuals point with great pride to the number of children, grandchildren, and even great-grandchildren they have, it is not likely that either grandchildren or great-grandchildren form a very active part of their social network. Unless these young relatives live nearby, occasional visits are realistically all that is experienced by most elderly persons. As long as adult children live nearby, more frequent interaction and possibly major dependence for certain services are more typical. When marital separation takes place, an increase in the need for such services, as well as for the emotional support of visits from family members, places major stress on the extended kin. Coupled with the sheer increase in the time demands that may occur is the lack of any clear norms about how one deals with the marital disruption of an aging parent or grandparent. Even if the adult children have experienced divorce personally or in the marriages of close friends or relatives, they are not likely to be able to approach this situation with much confidence. Furthermore, they are very likely to have unexpected and confusing emotional reactions to the event.

Economic issues hold special significance in the aging career period. Couples in retirement are most likely to be living on a combination of the husband's pension benefits, if any, and on federal government social security benefits. It is probable that retirement planning was based upon the assumption of the continuation of the marriage. While two cannot live as "cheaply as one," they certainly live more cheaply than two individuals! The division of income and property at this period of life is likely to introduce real economic stress for both individuals. Many pension plans, designed primarily to protect the rights of the worker, make no provision for assigning such benefits to a former spouse. While recent court decisions and legislation are beginning to recognize the claims of women to a portion of the retirement benefits of their husbands, this is still an area of considerable legal ambiguity. Especially if the wife has had no income-producing employment to provide her own retirement income, she may be left with minimal government pension benefits. As the probability of increased numbers of marital disruptions among the aged develops, we can expect increased legislative attention to this area. Meanwhile, we can anticipate some major adjustment problems, especially among women.

Adjustments in the division of labor for separated aging couples, while somewhat similar to those already discussed in midlife, are complicated by the increased possibility of physical disability or, at the least, reduced physical ability to handle the range of responsibilities for daily life formerly handled by two persons. The restructuring of habit patterns developed over a long marriage is difficult at best. One could expect that aged separated spouses would need to identify multiple resources to assist them in restructuring their lives in this area.

Finally, we again encounter the major concern for continued meaning in life. Like those separated in midlife, couples in this age cohort are likely to have found marriage to be a central meaning in life. Finding a replacement upon which to build a new life focus will be no small task. We can expect that the separated aged will turn to family and friends for primary meaning. Family, of course, can be expected to come to the aid of the separated individuals. Grandchildren and great-grandchildren can continue to provide important interests, even if new patterns of relating have to be developed. However, as we have seen, this will not be without its stressful aspects.

Friends may have more difficulty in knowing how to deal with this relatively new experience. Thus, one of the primary meanings for the aged may be denied to the separated — that of a network of friends in the same developmental cohort who have experienced over the years many things in common and, therefore, tend to view the world in a similar way. Widows and widowers are not people with a common basis for relationship with the separated. Regardless of the quality of the marriage broken by death, it is possible to reconstruct the history of that marriage so as to make it a topic for positive memories and comparative discussion with others in the same situation. Of course, remarriage for the aged separated is not an impossibility. As in midlife, however, it is likely to occur only after many difficulties have been overcome. Establishing new meanings in life for the aging who separate is no small challenge.

CONCLUSION

Almost half of America's families will experience marital separation. How they reorganize structurally and continue to perform the functions of family is the focus of the next chapter. Families face the task of reorganization without a well marked course. Nevertheless, either by default or by conscious decision, family members in all family career periods gain some personal autonomy. Newfound responsibilities can lead to an even more effective and orderly functioning in the family. As Golan (1978) points out, while crisis may be the initial experience, resolution of the crisis may reveal unanticipated internal and external resources. Such experiences can result in greater system morale and enhanced self-esteem in family members. It is such an outcome that makes it clear that marital crisis does not inevitably result in a negative experience.

FIVE

The Divorce Transition

THE MOVEMENT TOWARDS DIVORCE

As we have seen, the process of separation is primarily one of family disorganization. It is stressful for all family members, often bringing the family to debilitating crisis. How they cope with each stressor and the accumulation of stress determines how they will cope with the stresses of reorganization. There is probably no precise way of pinpointing when the separated family system may be said to be "reorganized"—nor can we set a criterion for the amount of time it will take to reach such a state. McCubbin and Patterson (1983) suggest that the degree of "fit" which prevails between family members and between the family and the community is a useful means for assessing the level of adaptation reached in the process. No "normal" family is free of stress or of occasional crisis. Likewise binuclear families are not immune from "normality."

Families going through this life transition do so with a minimum of societal support and without adequate guidelines for appropriate functioning. It is a hazardous journey, with no charts or stars for guidance. Further, unlike other major life transitions, divorce lacks rituals to mark the family's transition from nuclear to binuclear. We celebrate the beginning of nuclear families with elaborate ritual around the marriage. Each year the anniversary of that union is celebrated. The expansion of the family through the birth of a child is again treated with celebratory ritual. Even the death of a family member has its attendant ritual to provide structure for the mourning process.

Ritual is important, not only for those experiencing the transition, but also for the community. It provides a way for all to note that an important change has occurred. As a society we are very ambivalent about divorce. On the one hand we now have instituted laws that make it legally quite easy to exit a marriage, but we still hold on to the notion that divorce is deviant and a social ill. Marriage is clearly an indication of success, to be met with congratulations to the participants. Divorce has unclear connotations. Do we offer sympathy or congratulations to mark the event?[1]

Once control of the immediate tasks of separation has been gained, the family members may turn their energies to consolidating their position. The issue is no longer survival, but "getting on with our lives." The focus shifts from what the system has been like and what it is like now to what it should become. Family members become involved in assessing the basic orientation of the system and developing meaning for their relationships together. This assessment results in searching for the changes that are required in their role responsibilities and establishing ways for implementing these changes. There is less immediate pressure for solution and more time available for considering a range of alternatives. New patterns of relationship which result from negotiation and compromise may lead to new ways to support one another, thus enabling each member of the system to begin to live in a more satisfactory way—both individually and for the family group. Or the divorce can result in a severing of important attachment relationships, with profound implications for all family members.

The major goal of reorganization in families is centered on how the complex relationships of family members with each other and with others outside the family are structured to meet group and individual objectives. Some degree of orderliness and predictability is required in all social groups. Some require a minimal amount, while others demand a great deal. Most families fall somewhere between the loose organizational form of a planeload of passengers on a transcontinental flight and the high rigidity of a military organization. Nevertheless, patterns of relating in all functional areas within the family must be established.

As the old patterns are replaced by the new ones, there is a genuine process of *family redefinition*. New ways of relating within the family are established. New ways of relating to the estranged spouse are also worked out. It is no longer appropriate for the other partner to be called upon to play the old roles, but newly defined roles need to be introduced. In Minuchin's (1974) terms, new family boundaries need to be established. The *nuclear* family must be reorganized into a *binuclear* family. These new boundaries are effected not only in the immediate family members' interaction, but also in transactions with extended family, with friends, and with a number of other external systems — the school, religious organizations, businesses, and governmental agencies.

DIVORCED FAMILY REORGANIZATION:
AN OVERVIEW

Divorce is an "event" that sets in motion a process of drastic changes in family structure and membership, culminating in a complex redefinition of relationships within the family. Although the structure of postdivorce families varies, some basic tasks must be accomplished in this transition. In this chapter we identify the transitions that the family members go through as they reorganize and redefine themselves as part of a divorced family, while in the next chapter we will identify some of the different issues faced by families at various periods in the family career.

The major feature of the reorganization process is the interweaving of the tasks of establishing separate independent lives while simultaneously carrying out the functions and obligations of the original family. Although divorce is now a common transition in family life, role models for family life after divorce are still confused, unclear, and often in conflict. While divorcing partners are struggling with disorganization and loss, they must simultaneously figure out a method to continue their childrearing and parenting functions. The recent rapid changes in custody legislation are a direct result of the legal system's attempts to accommodate and facilitate the reorganization process. As we shall see, however, although the movement toward joint custody legislation in most states is philosophically sound, it does not yet provide practical and functional guidelines for families. Divorced partners are left to struggle with the very complex process of terminating their marital relationship while still continuing their parental relationship — with few guideposts along the way.

Anthropologist Paul Bohannan (1971) has identified six overlapping experiences of divorce:

1. the emotional divorce, which centers around the problem of the deteriorating marriage;
2. the legal divorce, based on grounds;
3. the economic divorce, which deals with money and property;

4. the coparental divorce, which deals with custody and visitation;
5. the community divorce, surrounding the changes of kin, friends and community that every divorced person experiences; and
6. the psychic divorce, with the problem of regaining individual autonomy.

In the preceding chapters on separation we have touched upon each of these areas but focused mainly on the process of emotional separation. In this chapter the major focus of our attention will be on the coparental divorce, for, as Bohannan notes, this is the most painful and complex experience of the divorce process. It is in this continuing kinship relationship and familial obligation that many of the unresolved issues of the other "stations of divorce" get played out. It is the presence of children from the marital union that requires some continuity of relationship based on kinship. Continuity of partner relationships after divorce for childless couples may occur because of emotional attachments, but does not require the ongoing complex interactions that the presence of children requires.

Once a family has established some ground rules for living separately (for example, where the children will reside or how visitation will be arranged), the family needs to clarify rules for relating within and across the various subsystems within the family system, for example, the parental or the parent-child subsystem. The relationship between the spouses lays the foundation for how the divorced family will redefine itself anew; this relationship also determines the emotional climate in which this redefinition will occur. Divorced spouses who want to maintain their parenting rights and responsibilities have the complex task of terminating their spousal roles while redefining their parental roles.

The concept of family boundaries, rules which determine the parameters of the family systems, helps us to understand a major stress of this transition. As Minuchin (1974) notes, clear boundaries result in "proper family functioning." In the earlier transition, the absence of clear boundaries creates much of the confusion and stress; in this transition, the *clarification* of boundaries generates the distress.

Minuchin stresses the importance of two separate subsystems for married parents—the spousal and the parental. Although in theory these two subsystems are separate, in practice, for most married couples, there is considerable overlap between the two systems. When a marriage is failing, the spousal subsystem ceases to meet the needs of both partners; it may decrease in importance for them or become so enmeshed with the parental subsystem that the boundaries between the two are diffuse and unclear. When these subsystems become enmeshed, it is difficult for separating spouses to define where their spousal relationship ends and where their parental relationship begins.

To reduce the contamination of parental roles by spousal conflicts, the boundaries between the subsystems need to be specified. This is one major task for the divorcing family, especially if a young child is involved, since these rules affect the parent-child relationship as well. How will each of the parents relate to the child? How will the parents relate to each other? Each subsystem needs greater clarification than is usually necessary or present in the married family.

Rules defining when and how each of the parents continues to relate to the children are critical to the child's understanding of the divorce and to the consequent stabilization of the parent-child relationship. Each parent must establish an independent relationship with the child to pass this transition successfully, but the continuation of each parent-child relationship unit requires the continued interdependence with the former spouse. This paradoxical and intricate process requires the clarification of roles and boundaries between parental and spousal subsystems. Within this continued interdependence, new rules and behavior developed by former spouses toward one another can be expected to have repercussions for all family members. The lack of role models and the absence of social norms for a continuing relationship between divorced parents complicate this transition.

SINGLE-PARENT FAMILIES: A MISNOMER

The final stage of divorce adjustment traditionally has been the exclusion of the "problem member" from the family system. This process of "freezing out" (Farber, 1964), "closing ranks" (Hill, 1949), or "closing out" (Boss, 1977) is functional only when the father remains absent in the system. While the literature has not directly identified this final stage as part of the divorce process, ample evidence suggests that this coping strategy has been common both to divorced families and to our thinking about them. Clinical literature often cites a healthy adjustment to divorce as associated with termination of relationships between former spouses (Kressel & Deutsch, 1977). The label "single-parent family" as a descriptor of divorced families indicates the assumption that divorce results in one parent's leaving the system. The prevalence of this labeling has led both researchers and clinicians to proceed on the premise that all divorced families are so characterized. This has led to a body of research on "father absence" which assumed that fathers were either present, as in nuclear families, or absent, as in divorced and widowed families. Clinicians, following the same path, formed treatment strategies based on father absence.

Recent research, however, reveals that this pattern of coping with postdivorce family reorganization results in increased individual stress and family dysfunction. The more the noncustodial father is "closed out" of the system, the more dysfunctional stress the system experiences. Noncustodial fathers with infrequent postdivorce contact with their children report more depression (Greif, 1979), more dissatisfaction in their relationships with their children (Ahrons, 1979), and more stress regarding role loss (Keshet & Rosenthal, 1978; Mendes, 1976). Mothers with sole custody report more depression resulting from the overburden of responsibilities (Brandwein et al., 1974; Hetherington et al., 1976). And children with very limited or no father contact suffer the most severe developmental and emotional distress (Hetherington, 1979; Wallerstein & Kelly, 1980). The nuclear family's reorganization in divorce creates single-parent families *only* when one parent has no further contact with the family and no longer performs parental functions. More frequently, the reorganization process results in interrelated maternal and paternal households forming one binuclear family system (Ahrons, 1979, 1980a, 1980b). How the family reorganizes structurally and redefines itself socially and emotionally is a key determinant for how the family copes with and masters this important transition. This process has profound implications for the future development of all family members.

Before we examine in greater detail the nature of postdivorce spousal relationships, we need to examine the way that child custody issues and the legal divorce process affect these relationships.

CHILD CUSTODY AND THE RELATIONSHIP BETWEEN FORMER SPOUSES

Although the study of divorce is a growing area of study, the relationship between former spouses did not receive the attention of social scientists until controversy over child custody issues came to the fore.

Prior to the middle of the 19th century, children were considered the property of the father and custody was arbitrarily awarded to him. Gradually, changes in societal views, reflected in the doctrine of "tender years," shifted the court presumption of custody to the mother. Although the "tender years" doctrine was meant to apply only to children up to six or seven years of age, the mother has become the generally favored parent, even in custody disputes involving older children. As a result, during the 1960s and 1970s approximately 90 percent of the custody awards were given to mothers.[2]

During the mid-1970s a new arrangement, joint custody, began to emerge. The desire for shared custodial arrangements probably arose from a combination of factors, the most important of these being: a trend toward a more egalitarian approach to role-sharing in marriage; the increase of women in the labor force; the women's movement; and a new emphasis on fathers' role in child development accompanied by more involvement of fathers in the birth and care of their infants.

The joint custody movement first began in California at a grass roots level. A small group of fathers, in objection to the prevailing court mandate of mother custody, organized to assert their parental rights. At the same time, there emerged a small group of divorcing spouses who chose joint custody as an agreement outside of the legal decision. Emanating from that, new legislation in some states was enacted to permit a shared or joint custody arrangement.

Now, in the mid-1980s, in virtually every state in the United States and in Canada, as well as in many European countries, joint custody is a permissible legal custody arrangement (Folberg, 1984). A very recent trend toward joint custody as the *preferred* arrangement is currently emerging. Several states have recently enacted legislation which makes joint custody a presumption or first choice; under this law divorcing parents must prove that joint custody is not in the best interests of the child—a complete reversal of the issue up until 1980.

As a philosophical concept, joint custody has won the approval of many legislators, judges, fathers, some mothers, and even many social scientists. However, as a functioning type of custody arrangement, it is a virtual unknown. How do divorcing families actually work out and carry through joint or shared childrearing after marital dissolution? What advice can we give them? Our ignorance is not surprising, given the newness of this type of shared parenting postdivorce, the "divorce as deviance" perspective, and the unsystematic nature of the samples upon which research is based. Ahrons, in the first study of joint custody on a sample drawn from court records, did not find support for the myth that all joint custody parents were amicable or that they shared responsibility equally for childrearing (1979, 1980c).

In sum, to date the joint custody research suggests that two parents who voluntarily choose to share custody may find it *possible* to do so, at least in the short term. Future research is needed to explore its suitability for different age and class groups, its feasibility over time, and the identification of characteristics of parents and families who are most able to handle successfully the complexities of this type of custody arrangement. Also, we need to look at the way that the process of determining custody influences the relationship between former spouses.

IMPACT OF THE LEGAL DIVORCE ON FORMER SPOUSE RELATIONSHIPS

Unlike marriage, with its lack of specified written contracts for the division of property, assets, roles and responsibilities, divorce in our society requires that partners divide up the "spoils" created by their marital union in a legal contract. For most couples, their first contact with the legal requirements of divorce introduces many realities not yet digested in their emotional decision to terminate their marital relationship. They are forced to consider seriously many of the dilemmas of severing their emotional ties and the kingdoms created by the institution of marriage. Our romanticized version of marriage usually does not include provisions for its termination. Hence, the discovery of the many details that must be considered and divided in some way creates additional stress. This may lead the divorcing spouses to use the legal arena to vent many of the emotional disappointments and angers that accompany a failed relationship.

The problems encountered in most legal divorces center on the division of property, continued financial obligations from the marriage, and the custody of children. No-fault legislation has been enacted in many jurisdictions over the past decade or so. While the issue of fault is no longer a legal issue, it is still very much an emotional one which may then be transferred, albeit transparently disguised, into the other legally acceptable arenas.

For most couples the division of assets and property stimulates some of the unresolved issues of the earlier separation stage. Couples must review their lives as they establish budgets, decide on who gets the livingroom furniture, who gets the summer cottage, who gets the remaining financial obligations. It forces an accounting of the marriage "balance sheet" in a much more detailed and specific way than most couples have needed to do in the past. While the emotional separation has involved a "taking stock" of the assets and liabilities of the relationship, the impact of the legal divorce requires them to relive that process and now attach dollar signs to it. Some couples move through this transition with a minimum of stress, having accomplished most of the emotional divorce prior to this stage. But for most couples this restimulates many of the old angers, grief, and anxieties. They must now come to terms realistically with what the restructuring of their family will cost them.

For many couples, encountering the legalities of divorce escalates their divorce crisis. This persists regardless of level of income and the abundance or lack of accumulated and current resources. Issues pervade of fairness, getting one's due, making up for past inequities, and anxieties about living on less. The traditional adversarial process is premised on protecting the rights of the individual, which most often results in conflicts of interests between the marital partners.

The central legal issue for over half of divorcing spouses (about 60 percent of those who divorce have minor children) is the issue of custody. Custody is a distinctive divorce issue, since in marriage both parents automatically have legal custody. Although custody is the determination of how parents will divide up their rights and responsibilities for the continuing care of minor children, it usually means that many of the other issues that couples must negotiate in divorce get enmeshed with the custody issue. The division of property, assets, and liabilities gets entangled with the custody issue in varying degrees. Furthermore, it is almost impossible to keep custody considerations from being contaminated by the emotional and financial issues of divorce. Who continues to live in the family home is often tied to the custody arrangement. The level of continuing financial support is governed by the needs of the children but entrusted to and exchanged between the parents. In this era of changing norms about custody and confusing and often necessarily ambiguous guidelines, these issues are difficult to separate. A clear indication of this is the case a few years ago in which the judge awarded the house to three adolescent children to resolve the financial disputes of the parents.

It is because of the movement toward joint custody, however, that the study of the relationship between former spouses gains importance. If, as joint custody presumes, divorced spouses are to continue their role as parents, they must share decision-making and childrearing. To do so implies continuance of some form of relationship. The prevailing assumption, however, is that divorce inevitably severs the relational bonds of the marital pair, just as it severs the legal bonds of matrimony. Given the perspective that divorce dissolves the family, there has been little attempt to separate out the relationship dimension from other aspects of the marital union.

FORMER SPOUSE RELATIONSHIPS

Although the process of termination of a marital relationship has received increasing attention from social scientists, the ongoing relationship between former spouses remains a neglected area of study. Yet this former spousal relationship has a dynamic history of shared experiences and familial ties that do not necessarily terminate with marital dissolution, particularly in those relationships to which children have been born.

Most of our current knowledge about the relationship between former spouses is derived from societal stereotypes and the clinical literature. Until very recently the clinical literature has considered a continuing relationship between former spouses as unhealthy. Contact between divorced spouses is usually perceived as an indication of unresolved marital issues or a "hanging onto" the marriage. It is interesting that while the general public, clergy, and mental health professionals decry the divorce rate and its familial implications, we nevertheless continue to view ex-spousal bonding as pathological or quasi-pathological. In a study which explored the attitudes of lawyers, clergy, and psychotherapists toward divorce, Kressel and his colleagues (1978, p. 138) found:

> With a few notable exceptions, there was a general distrust of the ex-spouses' continuing involvement with each other as friends, business partners, or lovers, largely on the grounds that such attachments reflect separation distress rather than realistic caring, and they drain emotional and physical energies that would more productively be spent in forming new relationships. Most respondents felt that for childless couples the best policy is to sever all ties.

The general distrust of a continuing relationship after divorce is reflected in the prevailing stereotype that former spouses must, of necessity, be antagonists — otherwise, why would they divorce? This stereotype is again reinforced by a bias in the available clinical material: Clinicians tend to see only the difficult or problematic former spousal relationships, while well-functioning divorced families are less apt to seek professional intervention.

The lack of language to describe the former spousal relationship, except in terms of a past relationship (e.g., "ex" or "former"), is another indication of societal lack of acceptance of it as a viable form. Margaret Mead's interpretation of the source of our discomfort in acknowledging a continuing relationship between former spouses may indeed still be valid. " . . . any contact between divorced people somehow smacks of incest; once divorced, they have been declared by law to be sexually inaccessible to each other, and the aura of past sexual relations makes further relationship incriminating" (Mead, 1971, p. 121).

A major conclusion that can be drawn from the available findings is that the former spouse relationship is a complex one with perhaps as many variations as we find between married spouses (Ahrons, 1981b; Goldsmith, 1980; Isaacs & Leon, 1986). In a recently completed analysis of her data, Ahrons found that somewhat over half of the sample do have relationships similar to ones depicted in the prevailing stereotypes (Ahrons & Wallisch, 1986). Although some of them do continue to have interactions, these are rare and are focused on the children. Some ex-spouses may be indifferent, but many still harbor the angers arising from the marriage and divorce. Not only is the marital union dissolved but so are their relationships. On the other hand, it was found that a large minority of the sample (approximately 40 percent) have what Duck (1982) has described as a "declined" relationship. These former spouses have at least a moderate amount of interaction, including shared information about issues related to the children and issues that also have a component of friendship.

In exploratory research more questions are raised rather than answered. One major question is whether a declined relationship is more functional than a dissolved one. To assign a value, however, to which type of relationship is better would require answering the question, "Better for whom?" If it is dependent children we are concerned about, then we can say with some certainty that they will fare the divorce better if their parents remain amicable. Recent longitudinal studies examining

the effects of divorce on children conclude that the children who
suffered the most psychological distress were those who experienced
the continual conflict of their parents and those whose fathers had
minimal or no contact with them (Hetherington et al., 1978; Wallerstein & Kelly, 1980). Given that Ahrons' findings suggest that over half
of divorced spouses have dissolved relationships with continuing conflict and anger, which is negatively correlated with continued involvement of the noncustodial parent, we can assume that those relationships are not in the best interests of children. Although there is little
research available on the effects on adult children, it seems reasonable
to hypothesize that their distress about their parents' divorce might be
lessened if their parents had a declined rather than a dissolved relationship.

For the divorced spouses themselves, assigning a value to which type
of relationship is better is more difficult. The clinical literature addresses the relationship in terms of its importance for children. Given
that for most of Ahrons' sample the ideal was to have a relationship
that was more amicable, we can only assume that they would be happier
if it were so. Certainly for former spouses who have to continue to
see each other because they live in the same community or have familial
obligations that require some contact, it would be much more comfortable to be at least on speaking terms.

The findings here are quite positive, however, given the numbers
of divorced spouses who have declined as opposed to dissolved relationships. It should be noted, however, that the study probably found
a somewhat higher percentage of declined relationships than might be
found in the general population, given the criteria used for inclusion
in the study. Nevertheless, it is clear that it is possible for former
spouses to continue to relate in constructive ways. This in itself is
surprising, since they do so without the support of the community and
without adequate role models. The respondents themselves noted that
they were very unsure of "appropriate" ways to relate, often asking
the interviewer how they were "supposed" to relate.

THE FORMER SPOUSE RELATIONSHIP:
FIVE RELATIONSHIP STYLES

We have discussed some of Ahrons' findings in terms of declining
and dissolved relationships. More recent analysis of her data suggests
that there are four distinct types of relationships. She has labeled these

"Perfect Pals," "Cooperative Colleagues," "Angry Associates," and "Fiery Foes." Since all of her families did have some sort of relationship, there is a fifth logical type which needs to be added to these — the "Dissolved Duos" who have not continued any kind of contact after divorce. Ahrons' four types span interactional styles that range from very friendly to very hostile. Much as researchers have identified a range of relationship styles in married couples, so divorced couples show a variety of relationship styles.

Perfect Pals

In the past there has been some disbelief that divorced partners can have an amicable relationship. Given our assumption that people who divorce must of necessity be bitter enemies, the usual response to a "friendly" divorce is: If they can get along so well, why would they divorce? The answer to this question is complex; there is no single answer. Nevertheless, there appear to be some spouses who, although they have decided to divorce, still remain friends. For some of these couples the decision to divorce has occurred over a long period of time and may be related to certain lifestyle decisions. Craig and Cynthia fit this style:

> *Cynthia*: Craig and I have always been good friends. Craig was my first boyfriend and we married during college. Over a period of ten years and two children we found ourselves going in different directions. We never had many disagreements but we slowly grew apart in our interests. It just seemed to happen gradually and almost without our being aware of it. We found ourselves doing less and less together although we spent a lot of time together with the children in family activities. I am a quiet person who likes to spend a lot of time with one or two friends, going to a movie or just sitting and talking. Craig, on the other hand, is very outgoing and likes sports and active things. We spent a lot of time talking about our different desires for our lives.
>
> At first we supported each other's wish to do different things but then we began to get angry with each other for not being willing to compromise or accommodate to each other's interests. Somewhere along the way the anger just turned into acceptance and we talked about separating for a while. The actual separation was difficult and we both felt very sad. Yet at the same time we enjoyed not feeling guilty about wanting different things from life. We lived separately for a couple of years before we decided to get a divorce. We still spent time together

with the children and had holidays together. When we finally decided to get a divorce it was not really a big decision, it just seemed like a gradual change.

Craig and Cynthia's relationship was basically a strong friendship with mutual respect that did not get eroded by their decision to live separate lives. Had Craig and Cynthia lived in an earlier generation they probably would not have divorced. The social sanctions at that time would have been too strong. However, divorce is now more acceptable and Craig and Cynthia chose the option of divorcing.

Not all the couples who had amicable relationships after divorce are like Craig and Cynthia, however. Consider Helen and Bob:

> *Bob*: It's hard to say what went wrong between us. We had some very good years and some very bad ones. Helen made a lot of changes in the 15 years we were married. She went back to school, got a law degree and became really excited about her work. She spent less and less time at home and I found myself resenting her involvement and missing the old Helen. We had a couple of very bad years, with me demanding that Helen spend more time with me and Helen feeling she had the right to pursue what she wanted to. We both sort of fell into having other relationships. At first we blamed each other but then we sort of accepted that we just didn't want to be married anymore. At first the separation was very hard, with a lot of resentments, but after the first six months or so we both felt more at ease and started to become friends again.

For the couples who established postdivorce relationships that were cooperative and friendly the road to achieving that was quite varied. Some, like Craig and Cynthia, had always been good friends, but others had stormier relationships. What appears to be similar among these couples was some sense of mutuality in the decision to divorce. They may not have made the decision simultaneously, but neither partner felt totally abandoned by the other. There also appears to be some equity in these relationships. What facilitated these amicable postdivorce relationships was a mutual respect for each other as people and as parents. Both partners perceived the other to be a responsible and caring parent. Although they had some anger with each other during the separation process and their interactions still involved some conflict at times, overall they genuinely liked each other and went out of their way to accommodate each other. Although they were unwilling to compromise themselves to stay in a marriage that wasn't satisfying, they were willing to compromise in divorce.

Perfect pals are not common in our society. They represent a small group of divorced spouses for whom the disappointments of a failed marriage appear not to overshadow the positive elements of a long-standing friendship. In Ahrons' Binuclear Family Study the couples who fit into this relationship style were able to manage a high quality shared parenting arrangement and all had a legal joint custody arrangement. They shared decision-making and childrearing much as they did in marriage, with many stating that they were even better parents after the divorce than they were in the marriage. They spent holidays together and kept relationships with each other's extended families. In summary, theirs was a broad-based relationship which, while focused on parenting, included much that was nonparental in nature.

Cooperative Colleagues

The main distinction between this group and the perfect pals is that these divorced spouses do not feel that they are good friends but are able to cooperate quite successfully as parents. They, too, traveled different routes before they negotiated a cooperative divorced relationship. We return here to the case of Nancy and Jim, whom we met during their separation in Chapter 3. Two years after the divorce she describes their relationship this way:

> *Nancy:* We had two kids and 11 years of marriage when we decided to separate. I wanted out of the marriage and Jim was very angry. He felt used and angry about losing his family as he saw it. We were fighting a lot in the last couple of years and we decided to separate to cool off. After a couple of months of arguing and a brief attempt at reconciliation, Jim finally moved out. We had trouble talking calmly with each other so we had to make some very rigid rules about the kids.
>
> Jim had always been a loving father and wanted to be with the kids a lot. I felt badly about wanting the separation and so I made it as easy as possible for him to be with the kids. We had a brief battle over custody and money but decided one evening to throw down the gauntlet and find a way to compromise on the issues we were both holding to steadfastly. After several months of haggling we sat down with our lawyers and settled things in one afternoon.
>
> We both love our kids very much and want to do what's best for

them. For me, that means having to accept some things that I don't like about Jim and to make a lot of compromises, both financially and about the kids, but it's working well. The tradeoffs are worth it. I can't always have David and Ellen with me when I want to, but then again Jim can't either. So, we alternate weekends and split the holidays. This past Thanksgiving we had dinner together with the kids and some close friends. It was a little awkward at times but there was also a nice sense of family for us all. I'm not sure I want to do that next year though.

Jim and Nancy are not atypical. It required some degree of maturity on both their parts to permit them to accept some of the compromises that are necessary in divorce. They have both learned to accept that they may not like each other in a lot of ways but that they need to compromise for the sake of the children and to achieve their own desires to be active and responsible parents. They still have some disagreements about financial issues and differences of opinion related to the children, but they are able to keep those conflicts from escalating into huge power struggles.

For many of the divorced couples who manage to achieve this kind of cooperative relationship it has taken considerable effort. Accepting the divorce without resorting to the need to punish by using the children has not been easy. There have been ups and downs in their divorced parenting relationship. But they are able to keep some fundamental issues clearly in their minds. In Minuchin's (1974) terms they have continued to keep the executive function in the family. They clearly accept their responsibility as parents and assume it is their duty to make decisions about the children. Foremost in their minds is a desire to minimize the trauma for the children of living in a divorced family and to continue being responsible parents.

Angry Associates

For this group of divorced spouses their anger with each other is still an integral part of their divorced relationship. Again, these couples have a variety of reasons for the divorce and still have bitter and resentful feelings about their past marriage, as well as resentment about the actual divorce process. Some of these couples had long and heated battles during the divorce process, often fighting over custody, visitation and financial matters. And, for many, the fights have continued for several years after the divorce. Consider Tom and Elaine:

Tom: Elaine will never forgive me for leaving her. She always needs to let me know in some way that the divorce was my choice and therefore I have to suffer. We're really not able to talk about anything without my feeling her hostility. It took us several years to work out my visiting with Jamie and I'm always worried about how she will be when I come to pick her up. I've learned to pick Jamie up without saying too much and hope we can avoid any hassles. I don't see Jamie as much as I want to but Elaine and I have a firm contract which took a couple of years to work out. It's not the way I would like it to be but it's the best I can hope for I think. She doesn't speak to Sandra, my wife, but she does let Jamie spend one weekend a month with us now.

For Elaine and Tom continued coparenting is difficult but they both still manage to continue parenting. They rarely discuss much of anything with each other; when they do an argument results. Although Tom's involvement with Jamie has diminished, he still keeps contact with her and hopes for more active involvement. These divorced spouses function in ways similar to marriages where spousal angers infuse family relationships. Children in these relationships often get caught in their parents' struggles and experience ongoing loyalty conflicts.

Fiery Foes

The major distinction in this category is that the ability to coparent is almost nonexistent. Their angers are so intense, even many years after the divorce, that their ability to accept each other's parenting rights is lost. For many of these spouses the other parent is the enemy. Indeed, for some, one or even both parents' ability to parent is limited. These divorces tend to have been highly litigious, with legal battles continuing many years after the divorce. They are unable to remember any good times in the marriage and cling to the wrongs done each other. Like couples in conflict-habituated marriages, they are still very much attached to each other, although they would be quick to deny it. Janine and Stewart provide a good illustration:

Janine: When I left Stewart it was after many years of unhappiness. He's just a self-centered, immature person. He drinks too much and he always has. We set up a visitation schedule but he was never able to stick with it. I want him to be a responsible parent but I can't count on him for anything. He only wants to see the kids on his time schedule, when it's convenient for him. He never sends his child support on time and there's no way he's going to see the kids if he doesn't support them. And I don't approve of his lifestyle and the women he sees. I have told him time and again that he can't see the kids if he has a woman in his apartment.

Stewart: I can never do anything right by Janine. She harangues me every time I come to pick up the kids. There isn't much that she doesn't complain about. My work is seasonal and I can't always come up with all the support money,[3] but she insists that if I can't then I can't see the kids. Sometimes I call the kids when she's working because its the only time I can talk to the kids without her interrupting. She's rigid — she always has been and always will be. I can't stand the fighting and it seems easier sometimes to just not see the kids.

For most of the couples who fall into this category the power struggle pervades the entire family. The children are caught in the middle, ofttimes taking sides with one parent or the other. There is still a need to place blame for all the disappointments in the marriage and the old angers are reignited with every reminder of the other. It is in this group that one of the parents, usually the father, sees the children less and less frequently over the years. Both parents blame each other for this declining contact and the children become pawns in their continuing battle.

Dissolved Duos

This category was not present in the Binuclear Family Research because of some initial criteria for selection for the study.[4] However, there are indeed divorced spouses who, after the separation and/or divorce, discontinue any contact with each other. Unfortunately, we have no data to even suggest the incidence of this in the general population. "Kidnapping" by noncustodial parents, however, has recently received much media attention and would be most likely to occur in this type of divorced relationship.

In these cases it is usual for one of the partners to geographically leave the area where the family lives. There are isolated cases wherein one partner, usually the man, actually disappears, leaving the other partner to carry the whole burden of reorganizing the family after divorce. Having no clinical or empirical data to draw on about this type of dissolved relationship, we can only speculate that for some people the only way they can cope with the stresses of a failing marriage is total elimination of the stressor by withdrawal, leaving the situation to be handled by the left spouse. It is this total withdrawal of one partner which leaves the true "single-parent family." It is only this type that we would classify as such — a single-parent family is one where there is no further presence of the former spouse except in memories and fantasies.

BINUCLEAR FAMILIES

As we have said, the term binuclear family is a structural concept implying nothing about the interaction patterns between spouses. It is only a term, comparable to the nuclear family concept, connoting the two households that form after divorce but still comprise one family system. Its purpose is to aid in institutionalizing the divorced family form and, therefore, to move beyond conceptualizing the divorced family as a dissolved unit.

We said we assume — as do many of the family theorists — that the relationship between spouses, and hence former spouses, lays the foundation for the emotional climate and functioning of the family. We have described briefly the major types of former spouse relationships that develop during and after divorce; now we will expand upon these types as they form the basis for the binuclear family styles. In later chapters we will develop these styles further as a new member is introduced into the system in remarriage. Although it is difficult to specify an actual chronological time for this transition, remarriage statistics inform us that most divorced spouses remarry within five years after the legal divorce (Glick, 1980; Spanier & Glick, 1980). The entry of a new family member creates sufficient stress and change of membership to alter the patterns of many binuclear families.

The relationship style of former spouses determines how the instrumental and emotional functions of the family are carried on. The differences among the four major types are quite distinct when we examine them from the perspective of family functioning. While the period of separation and early divorce is characterized by crisis and disequilibrium, the family begins to establish new patterns, frequently after much trial and error, which become more or less stabilized after the first year following divorce. It is not uncommon, however, for many families not to achieve stabilization because a new partner enters the system prior to the family's having time to develop a stabilized pattern of relationships. Nevertheless, for this section we will focus on the reorganization and redefinition of the family into a binuclear system.

Perfect Pals

The structural changes in the family created by divorce demand that all family members shift role behaviors. For parents, this means they will have to add new role behaviors, as well as lose certain aspects of their old roles, as they adapt to part-time rearing of children. In the perfect pals typology the role changes may be quite minimal, in that the former spouses are likely to try to continue their parent-child relationships and their parent-parent relationship much as they did in the married family. But even then, with the division of labor distributed between two households, some changes must of necessity occur. Perfect pals form a semi-open binuclear system and some creative ways are devised to maintain as much similarity as possible to the formerly married system.

These are the postdivorce parents who are likely to be seen together enjoying one another, as well as their children, at a wide range of family events — bar/bas mitzvahs, confirmations, graduations, music and dance recitals, Little League games, PTA conferences, weddings, holiday celebrations, funerals — the list is endless. They are not merely present at these events but they share both the planning and the joys and sorrows in a very real and intimate way.

The rituals of the married family are continued in these families. They are the ones who can address the financial issues, the children's schedules, behavior problems, and long-term aspirations with a sense of common purpose. Conflicts, when they arise, are more likely to be over the means for achieving a satisfactory solution than over the desirability of the solution itself. They share a common purpose to be as effective in their joint parenting as they can be.

As has been noted in the last chapter, custody is usually shared as they develop creative ways to divide the original household yet maintain open and flexible boundaries between the two reorganized households. A not too common pattern, but one devised to reduce the amount of reorganization, is what has been called the "bird's nest" (Wooley, 1978,

1980). Here both parents share equally in maintaining the original family nest by keeping the children in the family home and taking turns living "at home" with the children. Some parents have alternated their "at home" time weekly, biweekly, biannually or annually.

In these kinds of arrangements many of the functions of the family are still carried on mutually. For example, the distribution of money in the family is often flexible, based on the same formulas that were used in the married family. The financial equity in the family home is maintained, to be divided at a later date, usually when the youngest child reaches age 18. Parents continue to share, albeit in an alternating sequence, all the responsibilities of child-care and home maintenance. The other parent continues to play a very active role even when he/she does not reside in the household. The "changing of the guard" often includes some time together as a whole family unit. This type of arrangement requires considerable interdependence and, although it may increase in popularity, is not viable for most divorced couples.

Although we have no long-range data on this arrangement, it appears to be a transitional arrangement chosen by couples who are very child-centered and have an amicable, cooperative relationship. However, it is difficult in this arrangement for each individual to develop an independent lifestyle. Hence, it may be a temporary structural measure which for the time being eases the transition, thereby reducing the vulnerability of the family to crisis. We would speculate here that this arrangement may work satisfactorily until one of the partners establishes a new relationship, which requires more privacy and boundaries around the new system. Again, we have no knowledge about the children's adjustment in this type of arrangement, but it does provide the security of one home and the constancy of two parents. However, one might question whether it merely prolongs the fantasy of reunion between the parents or whether it permits the children to make a slow transition to restructured family life. Again, many factors may contribute to a child's adaptation to the changes necessitated through divorce (i.e., age, maturity, social development, etc.).

In addition to the "bird's nest" arrangement, couples have been known to buy houses in the same neighborhood and even to share a duplex arrangement. One couple managed to have houses with the backyards adjoining so the children could move between households without having to cross a street. There is undoubtedly a negative, though covert, response from some relatives and friends to this style of relating in their general day-to-day contacts, since it is so contrary to the prevailing view of how divorced couples "should" behave. While there may be begrudging admiration for their effectiveness as parents, there probably is also a strong sense of ambivalence in many of the social relationships of these couples. But we would venture to guess that we will hear more about these types of divorced couples as divorce becomes more institutionalized in our society.

More commonly, perfect pals are apt to structure some type of familying that permits more separateness yet still maintains many of the symbolic needs of the nuclear family. They may each set up their own households, with the children moving between the households on designated days. For some families the patterns are quite structured, whereas in other families flexibility according to children's and parents' needs can be accommodated. In general, the more amicable and co-operative the relationship between parents, the more flexibility that can be tolerated in the relationship.

Perfect pals, thus, can continue to use each other as resources in the full range of functional areas. This can be quite crucial, especially for the mother, in the socialization and care of children. In some of the other relationship types the mother may be left to cope with little assistance from the father. Child-care for small children, help during childhood illnesses, collaboration during the stressful adolescent transition of their children, and working together as children move toward maturity and make important decisions about education, career, and possible marriage—all of these can be part of a joint effort.

Cooperative Colleagues

For the cooperative colleagues, these types of arrangements are also possible, but usually take more negotiating. Many of these couples establish one home as primary, with the other as secondary, and divide time up more unequally than do the perfect pals. The parents need to have arrangements more explicitly and formally defined, since the friendship relationship cannot be depended upon as a safety valve if problems or disagreements arise. While some anger and hostility may occur in such circumstances, they are still able to keep in mind the ultimate objective of doing what is best for the children.

Thus, for example, custody arrangements will be clearly spelled out, but they will still probably not be so rigid as to disallow deviations to fit the convenience of one of the spouses or to respond to the request or need of a child. While these couples are less likely to opt for joint or shared custody, there will be a significant proportion who do so or who agree on a custody arrangement which allows for a high level of contact with each parent. The divorce decrees in this type of arrangement often do not state specifically the visitation times; rather these are subsumed under the heading of "suitable and reasonable" arrangements. These can run the gamut from the typical sole custody arrangement with every other weekend with the noncustodial parent, to a joint custody arrangement with fairly equal time spent with each parent. Consideration for the developmental needs of the child and the parents remains central to these relationships.

In this type, too, the instrumental functions of division of labor and decision-making, as well as the socialization function, will be handled with less stress than in conflictual families. There may be less willingness to be always readily available for the other, especially if these are areas which were sore points in the marriage. Assistance may be rendered under clearly defined agreements, rather than in the more casual manner of the perfect pals, but enough flexibility and respect for the other exist so that we can expect that neither partner will be left devoid of resources when really in need.

Major life events, as in the perfect pals' situation, will still probably be joint events, but not with the same camaraderie. Relationships with in-law kin and with mutual friends may still be carried on — usually separately and on a more selective basis. The in-laws and mutual friends will not feel much pressure to take sides out of loyalty to one of the ex-spouses. As a result, both parents develop a sense of success and competency without the kinds of major stresses and crises that arise out of unresolved spousal conflict. And, when a stress moves to crisis, it is more likely to be addressed in a manner that leads to satisfactory resolution, since both are committed to that task. Here we see the consequence of clear boundary definition and maintenance between spousal and parental roles. In many ways, the normal stresses of childrearing are dealt with in a way not unlike that in nuclear families who have developed competent parenting styles, for it is equally important for those "normal" parents to avoid the contamination of parenting roles with spousal ones. It is not surprising, then, that these ex-spouses report a high degree of satisfaction with their parental functioning.

In the early stages of this reorganization there are usually some changes, as parents and children try to accommodate to the continual and consistent change in household structure. Children may have some initial problems in adjusting to the disruption in their routines but often state they prefer this arrangement to not living with one parent at all. Again, this pattern requires flexibility for all family members, but over time, as a consistent patterns develop, it becomes routine. In nuclear families with parents whose work patterns require travel, family members must make a similar adjustment to change in routine.

The literature on the effects of divorce on children is consistent in reporting that the maintenance of both parental relationships in a spirit of cooperation mediates the stresses of divorce for children. So, although the arrangements made by many families in this category appear to be complex to most outsiders, this adaptation appears to fulfill childrearing obligations, parental role fulfillment, and children's emotional needs for stability of significant relationships. These arrangements require compromise and negotiation and ongoing resolution of conflict.

As we move to the next two categories it is important to note that the major differentiating factor is the management of conflict. Although conflict is present in the first two types, it is managed more effectively.[5]

Angry Associates

Probably the term "coparenting" is less applicable to the angry associates. There is less integration in the approach, making it much more of a "parallel" process than the integrated kind found in the two previous types, but still not one which involves the constant violent collisions observed in the fiery foes. There is a similar need for explicit negotiation and specification of arrangements, but much less flexibility in following those agreements. Also, the negotiations, as well as the process of carrying out the agreements, sometimes arouse old antagonisms rooted in the marriage relationship, since the boundaries are neither as clear or as firmly set. Children feel less free in their relationships with one or both parents, since they are aware of the more rigid limits which govern their relationships with them and at the same time are not always sure of what may precipitate an angry outburst. Major life events, which are approached much more positively by perfect pals and cooperative colleagues, may represent major stress, since they are likely to require special negotiations. There is generally more of a quality of "tiptoeing through a minefield" for all of the participants.

In both the angry associates and fiery foes custody is usually awarded to one parent. Continuing power struggles are characteristic. Usually the mother has control over the children and the father has control over the money. A typical scenario that may be replayed for years is father's late or incomplete support payments and mother's withholding or altering visitation. Often subtle and cyclical, this pattern keeps the couple and the children enmeshed in continual strife. If either parent is asked about the reasons for his or her reduced money or visitation, he or she will automatically reply that it was started and aggravated by the other parent. Mental health professionals and court counselors spend many frustrating hours trying to unravel the escalating process.

It goes something like this: Dad is scheduled to pick Jamie up at noon on Saturday. At 11:00 Mom calls Dad and says Jamie has some chores she must finish before she goes with Dad so she can't leave until 2:00. Dad arrives at 2:00, angry about the change in plans and Mother's control over his relationship with Jamie, and is met at the door by mother, who announces that Jamie is not quite ready. She uses that time while Jamie is anxiously getting herself together in the next room to argue with Dad about his irresponsibility about child support and the increasing financial needs of Jamie. A fight ensues and Jamie and Dad leave in anger, with Mother reminding them to be home precisely at 8:00 that night. At 8:00 Mother is watching at the window waiting for Dad and Jamie to arrive and growing increasingly angry as Dad and Jamie arrive an hour later. Jamie runs into her room after hugging Mom while her parents continue the fight started earlier in the day.

Next month Dad sends half the child support or sends it a couple of weeks late. Usually, one or the other of the parents will contact his/her lawyer to grieve about the lack of compliance of the other parent, and the legal system and/or helping professionals will intervene. The immediate symptom will be temporarily abated, only to pop up again around another similar incident, which sets the whole process off again.

Relationships with ex-in-laws and former mutual friends are also not likely to continue on an amicable level. Knowing of the continuing anger, the couple's parents, grandparents, adult siblings, and friends will be reluctant to initiate or respond to opportunities for social interaction with the estranged partner. Or they will find themselves enmeshed in the couple's continuing power struggles and firmly taking sides with one or the other. Their loyalty will be appealed to and frequent or intimate contact with the other partner will be defined as a violation of that bond.

Thus, this binuclear family form exhibits a loss in resources when faced with the normal stressors of childrearing, not only because the other spouse is less likely to be called upon for assistance or to respond if asked, but also because others may not feel able to assist. It can be expected that certain situations may continue to be "sore spots," almost always representing stress, subject to repeated negotiation, and never completely resolved. The consequence is likely to be less ability to cope with stress and more crisis events. Thus, children in such relationships, as well as parents, will find their experience much less satisfactory, just as children in nuclear families suffer when there is frequent unresolved conflict between parents.

Fiery Foes

For the fiery foes we see shifting and overlapping boundaries, barriers raised, attack and counterattack — all characteristics which dominate parenting for these ex-spouses. The custody agreement, undoubtedly reached after difficult and wrathful litigation, remains a battlefield. Custody will almost always be to one of the parents. (If joint or shared custody is imposed by the court, it is unlikely to function in the manner intended and is most likely to be another major source of antagonism.) Access to children by the noncustodial parent will be a source of continued strife. When visitation rights are exercised, one or both parents are likely to use these times to identify recurring or new provocations. Support payments by the noncustodial father, if paid at all, will be delayed, underpaid, and/or seen as exorbitant or misused. The custodial mother will have her own set of complaints about them. Indeed, all aspects of the custodial settlement are used as weapons in the continuing struggle.

Nearly all aspects of normal family functioning carry potential for a new hostile engagement. The highlights of children's lives — birthdays, weddings, holidays, and other ceremonial occasions — often lose their celebratory character in the struggle for control and/or in the exclusion of one of the parents. No smiling group photographs will appear in family albums for this type! Extended kin and friends will also find themselves shut out if they are on the "wrong" side. Indeed, a major theme of such binuclear family forms might be seen as exclusion, rather than parallel or inclusive functioning.

This is a family form that is highly vulnerable and in which stress is very likely to end in crisis. Commonly agreed upon goals and means for attaining them do not form a foundation upon which other resources may be brought to bear. And, of course, the range of resources is reduced significantly by the exclusion of so many possibilities.

Dissolved Duos

We have said that data on dissolved duos is almost nonexistent. However, our theory tells us that these ex-spouses do continue to have to take each other into account. The fact that there is no personal contact between the ex-spouses — and in many cases no contact of any kind — does not negate a basic social psychological fact. The marital and parental histories have set a foundation for the current and future lives of both.

The noncustodial parent, probably most often the father, must face the reality of being completely cut off from his child(ren). Unless and until he establishes another marital or marriage-like relationship, he is very much on his own and must meet his own functional and emotional requirements from his own resources. Aside from the basic need to meet the daily demands of life in terms of food, clothing, housing, household demands, and the like, it is probable that a major task for him is redefining the meaning of family in his life. Extended kin may provide some of that meaning and he may establish kin-like friendships. It is often true that such men will have moved to another city, thus cutting off the support resources which may have been built up during the marriage.

Meanwhile, we are quite aware of a substantial portion of the dissolved duo families which are accurately labeled "single-parent families." Again, however, our knowledge may be somewhat distorted. Focused as it has been on those who are in difficulty of one sort or another, we have little insight into what may be another invisible group of substantial significance — those who *do* function competently. Once more, while many of us may know such families, we have very little systematic knowledge of their reorganization processes.[6]

Summary

An important developmental rite of passage in a child's life, such as a high school graduation, provides a good illustration of how these differing patterns may influence the nature of that event for parents and children. The perfect pals would plan festivities to celebrate the graduation together as a family unit. They might plan a lunch or dinner together, sit together at the graduation, and perhaps even give their son or daughter one gift. The cooperative colleagues would be less likely to plan the festivities together, but both would attend them. Perhaps mother would plan a dinner and invite father to join them. They might sit together at the graduation, but interactions would be more strained and formal.

The angry associates would celebrate separately with the child, perhaps one taking the child to dinner the evening before and one having lunch after the ceremonies. They would sit separately at the ceremonies and avoid contact with each other as much as possible. It is very likely that in the fiery foes one parent would be excluded from the celebrations surrounding the event and even not be invited to the graduation. The excluded parent would be aware of the event and feel angry and hurt to be left out. In the dissolved duos the noncustodial parent would probably not even be aware that his or her child was graduating and, if he or she was aware, would not acknowledge it in any way.

FUNCTIONAL AND DYSFUNCTIONAL BINUCLEAR FAMILIES

As we said in the first chapter, "successful" divorces have only recently entered our realm of thinking. In the past few years criteria for a "constructive" or successful divorce have been developed by a number of social scientists (Kaslow, 1981; Kressel, 1985; Volgy & Everett, 1985). Kressel's definition as it emerged from his study of clinicians' attitudes toward divorce provides a good summary:

> A constructive divorce is one in which the process of psychic divorce has been successfully completed. There was consensus that psychic divorce has occurred when certain conditions prevail with regard to the attitudes and behavior of the former spouses toward one another, the

welfare of children, and the level of functioning of each of the ex-mates as a newly single person (1985, p. 76).

The current research examining the effects of divorce on children concludes that a constructive divorce in a family with children requires minimizing the psychic injury to children through continued relationships with both parents and an atmosphere of support and cooperation between the parents.

Rather than using the terms "successful" or "constructive," we prefer here the concepts "functional" and "dysfunctional" as they relate to the disorganization and reorganization of families in the divorce process. A functional divorce is one in which spouses are able to move through the transitions of disorganizing the nuclear family without creating severe debilitating crises for themselves and other family members. Additionally, they are able to move through the transitions of reorganization without suffering significant relational losses to children, extended kin, and friends. A dysfunctional divorce results in an enmeshment of familial relationships in the spousal relationship. This type of divorce most frequently sets the stage for prolonged and permanent psychic injury to one or more family members.

The limited knowledge we have to date suggests that about 50 percent of the families emerge from the divorce process exhibiting some dysfunction in at least one member of the family; we interpret this to mean that 50 percent of the divorcing families reorganize into *functional* postdivorce family systems. Due to the equating of divorce with pathology, we know much more about the dysfunctional aspects of the divorce process than we do about the functional ones. Since one of our major goals in writing this book is to provide a more balanced view of the current situation of divorce in our society, we need to explore the functional, as well as dysfunctional, processes that divorce produces.

As we analyze the five styles of former spouse relationships, we will categorize the first two as resulting in functional binuclear family reorganization and the last three as resulting in dysfunctional systems. Unraveling the causes for functional and dysfunctional family relationships postdivorce is beyond the scope of this book. For some families merely recognizing and even learning appropriate behaviors will not be sufficient to achieve a functional reorganizational process; their dynamics are too firmly rooted in the individual personalities of the former spouses and the intergenerational dynamics of their family. As noted by Volgy and Everett, "It should be recognized that dysfunctional patterns which were present in the prior nuclear system will continue at differing levels of intensity through this structural decoupling and recoupling process" (1985, p. 88). We are not attempting to understand causes here as much as we are trying to distinguish descriptively the behaviors that result in divorced family dysfunction. As we stated early on, the transitions of divorce result in a wide variation on the continuum from healthy to unhealthy adaptation.

When angry associates and fiery foes go through the transitions of divorce they are likely to involve many of their family and friends in the stormy process. When they separate they are likely to have mastered few, if any, of the tasks of the emotional separation process. Their decision to divorce is likely to be a one-sided decision polarizing into a leaver and a left, a "good guy" and "bad guy."

The separation crisis is usually preceded by angry, retaliatory outbursts and a precipitating crisis such as uncovering an extramarital affair of one partner. They select as their lawyers persons identified in the community as excellent matrimonial lawyers and often proceed with the divorce negotiations only through their attorneys, while marshalling the support of extended family, friends, and frequently the children.

The legal divorce process turns into a win-lose battlefield, leaving new bruises and wounds to add to the already existing marital history scars. When there are dependent children, the issues of custody and visitation become the primary arena for all the unresolved emotional issues between the spouses.

For the fiery foes the legal divorce process may get protracted over years, as they each vie for custody or changes in visitation rights. Usually a sole custody arrangement with varying amounts of time for visitation is settled on. Family court calendars around the country are overloaded with these families, who return to the courts for intervention and arbitration over each visitation agreement. The specifics of what an out-of-home parent may do with the child — how many hours that parent may see the child on the weekend, the exact time of pickup and return of the child, and so on almost endlessly — may need to be spelled out over and over again throughout the child's dependent years.

Angry associates will also exhibit some of these patterns, but not usually to the same degree. They may be able to rely on negotiations between the attorneys rather than court arbitration to resolve their differences. But for both types of couples each decision related to childrearing will be a cause for dispute. A major difference between these two types is that, in the angry associate relationship, both parents are able to maintain involvement, although the out-of-home parent (usually father) is apt to decrease his involvement with the children over time. In the fiery foes the out-of-home parent tends to have only minimal involvement from the outset and may then cease to be involved at all.

Although we would still call these types of families "binuclear," the parenting is more like parallel parenting than it is coparenting. Issues about the children are rarely discussed and decisions are made unilaterally. Children are usually the ones who suffer the greatest psychic injuries. Each crossing from one parental household to the other is marked with anxiety. They feel torn between the parents, are often forced into alliances with one or the other parent, and are made responsible for decisions that should be the functions of the parents. Mental health professionals are most familiar with these families, since children often present symptoms of stress which require professional intervention.

In contrast, perfect pals and cooperative colleagues follow a different path from disorganization through reorganization. Perfect pals, although they experience emotional turmoil and pain, move through the transitions at a more moderate pace, having the coping abilities to resolve their differences with less acrimony. Unlike the two groups described above, they are more likely to have some degree of mutuality in their decision to divorce, even though the initial decision may have been initiated by one partner. They usually make the necessary decisions for disorganization of the nuclear family themselves, using a mediator or one lawyer and/or accountant to assist them in the legal details. They may experiment with a number of different child-sharing arrangements, shifting them to meet the needs of both parents and children. Always present is their genuine respect for each other as parents and concern for the children's welfare. The hurts and angers in the spousal relationship are contained and do not spill over into their parental functions. Their reorganization process is characterized by continued involvement of both in the children's lives and a continuance of the parental executive functions.

Children in these family types tend to be free of dysfunctional loyalties and alliances. They experience stress as part of the transition of a changing family structure, but these stresses are situational and do not result in long-term emotional injury. They may take longer to accept their family reorganization and, depending on their developmental stage, they may experience some temporary distress. It may well be that the children in these families have to defer some of their own developmental needs as they focus some of their energies on pleasing both parents. Perfect pals try very hard to make their arrangements work in the best interests of the children, which in turn may exert pressure on the children to make sure the arrangements do, in fact, work.

Cooperative colleagues are less easy to describe as a group as they move through the transitions. Some resemble perfect pals in the reorganization process, but others behave like a milder version of the angry associates. This latter group, however, is different from the angry associates in that they eventually are able to separate their spousal conflicts from their ability to continue to share parenting. They may start with an adversarial process, but they are less likely to prolong that process and let it fuel their anger. Custody and visitation issues often result in some conflicts. Once settled upon, however, they are usually adhered to.

Over time, as they reorganize, cooperative colleagues are able to find a satisfactory arrangement that requires modification every now and then, either by themselves or with the help of a mediator, counselor, or therapist. Some will settle on some variation of joint custody, perhaps with primary physical custody going to one parent. Some will choose a split custody arrangement, whereby one child may be more with one parent than another child. Still others will agree to sole custody, with frequent visitation of the noncustodial parent.

The major similarity across the families in this category is that, for the most part, they are able to share major decisions about the children. They do not have much, if any, personal relationship, but they do share in varying amounts the joys and problems of parenting. Children in this type of arrangement are not used as pawns in their parents' disagreements, although they are very aware of the existing differences and areas of conflict. However, because the parents are able to keep separate their parental and ex-spousal subsystems, so are the children.

There is no way that we can expect all divorcing spouses to reorganize as healthy, well-functioning binuclear families. But just as models and paradigms for healthy nuclear family functioning are being developed, we offer here models for healthy, well-functioning binuclear families. Characteristically, a healthy binuclear family is one in which boundaries are clearly separated between spousal (or nonparental) roles and relationships and parental ones. Issues of the marital relationship may not be completely resolved, but they do not contaminate the interactions in the binuclear family.

We differ from some of the writers in this field in that we tend not to believe that a functional divorce requires the resolution of all the marital issues. A more realistic goal is to learn to live with some of the ambiguity and ambivalence that accompanies a failed marriage. In so doing divorced spouses retain some of the old attachments, the painful and the pleasant ones. But over time they come to accept their own and their partner's mistakes and shortcomings, and are able to separate and repair sufficiently from the rupture to move on in their lives as separate adults.

CONCLUSION

We have noted frequently in our discussions that much of what we know about the long-term process of divorce is tentative, with little empirical evidence to permit statements of fact. Nevertheless, amidst the lack of conclusive evidence, in the growing body of divorce research, flawed as it is, some tentative guidelines are beginning to emerge. In Ahrons' Binuclear Family Study about 50 percent of the couples fell into the first two categories. Although the sample most likely underrepresents the very hostile divorces, these figures are consistent with those of other studies. As noted by Kressel, "the overall estimate of destructive conflict for all divorcing couples, with and without children, averages out to between 40 and 50 percent" (1985, p. 10). He asserts, and we concur, that at this point in time this can only be an "educated guess." It is also important to note that most data are based on the initial stages of the divorce process, when it is assumed that the anger is the highest. Both Wallerstein and Kelly (1980) and Hetherington et al. (1978) note a decrease in anger over time, which is consistent with the findings of the Binuclear Family Study.

The categories we have described for divorced couples are not as discrete as they may seem in this presentation. Nor are they static. In reality they form a continuum with wide variations among divorced couples. And although we are not able to state with any certainty what percentage of the population falls into any one category, nor are we able to chart the changes in relationships over the life span, we can use these categories as tentative guideposts to learn more about the nature of postdivorce family relationships. The current work in mediation suggests that not all divorced couples will be able to have a constructive divorce, just as not all marriages provide a healthy environment for the partners or the children. But we have made considerable progress in the last decade to even consider the potential for healthy families after divorce.

What seems to differentiate constructive divorces from destructive ones? In general, it appears to be the ability of the divorced spouses to accept their past failures as spouses and to move forward in their relationships with each other in the best interests of their continuing family. For some, the passage of time will bring resolution of the emotional divorce, the ability to grow psychologically and to build new, productive lives. For some, the result will bring cooperative, and perhaps even caring, kin-like relationships. For others, the passage of time will result only in a more entrenched pattern of hostility toward the former spouse. And for still others, as time heals the wounds, indifference may replace the earlier affect.

Although there is no research to support the complex interweaving of factors that may contribute to the process of divorced family reorganization, it is likely that some are related to personality and coping styles of the participants. For example, if someone generally deals with conflictual relationships by withdrawing and cutting off relationships, he or she is likely to react to a divorced spouse in the same manner. For another example, how a person coped with a conflictual relationship with his or her sibling or parent might be similar to how he or she copes with a relationship with a former spouse. We would venture to guess that, if one were to study the personal history of a divorced spouse who had a dissolved relationship with a former spouse or a discontinued relationship with a child after divorce, we would find other examples of significant relationships in his or her life that were dissolved as a way of coping with the conflict and ambivalence.[7] Therefore, we make the assumption, although not supported by empirical data, that the relationships that divorced spouses develop resemble other resolutions to conflictual relationships in their lives.

Our earlier discussion of boundaries in families helps us to understand some of the major characteristics of relationship types we have presented. In the cooperative colleagues the boundaries seem to be very clear. Spousal issues are separate from parental ones, permitting the partners to cooperate parentally while not always resolving the spousal issues. In the latter two categories these boundaries are less clear and anger over nonparental issues infuses the parental arena. For the perfect pals, this is less clear. In this smaller group of divorced families it is uncertain whether their friendship represents a continuation of the marital relationship or a new relationship based on some old attachments that are positive for the partners.

The study of attachment has thus far focused primarily on the negative aspects, with an assumption that continuing attachment to one's former spouse is a sign of an incomplete emotional divorce (Berman, 1985; Bloom et al., 1985; Kitson et al., 1985; Weiss, 1975, 1979). We are suggesting an expanded view of attachment here, hypothesizing that some aspects of attachment to one's former spouse may have positive consequences for the divorced family. The Binuclear Family Study sample and clinical experiences suggest that a positive attachment between former spouses can be healthy, permitting them to incorporate the good parts of their relationship. We are not suggesting that even a majority of the divorcing are able to do this, but we are cautioning against assuming that all attachment between former spouses is inherently negative. Since we have no studies of divorced spouses 30, 20, or even 15 years after the divorce, we cannot even speculate at this time about the changes that may occur in the relationship.

As Ahrons has presented the results of her research over the past few years, she has been surprised at the number of people in the audience who have related life histories involving tender reunions of ex-spouses many years after the divorce. It is clear that the intimate relationship between marital partners who have divorced continues to hold an important place in one's memories. For some old pain and anger prevail for a lifetime and cancel out any positive qualities that may have been present, but for others the pain and anger have disappeared and some fond memories remain. It is like the old adage, "Don't throw out the baby with the bath water." Indeed, it may be a sign of a functional divorce when the partners can remember, and even savor, the warmth and loving feelings that were present at some time in most marriages. Even the endearing qualities of an ex-spouse may be remembered as a link between the past and the present.

SIX

Family Career Implications of the Divorce Transition

Having identified five possible developmental paths for postdivorce family reorganization, we now look at the different implications of these patterns for families at varying periods in the family career. As we saw in Chapter 3, reorganizing after a crisis can mean very different things to families rearing small children than to those in midlife. Once again we need to be conscious of the six areas of family functioning: reproduction/recruitment, maintenance of biological functioning, socialization, division of labor, maintenance of order, and maintenance of meaning. However, some of these will have considerably more salience than others during this transition. As in Chapter 4, we will not address the childbearing and childrearing family career period, since that has been the focus of Chapter 5.

CHILDLESS COUPLES

The relationship types that we have identified (e.g., perfect pals, angry associates) are based on data from couples with children. Consequently, when we apply these types to the childless couple category our scenarios are highly speculative. Nevertheless, it seems logical that these types may well appear among divorcing couples in this family career period, and the use of the typology provides a useful means for more specific speculation about the characteristics of postdivorce reorganization for them.

Perfect Pals

The childless couple has the least in the way of continuing bonds to hold them together. Without children, the ties which may have been built up with in-laws and mutual friends are less likely to be sustained.

Most of the divorces in this stage occur after a short-term marriage, so that family ties with in-laws have probably not become an integral part of the individual's life. However, some childless marriages follow several years of friendship, and aspects of that friendship may well continue in some fashion following divorce. Since, by definition, perfect pals like and respect each other as people—even if they have decided that they ought not to be married, they may continue to share a number of aspects of their now separate lives. They apparently use the assimilation coping style to deal with the stresses created by the differences which led to the divorce.

Thus, it is conceivable that perfect pals may continue to share some of the more intimate aspects of their new situations. They may discuss experiences they are having with potentially new partners and even seek advice from one another about how to deal with issues that may arise in these new relationships. After all, the experience of marriage, and of the breakup of that marriage, gives the former partner a special insight into how the other feels and behaves in a variety of circumstances. This may also be a time for former partners to suggest some changes in the way the other does certain things, based upon the unsatisfactory—as well as the satisfactory—experiences of the marriage. There is still a high potential for anger and conflict; however, given the basic respect and trust which are key in this pattern, the former spouse may represent a valuable resource, even if there is some risk of old conflicts showing up in such discussions.

It is even possible that perfect pals will find occasions to relate socially with their former spouse's potential new partner. Especially for those who live in small towns where both may keep the same friendship network, socializing together may be required at times. In fact, their continuing relationship may be quite similar to many of the "steady" or cohabiting relationships that continue even after the romantic love has waned and the living together has ceased. At the same time, given the stereotypes carried in society, new partners may have some difficulty in understanding how the former spouses can continue to relate and may exert pressure to have the old relationship totally severed.

While there is no longer any requirement that former spouses continue to assist each other with some of the daily problems of living, perfect pals are quite likely to carry on providing such help. If they had developed a specialized division of labor in the marriage, the former spouse may again represent a ready and reliable resource—at least in the period of transition to the new single state. And, since issues of power in decision-making are less salient, ex-spouses may be more willing to accept the greater competency of the other in certain areas. We can imagine more calls for help in those areas that are often sex-typed—household repairs, cooking, economic decisions, or dealing with the landlady. We can also imagine continuation of some joint ventures in these areas—at least until each is well established in their singleness.

Perfect pals are also most likely to maintain certain joint relationships with kin and mutual friends. While this may cause some discomfort for parents, grandparents, and some of their friends, the evidence that the former spouses still find each other to be important in their own lives may have a great deal of influence on these other relationships. If kin and friends find that they are not called upon to take sides and if the relationships have been something more than obligatory because of their association with one of the ex-partners, a new pattern of relating may well develop. A wife who has developed a close relationship with her mother-in-law may very likely continue that relationship after divorce.

Finally, perfect pals seem most likely to continue to see their relationship as having high meaning in their individual lives. They have faced the fact that they could not relate effectively in marriage, but they have also retained aspects of the relationship which are clearly important to them. It could well be that a firm and lasting friendship of considerable significance will result, even after one or both have established another love relationship.

Cooperative Colleagues

While perfect pals have a highly affective relationship—chiefly positive—we would expect that cooperative colleagues will relate in much more instrumental ways. Indeed, without the bonds of either children or personal affection, one might wonder if this type would appear frequently or have any durability when it did appear. There does remain the factor of respect for the other and, given the many aspects of adjustment that are required—especially in the beginning postdivorce period, we could expect some continued relationship. These most likely revolve around needs related to division of labor.

Sharing intimacies around new relationships, continuing to relate to in-law kin or mutual friends together, or depending on one another for help in decision-making is considerably less likely. And, because there is likely to be less central meaning to the former spouse relationship, it can be expected that cooperative colleagues will move further apart as new patterns of living replace old ones. Unless such couples discover a new basis for friendship, thus moving more towards the "pals" (though not *perfect* pals") style of relating, we could anticipate that their interactions would become less and less frequent as time goes by.

For both the perfect pals and the cooperative colleagues, the decision to divorce is probably fairly mutual. The legal divorce itself is likely to be a simple process completed frequently without the aid of lawyers. "Pro se" divorce, handled by the parties themselves, although not encouraged by the courts or highly publicized, is an option available to people who have little in the way of assets or liabilities to divide.

Angry Associates

Angry associates *do* have a basis for continuing their relationship — albeit a negative one. There are aspects of postdivorce life which inevitably bring the former partner back into one's sphere. A wedding of a mutual friend or a high school or college reunion may force the contact of former spouses who would otherwise not choose to be together. Or, given that the anger has not abated, learning of certain events can precipitate contact in order to express that anger. Learning of a new relationship ("I always *knew* that you had something going with him/her!"), encountering a financial problem that has its source in the marriage ("You told me you had taken care of that!"), hearing of something that was said to kin or friends ("Still trying to drive a wedge between us, aren't you?"), or other such events can lead to a rekindling of the anger and resumption of contact with the former spouse. The basic meaning of such a relationship probably lies in a continued attempt to "right the wrongs," "balance the scales," or justify one's position around some issue that was part of the marriage. Since, at the same time, there are fewer reasons to learn about such events and to react to them, we would again expect that these relationships would not endure as the anger dies out and as new relationships replace the old ones.

Fiery Foes

Perhaps the distinction between this type and the angry associates would be in the initiative taken to enter into battle. One might expect that fiery foes would be constantly on the alert for anything which would justify yet another engagement in the ongoing war. The issue would not be as important as the opportunity to once again attack and attempt to wound. And, indeed, the meaning of the relationship would be found primarily in the ability to continue to make life miserable for the former spouse. In this case, it is possible that one could expect the relationship, pathological as it might be, to continue "until death do us part"!

For both angry associates and fiery foes, it is most likely that one partner has chosen divorce. A new love relationship may have prompted the decision to divorce, leaving the other partner feeling rejected and angry. These feelings then are carried over into the legal process and escalate the anger even more. The lack of children does not automatically imply no battles over custody. Legal custody battles have been known to ensue over a family pet or a valuable piece of property. Reported in the Los Angeles *Times* recently was an article titled "Ex-wife mistreats the Rolls, so hubby gets joint custody." As explained by an exasperated judge: "She gets the car for four weeks and then he will get the car for four weeks. It was the best thing I could do." Similar decisions have been made about family pets.

Dissolved Duos

This category is the one which most fits our stereotype for divorced spouses in this developmental stage. Yet the relationships that fit here probably were short-term and highly conflictual. Some may have had short courtships which resulted in impulsive marital decisions. By definition, these ex-spouses have intentionally severed their relationship in all its aspects. While there may be unresolved issues and much potential conflict, they have taken the path of avoiding each other rather than dealing with them. Thus, without children to force them to have to take account of one another, they are quite likely to be successful in not engaging each other in any way after divorce. In a very central sense, the relationship has become meaningless. In fact, many of these divorces may not even be mentioned by the participants in their later life. One of the authors knows of several situations in which an adult child found out at the time of his or her own marriage that one parent had been married for a short time before the current longtime marriage. Many people in this category discount that early marriage and divorce, preferring to pretend for most of their life that it was nonexistent.

MIDLIFE COUPLES

As we move to the remaining two family career periods, we reiterate that our types were derived from childrearing postdivorce family data. As we have repeatedly noted, divorce research has not been addressed to the increasingly significant number of couples who sever their marital ties after childrearing. There is no reason to believe, however, that they would not fall into similar categorical types.

From this point on in the family career the fact of children as a part of the family structure carries a central significance for these relationship types. Even assuming that marital issues are no longer relevant, parental issues and the kinship implications that they have make some sort of relating inevitable.

Divorce in midlife leaves the couple with a long period of life to anticipate. In the "prime of life," with all of the activities and involvements of people of this age, the dissolution of the marital bond leaves a major void. Even for those close to retirement, who may have spent a lot of effort around planning for that time as a couple, it is necessary to develop a new life organization. Family and old or new friends may play a major role in that new organization, but there are also a number of aspects of daily life which will require close attention. The character of the relationship that is developed with the former spouse plays a critical role in that development.

We have a small body of research that gives us some information on the divorce transition among midlife couples.[1] The most relevant is the work of Hagestad (Hagestad & Smyer, 1982; Hagestad et al., 1984) which we discussed in some detail in Chapter 2. Hagestad's findings make it clear that there are a range of styles to restructuring the family in midlife divorce. It gives us some confidence that the types which Ahrons found in her childrearing couples are probably equally applicable in this family career period.

Perfect Pals

It is tempting to assume that couples who divorce in midlife are composed primarily of those who have stayed together "for the sake of the children." Since we really don't know how accurate such an assumption is, we think it unwise to base very much speculation on it. However, midlife divorce has an intriguing character to it, since post-childrearing is often characterized as that period in marriage when the high quality of spousal companionship, to which so many couples aspire, can finally be experienced. That being the case, the "perfect pals" pattern in postdivorce is an even more intriguing phenomenon — if, as we assume, it does exist. We would speculate that it finds its roots in perhaps four factors: (1) the long-term relationship experienced by these couples, in which a good deal that is positive has occurred; (2) a strong desire to maintain family ties — especially ties with children and grandchildren — and not to have those ties disrupted by personal animosity; (3) a continuing need to meet certain functional requirements which have been met in the past in their marital relationship; and (4) the reticence of individuals in this age cohort to return again to the courtship experience. Having decided to sever the marital relationship for whatever reasons, there is much that motivates them to develop the perfect pals pattern.

There is a high potential for resources to be available to both individuals in meeting a number of their functional needs. Like their childless counterparts, should they develop another love interest, they may indeed use the former spouse as a confidant in dealing with that relationship. Then there are the routine needs, many of which are gender-typed in this age cohort — the good home-cooked meal prepared by the woman and the routine household repairs and maintenance carried out by the man. They may consult about decisions around finances, occupational issues, needs of aging parents, or preretirement plans for themselves. They may engage in mutual socialization in developing an effective single life in which there is less dependency and more autonomy. All of these are solid reasons for continuing to relate to the former spouse.

It is perhaps in the "maintenance of meaning," however, that the perfect pals find continued richness in their relationship. Family and mutual friends can remain a focus for much of their relating. Continuing to share the joys and sorrows of adult children and grandchildren and the relationships with their own aging parents provides a strong mutuality. Recall that this is the "middle generation," which Hill (1971) found to be the focal point of much intergenerational exchange — the generation doing much of the giving and supporting. These kin may have some difficulty accepting something as unorthodox as friendship between the ex-spouses; however, given the fact that the couple is not requiring divided loyalties, a creative and satisfying kinship style can result. Divorce does not mean losing access, only revising the form of that access. We can expect, of course, continuation of many joint family ceremonial occasions, which tend to carry increased value in midlife and later.

Similar continuation of more intimate friendships could occur. Longstanding bridge partners, camping companions, bowling league friends, or people with whom the spouses have shared season tickets to the theatre or symphony need not be shut out of their lives. Church, temple, or club memberships may be continued, though these more formal organizational ties may be somewhat more difficult to maintain. This violates the societal stereotypes. However, if childbearing couples manage to develop such a style, there seems more reason for it to be possible among those who no longer have the complications of minor children as part of their relationship. But to achieve such a relationship at a time of life when gender inequities are likely to be most prominent may require mutuality in the divorce decision. Both partners would have to have fairly equal resources or at least the potential for them to feel they can comfortably succeed in their single lifestyles. One can imagine a divorce of this type occurring in a dual career couple whose interests have been growing more separate over the years. The launching of the children may signal the awareness of their divergent paths in life and of the absence of reasons to continue to live together.

Cooperative Colleagues

This group in midlife is likely to show a somewhat more restricted pattern of relating. We cannot expect the same kind of continuity of patterns in many of the functional areas. We would not anticipate much consultation or assistance around daily activities or about major life changes or plans. Indeed, we would expect that the primary focus of their association will be around family members. They are quite likely to confer on family matters which affect them both to a greater or lesser degree. There may be some continuation of the caretaking activity for the aging in-law parents — or, at least, discussion of major needs affecting them.

Around married children and grandchildren there may be considerably more contact. Routine joint celebrations of birthdays and holidays are unlikely, but the major transition ceremonies — graduations, weddings, christenings, bar/bas mitzvahs, and funerals — may well continue to be shared, with minimal stress. These events, while very significant, do not require intimate or extended interaction. Since many married families experience some conflict on such emotional occasions, reality requires that we recognize the somewhat greater potential for it among the cooperative colleagues. At the same time, as in married families, there is a strong pressure not to "spoil" the occasion and to keep differences under control.

The maintenance of meaning for cooperative colleagues may require some major revision. Focusing on the marital and parental relationship as a central concern of the pair may give way to a pattern of shared significance in some limited areas of family. Both individuals, however, will need to seek out new elements to replace the centrality of the marriage in their former lives. New relationships, new or redirected emphases on work or domestic activities, and new recreational and intellectual interests will need to be found to fill the "empty" place. Again, what these replacements and revisions are and how this happens remains to be learned in future research.

Unlike perfect pals, cooperative colleagues may not have made a mutual decision to divorce. But, as we have noted about this group in our prior discussions, they have been able to separate their spousal angers from their parental responsibilities. Familying is still an important function for this group, even though the children no longer reside at home. They may still want to continue some family rituals together, although they are likely to split up the holidays between them rather than spend them together. But their relationship still remains child-centered, and they are able to keep their anger contained so that it does not infuse their child-related interactions.

Angry Associates

We noted in reporting the data on the childrearing sample from which the types were developed that we were dealing with more of a continuum than four clearly defined groups. Again, because there are no minor children to provide a ready reason for contact and for the expression of residual anger, we would anticipate that angry associates differ from cooperative colleagues primarily in the degree of contact and the level of conflict that occurs during that contact. We could expect, as well, that kin and friends would not initiate occasions which would precipitate opportunities for conflict. One can imagine married children carefully considering whether to tell Mom and Dad about some event because of what could develop between them. And, we can anticipate careful planning for major ceremonial events to reduce the potential for an emotional outbreak. The adult child of recently divorced parents, for example, in planning a bar mitzvah dinner, might need to take special care to keep parents separate. "Let's have Mom sit at the table with Rachel and her family. Mom can gripe to Rachel about Dad without getting into an argument. Dad can sit at the table with Uncle Ben and Aunt Lou. They'll want to hear about Dad's fishing trip to Colorado and Mom was never very close to them any way. And we'd better not have any of the grandparents light candles on the cake!" Such attempts at lack of favoritism and keeping the former spouses apart are probably typical.

Minimal and episodic participation in family occasions leaves the angry associates to work out new meaning for their individual family relationships. For them, to an even greater degree, meaning will have to be sought in new interests.

Fiery Foes

Now the tables are once again turned. In this extreme type of post-divorce couple the areas of functional need provide a multitude of opportunities for hostile encounter. Given that there may be a considerable accumulation of joint property, the division of the spoils can provide a continuing source for disagreement. Family, especially married offspring, can be both a source for reopening old issues and a ready target for complaints. Daughters and sons may find themselves desperately seeking ways to avoid having to hear the account of the latest offense, real or imagined, of the other parent. Children, although grown and independent, can still be used as pawns and weapons in the endless conflict. The consequence of this may be alienation from adult children, since they are no longer at the mercy of their parents. It is likely that even the major family ceremonies will exclude one or both of the divorced parents. Some method of alternating participation in birthday and holiday celebrations may be developed, if they are observed with divorced parents at all.

As in the other family career periods, fiery foes will probably find the major meaning in the former relationship to be initiating or winning the most recent skirmish. Rather than directing their energy to the development of new meanings in their lives, they are likely to be obsessed with continued attempts to punish the ex-spouse. Little of a constructive nature can be found in such a pattern, and one of the tragic elements in it may be the increasing isolation of both individuals from most of their former relationships. The consequent loneliness can only further exacerbate an already bad situation.

Mutuality in the divorce decision would be rare in these last two types. More likely would be the situation where one spouse initiated the divorce, thus setting the pattern for the usual feelings of the leaver and the left. Leavers usually feel guilty, while the left feel angry or depressed. "Displaced homemakers" fit in this category. They have spent most of their lives in unpaid employment as homemakers, often finding their role fulfillment as mother, wife, and supporter of the husband's career.

An example of this is the doctor's wife who, when her physician husband of some 25 years leaves her, finds herself without many resources or even purpose in her life. The children are grown and most of her community activities have centered on her husband's profession. She suffers extreme role loss at the time of divorce and in midlife must find new ways to fulfill herself as a single person. Or, the man whose life career has been centered on being a breadwinner and "family man" finds himself without anything but his work when his wife, upon finding new direction in her life, decides to divorce. These individuals, unprepared for living life without their spouse, suffer severe distress. Many are not able to restructure their lives in meaningful ways and cope with the anguish of the transition by clinging to their anger at their former spouse for wreaking such havoc unnecessarily in their lives. Adult children in these types of families often ally themselves with the more distressed parent and may have to take on the responsibilities of parenting their parent.

Dissolved Duos

As we have seen, it is only this postdivorce type which totally removes the former spouse from the development of a new life organization. Having solved the basic conflict by avoidance, these couples will probably continue a similar pattern. It is unlikely that these couples will maintain relationships with any mutual friends. But, because they do not need to carry on any battles and have abandoned any requirement to be tied to old relationships associated with the marriage, they may quite successfully develop an entirely new set of patterns. Of course, they will have to develop these in most of the functional areas.

As to family ties, contacts with former in-laws are very unlikely. On the other hand, association with their own siblings and parents may change very little. How they develop new relationship styles with married children and grandchildren all probably vary from continued and wide-ranging relationships that do not include the former spouse, to carefully planned events excluding their ex-partner, to no contact at all. It is possible that such couples develop a new pattern of meaning in life which maintains a strong element of family involvement. It is also possible that they create patterns with no family element at all. As we said about the "perfect pals," if they are out there—and we think they are, we'd like to know more about them. Without empirical evidence, our theory helps very little in characterizing the developmental patterns for this type.

The research on midlife divorce, as we have said, is quite limited. This is especially so with respect to the impact of divorce in midlife on adult children. There appears to be a general assumption that, because they are adults and less dependent upon their parents, they experience little impact from parental divorce. However, the contrary appears to be true from what little research evidence we do have.[2] At least with respect to the initial reaction to the crisis, these young adults have a range of reactions similar to those of minor children—anger, sadness, and relief. Although not residing with their parents, young adults may still be financially dependent on their parents, still tend to view the parental residence as "home," and continue to find comfort in family rituals. These all become central issues of concern in the transitions of family disorganization and reorganization.

AGING COUPLES

Fiery Foes

We have reversed the order of presentation somewhat in this family career period to discuss the most probable types first. It takes major differences to precipitate divorce at this age. Therefore, we can be more confident that, when it does occur, the resulting postdivorce relationship will take this or one of the next two forms. Contemplating this type in the later years of life brings forth all of the stereotypes attributed to the aging as difficult, cantankerous, and demanding. Much as we reject these stereotypes, it seems realistic to expect that these terms would be quite applicable to this group.

The primary impact of much of the hostile interaction between aging fiery foes is on the younger generations. The dilemma for them is intense. We have speculated that fiery foes in the earlier family career periods will often find themselves increasingly isolated from other relationships to the extent that their continued warfare is inflicted on kin and friends. Yet, for the younger generations there is a strong pressure not to allow aging parents and grandparents to be neglected. But if the primary experience when in touch with them is to receive the latest "battlefield bulletins," they are likely to avoid their estranged parents or to see them begrudgingly and only out of a sense of duty. The inevitable result, it would seem, is decreasing contact and emotionally unfulfilling experiences when they do occur.

As for the maintenance of meaning, another stereotype of the aging comes to the fore. Older people are often seen as getting their greatest pleasure in complaining. If the continuing conflict becomes a central meaning in life and the shortcoming of the former spouse a primary focus, aged fiery foes are again likely to confirm that stereotype. In the process they are likely to lose the opportunity to find creative and constructive new goals in life. One is hard-pressed to find much that family or friends might do to help these divorcees redirect their energies towards a less dismal pattern.

Angry Associates

Considering their long marital history, continued contact for aging divorced couples is quite likely. This contact around continued physical or financial needs or around extended family events may bring forth angry exchanges. Because of the aged's increasing dependency on the younger generations for various kinds of assistance, even if financial concerns are not important, the married children and grandchildren are likely to be a party to many of these exchanges.

Indeed, we would think that the major impact of divorce reorganization in aging might be on the younger generations, as they work out means for dealing with Grandma and Grandpa. Having been unsuccessful in getting the aging couple to stay together (an effort to which we suspect they gave much energy), they will have little in the way of previous experience or role models for guidance. Indeed, they may see the whole situation as having complicated *their* lives much more than it did the lives of the divorcing couple! Physical care and economic needs will demand more resources in energy and money.

Without the central meaning of a continued marital relationship, the maintenance of meaning in life is also likely to fall heavily on holding onto extended family relationships. Perhaps there is not a great deal of difference in the handling of familial celebrations from that in the midlife angry associates type. However, family may have been the primary focus for meaning in life for some period of time. It will be much more difficult, therefore, to reduce the aging ex-spouses' involvement in such events. To exclude them would seem almost impossible. If angry exchanges are frequent at such times, the younger generation does indeed face a major dilemma! And most certainly for the couple the bittersweet experience of participating in these events must be less than what they might have anticipated in earlier years. Alternative sources of meaning in life appear to be considerably reduced, assuming the normal decrease in physical energy and the probable reduction in financial resources to pursue travel or other similar activities. Here again, we are frustrated by our inability to call forth empirical evidence which might help us identify more positive patterns.

Cooperative Colleagues

When divorce occurs in this age group, we would expect that it would be as a result of such strong feelings that it would be difficult to maintain a cooperative postdivorce approach. Nevertheless, we think that this is still a more likely type than the perfect pals one. One can speculate that there are couples who, having found the marital relationship no longer worth maintaining, may nevertheless continue a reasonably amicable relationship around specific areas. Development of economic arrangements which provide some degree of adequacy for both is certainly quite likely. (It must be remembered that for this age cohort the woman is probably highly vulnerable in the economic sphere.)

We would expect that familial relationships would also exhibit cooperative concerns. In addition to the help which may come from married children and grandchildren, the key area of ceremonial family events would call for a cooperative approach. Respect, even in the face of high marital discord, would call forth behavior designed to insure that the former spouse received adequate care and appropriate support. Much of this, we suspect, would be in the form of insuring that extended family kept aware of needs that came to the former spouse's attention. We can imagine consultations about important decisions or events that might arise. And, from the extended family's point of view, we can expect much contact and communication around assuring one former spouse that the needs of the other were being met. Once again, however, we are reminded of the likely values of permanence and "taking the good with the bad" held by this generation. As a result, we cannot be confident that the type will be found with any great frequency.

Dissolved Duos

Much that was said concerning the midlife dissolved duos applies to the aging career period. The potential to develop more positive life patterns exists. However, the reduced resources, material and non-material, of the aging again place a greater pressure on the extended kin. Nevertheless, for these couples, free of the conflict-ridden nature of the fiery foes and angry associates types, the working out of a satisfactory postdivorce life pattern seems at least possible.

Perfect Pals

Of all the types in all of the family career periods, this one seems least likely to occur. Given the centrality of marriage and family — especially the place of marital companionship in old age — in this group, the value of permanence in marriage, and the long marital history which they will probably have experienced, the question, "Why would they divorce at all?" becomes extremely salient. We read in the newspaper or hear of aging couples who, under the stress of financial demands related to extended illness, divorce in order to qualify for care facilities not available to them as a married couple. But this is an indication of the failure of the society to develop appropriate means for providing for such family needs, rather than a genuine severing of marital ties. While we may be wrong in our assessment, we think it so unlikely that this postdivorce couple exists empirically that there seems little need to attempt an analysis of what implications it may have.

SUMMARY

Postmarital family reorganization is a highly diverse process. Our inability to present detailed analyses of these potential types in the three non-childrearing family career periods underscores the need for more empirical work on these divorced family groups. When taken out of its clinical and pathological context, divorce emerges as a complex mosaic of multiple possibilities. As we turn to the transition of remarriage, we maintain our view that a better understanding of the normative and nonpathological aspects of the divorce process will lead to achieving the kind of full and satisfying lives that we covet for all families.

SEVEN

The Remarriage Transition

The family change process set in motion by one marital disruption boggles one's mind. It frequently requires complex computation to chart and understand the kinship relationships. Even though the current remarriage rates show a continuing decline (Appendix Table 3), the vast majority of divorced families will move through the series of stressful transitions and structural changes brought about by the expansion of the family postdivorce. The structural changes in remarriage give rise to a host of disruptions in roles and relationships, and each transition may be mastered with varying amounts of stress and turmoil.

Projections from the current trends indicate that between 40 and 50 percent of the children born in the 1970s will spend some portion of their minor years in a one-parent household. Given the current remarriage rates it is also projected that approximately 25 to 30 percent of American children will live for some period of time in a remarried household. Although we do not have as adequate cohabitation information as we would like, we can assume that many of these children will also live for some period of time in a cohabiting household, which may or may not become a remarriage household.[1] This means that at least 25 to 30 percent of the children will have more than two adults who function simultaneously as parents. Rates of redivorce are also increasing, resulting in even more complex kinship structures.

Consider the following case example of the Spicer/Tyler/Henry binuclear family. We have followed Nancy and Jim Spicer through their separation in Chapter 3 and their divorce in Chapter 5. Their new spouses are also familiar to the reader from Chapter 5, where we used as case examples several of their former marital relationships. Here we chart their family transitions through remarriage. Figure 2 provides a map of these complex family relationships.

154

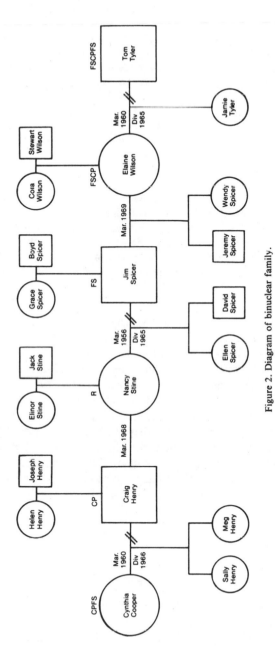

KEY:

R   Respondent
CP   Current Partner
FS   Former Spouse
CPFS   Current Partner's Former Spouse
FSCP   Former Spouse's Current Spouse
FSCPFS   Former Spouse's Current Partner's Former Spouse

Figure 2. Diagram of binuclear family.

When Ellen was eight and David ten, their parents separated. They continued to live with their mother, Nancy, spending weekends and vacations with their father, Jim. Two years after the divorce their father married Elaine, who was the custodial parent of her daughter, Jamie, aged six. Ellen and David lived in a one-parent household with their mother for three years, at which time their mother remarried. Their new stepfather, Craig, also had been divorced, and he was the joint-custodial parent of two daughters, aged six and 11. His daughters spent about ten days each month living in his household. Within the next four years, Ellen and David's father and stepmother had two children of their own, a son and a daughter.

When Ellen and David are 15 and 17, their family looks like this: They have two biological parents, two stepparents, three stepsisters, a half-brother and a half-sister. Their extended family has expanded as well: They have two sets of stepgrandparents, two sets of biological grandparents, and a large network of aunts, uncles, and cousins. In addition to this complex network of kin, they have two households of "family."

Ellen and David also experienced two major household transitions as their family reorganized. First, they experienced the transition from living in a nuclear family—a two-parent household—to living in a one-parent household. During this adjustment they had to develop independent relationships with each parent, seeing their father, Jim, only on weekends and vacations. Living in a one-parent household with their mother involved a number of major role changes, as the family reorganized to fill the roles that had been Dad's prior to the divorce. After Ellen and David adjusted to this living arrangement for three years, their mother remarried and they again had to make another major household transition. Again roles had to be shifted to accommodate a new adult, Craig, into the household. In addition, Ellen and David also had to make changes to accommodate Craig's children as members of their household.

BINUCLEAR FAMILY REORGANIZATION
THROUGH EXPANSION: AN OVERVIEW

The expansion of the binuclear family through remarriage involves the addition of new family members in all three generations. The recoupling of one of the former spouses requires another reorganization of the former spouse subsystem and each of the parent-child sub-systems; a recoupling of the other former spouse requires still another reorganization of the whole system. Each of these transitions has the potential of being highly stressful for family members. The way in which the family reorganizes itself will determine whether the binuclear family emerges as a functional or dysfunctional system.

The structural complexity of remarriage, combined with the lack of appropriate norms, makes the binuclear family highly vulnerable to a number of stresses. Pasley and Ihinger-Tallman (1982) identify three main causes of stress in stepfamilies: (1) the possible clashing of two different family cultures; (2) the differing perceptions of how the family's time, energy, material goods and affections should be shared; and (3) the feelings of loyalty to current and prior family members. Although these sources of stress are potentially present from each individual's family-of-origin history in the first-marriage family, they are compounded in remarriage by the additional, and more currently potent, divorced family history. The presence of children in the binu-clear system adds a unique dimension, which contributes more sources of potential stress.

The type of relationship style that former spouses established in the earlier transition to divorce lays the foundation for their relationship when one or both join with a new partner. Although remarriage has been noted as a stressful transition, with different systemic properties than a first marriage, there are no established or socially accepted rules of relationship for the family members of the continuing binuclear system.[2] We do know that the rules for relating undergo substantial revision when one of the former spouses remarries. For example, where it may have been acceptable for a divorced mother to call upon her former husband to do certain household tasks like fix a broken garage door, it may not be acceptable once he has remarried. His recoupling requires them to negotiate new rules to integrate his new partner, as well as other members of his family unit, i.e., the new wife's children from an earlier union and/or her extended family.

The binuclear family system also takes on new properties when one of the spouses has a significant new partner who is involved with the child in some kind of adult-child role. For example, if father remarries, then mother may feel that she has to deal with two people instead of one on any issues related to the child. Also, as the father is forming a new family, he has to meet its needs as well as his first family's needs, which may cause new conflicts and negotiations. New rules need to be constructed for the coparental relationship, as well as new rules for the relationship between first and second spouse—mother and stepmother, father and stepfather. Many of the old angers and conflicts may arise again at this time. If the child was used in the struggle for power between the parents in their divorce, he or she will probably be put in that role again as the family juggles positions and roles to establish a new equilibrium.

The variations in family structure that result from remarriage in binuclear families almost defy categorization.[3] Although several writers have categorized the remarried subsystem into types of family structures ranging from simple to complex, with many variations in between, to do so with the binuclear family system with remarriage partners would involve so many permutations that the categorization would lose its original purpose.[4] Structural variations are determined by the marital history of all the adult parent members. For example, whether new partners were married before, whether there are children of those earlier marriages, and if so, the custody and visitation arrangements—all these become variables which affect the family structure. Add to these the same kind of variables for the formerly married pair and what emerges is an incredible number of possible structures.

Our purpose in this chapter is to examine the transition of family expansion created by remarriage by focusing on relationships within and across subsystems. So, for example, we will look at the former spouse subsystem and the remarriage subsystems and some of the factors that have an impact on the interrelationships between them. Because of the addition of children in many binuclear expansions, we will also discuss the child subsystem as it develops and interfaces with the parent subsystems. Further, because the grandparent generation also expands for the binuclear family, we will address the impact on these intergenerational relationships. Our primary interest in this chapter, however, remains consistent with the preceding chapters: We will focus on the relationship patterns that undergo change in this transition and have their roots in the former spouse relationship. In the following chapter we will again look at the variations that can be expected in the family career.

We are very much hindered by the inadequacy of current language in our discussion of the binuclear family in remarriage. For most of the relationships between family members in this expanded system there are no formal labels or role titles. What does one call one's former mate's new spouse? Or the children or parents of the new mate who have a relationship with one's child? Even the former spouse relationship has no current title, which requires that we continue to speak of it as a past relationship. Although ex-spouses with children may refer to each other as "my daughter's (or son's) father (or mother)," this does not capture the ongoing nonparental relationship between the divorced couple. So, of necessity, as we struggle to analyze some of the components of this complex system, our language suffers from being cumbersome and we will occasionally resort to inadequate terms that have emerged in the process of studying these families.

Former Spouse Subsystem

The former spouse relationship, with its many possible relational variations, becomes even more complex when one or both partners remarry. The timing of the remarriage further complicates the dynamics of this highly ambiguous postdivorce relationship. In McCubbin and Patterson's (1983) theoretical formulation of the pathways and mediating factors leading from stress to crisis, accumulating stressors, or "pileup," increase the potential for crisis. Consequently, if one of the ex-spouses remarries before the binuclear family has adequate time to establish new patterns for its reorganized structure, the potential for dysfunctional stress is high. Given the statistic that about 62 percent of men and 61 percent of women remarry within two years after divorce (Appendix Table 5), many families will experience the added stress of incorporating new family members in the midst of struggling with the complicated changes produced by the divorce.

Even if remarriage is delayed until the divorced family has had sufficient time to reorganize and stabilize, shifting of roles and relationships is necessary when a new member is introduced into the family system by remarriage. The family has to struggle with the role of the new family member while allegiances, loyalties and daily relationship patterns undergo transition. For many families, just as they are adjusting to one new member, the other ex-spouse remarries, which causes another transition requiring a shift in the family's tentative equilibrium. The length of time between one ex-spouse's remarriage and the second remarriage will influence the severity of stress experienced by all family members as they are required once again to cope with reorganization.

For the single ex-spouse, the remarriage of a former mate irrespective of the timing, may stimulate many of the feelings unresolved in the emotional divorce. If there are any lingering fantasies of reconciliation, the remarriage brings the sharp reality that reunion is no longer a possibility. It is not unusual for the single ex-spouse to feel a temporary loss of self-esteem as he or she makes comparisons to the new partner. Feelings of jealousy and envy are normal, even for those who thought they had worked through these feelings at the time of the divorce. Seeing an ex-spouse "in love" with someone else often rekindles the feelings of the early courtship and romantic phase of the first married relationship and a requestioning of the reasons for divorce. For a single ex-spouse who did not want the divorce, the remarriage has the potential of creating a personal crisis that closely resembles the experiences of the divorce. But even for those ex-spouses who may have initiated the divorce, the remarriage usually stimulates old feelings and resentments.

> *Nancy*: When Jim told me he was getting married I reacted with a cutting comment, saying I hoped she was better prepared for long evenings alone than I was. But what I was really scared about was that he would be different with her than he was with me. What if he had *really* changed? I realized that I wanted his marriage to fail. Then I would know that I was right in divorcing him.

Jim's remarriage resulted in Nancy's returning to therapy to work through many of the unresolved issues of the divorce. Jim's new wife was younger than Nancy and had one child by a previous marriage. Nancy and Jim had become cooperative colleagues in their divorced parenting relationship and she was fearful that she would have to give up many of the conveniences of their shared parenting as Jim took on the responsibilities of a new family.

The remarriage of one or both of the former spouses might be expected to decrease the amount of coparenting between former spouses, since a person involved in a new relationship may have less time to spend, or interest in, relating to his or her former spouse, or may perhaps feel pressure from the new spouse to decrease his or her involvement with the first spouse. For Jim, the conflicts were many.

> *Jim*: When Elaine and I decided to get married I felt guilty and like I needed to tell Nancy immediately. I dreaded telling her. When I did

tell her she didn't say much but I knew she was feeling upset. I wanted the kids to be part of the wedding and I knew Nancy was going to feel jealous and left out. I'd feel much better if she had someone else in her life. Elaine's relationship with her ex-husband is nothing like my relationship with Nancy and she didn't understand my wanting to ease Nancy's pain by not flaunting my new life at her.

Jim's marriage to Elaine initiates a complex cycle of changes for all participants. Nancy needs to adjust to Jim's sharing of his life with a new partner and a child, while both Jim and Elaine need to cope with two ex-spouses who will continue to be part of their future lives. Six months after Jim's marriage to Elaine, Nancy summarized it this way:

> *Nancy*: Things have changed a lot since Jim remarried. He's less willing to accommodate when I need to change plans around the kids. He always has to check with Elaine first. I really resent that — the kids should come first. I invited Jim to Ellen's birthday party but he couldn't come because of plans he had made with Elaine and her child. And I feel uncomfortable calling him at home about anything. Elaine usually answers the phone and I feel like she's listening the whole time. Jim has asked to take the kids on a week's vacation to visit Elaine's parents over Easter. I know it's his time with the kids but I think he should give them some special time and not make them spend it with Elaine's family.

For Nancy it is difficult for her to see her children's family extending to include more members not directly related to her. And in these early stages of his remarriage Jim is having difficulty coping with the conflicting demands that his increasing family membership causes.

> *Jim*: I knew Nancy would be upset about our plans for the Easter vacation. Sometimes I wish I could just go off with the kids skiing like we did the first year after the divorce, but I know Elaine wants to visit her parents. There's no way I can please everyone.

Nancy and Jim's relationship is in the process of undergoing considerable change. They talk less frequently and anger sparks up more often now as they try to make decisions about the kids. Jim feels more anger at Nancy now because she is "not understanding" his new responsibilities, and Nancy feels more anger as she has less access to Jim. They are traveling the bumpy road of this transition as they redefine their relationship again, dealing with the changes brought about by Elaine's entry into the family system.

In Ahrons' Binuclear Family Study a deterioration in coparental relations after remarriage did occur among the respondents. This was especially true if only the husband had remarried. For instance, the number and frequency of childrearing activities shared between the former spouses were highest where neither partner had remarried and lowest if only the husband had remarried. The amount of support in coparental interaction was highest and conflict lowest where neither partner had remarried, while conflict was highest and support lowest if only the husband had remarried. Also, if neither former spouse had remarried, they were most likely to spend time together with each other and their children, and least likely if only the husband had remarried (Ahrons & Wallisch, in press).

There are many possible variations on this theme, but for most divorced spouses the remarriage of one partner unbalances the system for some period of time. The degree of change in the system and the resulting stress depend in large part on the type of former spouse relationship that was developed prior to the remarriage of one of the spouses.

In the Binuclear Family Study, there were no remarriages among those who were categorized as Perfect Pals at three years postdivorce. It is difficult to imagine continuing that type of intimate relationship in the presence of a more intense intimacy. We would venture to guess that when a remarriage does occur in this pattern, the perfect pals might become cooperative colleagues. Cooperative colleagues shift in various ways with remarriage, but are most likely to continue sharing parenting, although their interactions tend to decrease. There may be fewer changes for angry associates and fiery foes. One would suspect that here interactions would be less frequent but still retain much of the anger that characterized them in the past.

If the other ex-spouse remarries it adds further complexity to the family system; however, this transition seems to be less stressful than the first remarriage. Remarriage of both ex-spouses appears to balance the former spouse subsystem, resolving some of the anger and guilt.[5] As we shall see as we look at the other subsystems, the nature of the new remarriage relationship, the relationships between new siblings (step and half), and the relationships between new extended family, including the ex-spouse relationships of the new partner, must all be entered into the transition equation.

Remarried Couple Subsystem

The transition to remarriage after a divorce of one or both partners is markedly different from the transition to a first marriage. Not only do the new spouses bring their families of origin into their extended system, but they also have relationships with their first married families which need to be integrated in some way. Remarried couples overwhelmingly report that they are unprepared for the complexities of remarried life.[6] Their model for remarriage is often based on a first marriage model. In contrast to the relatively impermeable boundary that surrounds a nuclear family, permeable boundaries are needed in households within the binuclear family system. These facilitate the exchange of children, money, and decision-making power. If one of the partners has not been previously married, he or she is particularly vulnerable to the dream of the ideal traditional family.[7]

In laying out our theoretical foundations in Chapter 2, we discussed Kantor and Lehr's emphasis on the importance of energy, time, and space in the distance regulation process. Their relevance to the reorganization of remarriage families is obvious. We have also discussed McCubbin and Patterson's view that the development of a shared definition of the situation is essential to readjusting and consolidating the reorganization after crisis. To these perspectives we add Klein and Hill's (1979) finding that the effectiveness of decisions reached in a crisis is dependent upon both the quality of the decision and its acceptability to those affected. Developing such shared definitions and decisions of high quality in two, or even three, family units linked by remarriage is a major undertaking, one that may present considerable difficulty.

When Elaine and Jim decided to get married, they talked about their divorce histories and their current relationships with their ex-spouses and brought their respective children together for brief periods of time. They fantasized about their plans for blending their family and perhaps adding a new child of their own to the picture. Although they were both aware of some potential problems, they felt able to cope because of the strong bond they had developed between themselves. But as they actually made the transition to remarriage many of the problems created more stress than they had anticipated.

> *Elaine*: When Jim and I decided to get married I was surprised by his feeling guilty about Nancy. I didn't have any of those feelings about my ex, Tom. When Tom remarried last year it didn't make much difference in my life. He hadn't seen much of Jamie anyway and he just

saw her less after he remarried. It was a relief not to have much to do with him. So, after living alone with Jamie for three years, I was really excited to have a family again and give Jamie more of a dad. But it's not working out that way. Jamie is angry a lot about not having time alone with me, which ends up with Jim and me fighting a lot. Jim feels badly about not spending enough time with his kids and when the kids are together, it just seems to be everyone fighting over Jim. And I feel resentful at not having enough time alone with Jim. Between every other weekend with his kids and the long hours we both work we never seem to have time alone together. Last Friday we were finally spending an evening all alone and, just as I was putting dinner on the table, Nancy called. Jim and I spent the next two hours talking about Nancy. It ended up spoiling our whole evening.

Elaine's feelings are not uncommon for second spouses within a complex binuclear family. The stresses of accommodating the existing bonds of first married relationships into the new stepfamily subsystem often turn the traditional "honeymoon stage" of marriage into a overwhelming cast of characters who share the marital bed. The reorganization required in moving from a one-parent household to a two-parent one often involves more adjustment than the single-parent expected. Roles and relationships require realignment and the addition of a new person in some type of parent role is stressful for all the family participants. A frequent complaint in new remarriages is the lack of time and privacy for the newly remarried partners. Jim expressed his disillusionment this way:

> *Jim*: Maybe we shouldn't have gotten married. When we were dating we made time for each other and spent many days and evenings enjoying things together. But after we got married Elaine felt guilty leaving Jamie with her mother or a babysitter very often. Jamie is very demanding — she always seems to want Elaine to do something for her. And Elaine can't seem to say no. Whenever I try to suggest to Elaine that Jamie should learn to play alone more, Elaine seems to get moody and quiet. Her resentment of the time I spend with my kids is hard for me to deal with. Sometimes I think she wishes I would stop seeing them or see them as little as Tom sees Jamie.

When the remarriage partners have been previously married, it is difficult for them not to compare their respective relationships with their ex-spouses. Their own former spouse relationship becomes the model for their new spouse's former spouse relationship. Elaine's expectation that Jim would have a similar relationship with Nancy as she had with Tom was shattered as she realized that Nancy was still very much a part of Jim's life.

The rise of dual-career marriages has resulted in a time problem for first marriages which is only exacerbated in the dual career remarriage. Add to this children and an ex-spouse or two and the issue of time becomes a very real problem. The usual marital issues of power and regulation of distance and intimacy are multiplied in the complex binuclear family. McCubbin and Patterson's (1983) focus on the need to utilize existing resources and to identify new resources in the reorganization process seems especially important for the dual-career remarried family. Space, time, and energy (Kantor & Lehr, 1975) also become especially critical.

As with divorce, and with marriage as well, the first year of remarriage has the most potential for crisis. The rate for divorce after remarriage is even higher than that for divorce in first marriages. Glick (1984) calculates that 54 percent of women and 61 percent of men who remarry will divorce. The timing of redivorce also differs from that of a first divorce. Remarriages have a 50 percent greater probability of redivorce in the first five years than first marriages (Furstenberg & Spanier, 1984).

Current empirical work also suggests that remarriage satisfaction is highly dependent on stepparent-stepchild relationships (Cherlin, 1977; Crosbie-Burnett, 1984; Duberman, 1975; Pasley & Ihinger-Tallman, 1982). How the crises are handled by the remarriage pair will depend on many past experiences and will define the future functioning of the family. Over time, and perhaps with some professional help, Elaine and Jim may be able to find ways to cope with their overcrowded lives. They will need to devise ways to protect and nourish their relationship without damaging the existing parent-child bonds. This will require developing a new model of familying which includes more flexibility, compromise, and fluidity of boundaries than they may have expected originally.

Parent-Child Subsystems

Remarriage is likely to be a more difficult transition for children than it is for adults. In the romance and excitement of a new love parents may minimize the distress children feel as they anticipate the many changes that accompany adding a new family member. For children, a parent's new mate is living proof that destroys the fantasies of their parents' reunion and the hoped for restoration of the original nuclear family. And after all, it is the *parent's* choice, not the child's, to expand the family system.

The stepparent role is perhaps the most confusing one in the binuclear family. The term "stepparent" itself connotes only negative stereotypes with no positive role prescriptions. For example, the question of whether stepparents should function as "substitute" or "additional" parents is a critical one in binuclear families. As we noted earlier, the tendency remains for remarriage subsystems to model themselves after nuclear families. Consequently, the expectations for the stepparent role are similar to those for the parent role. But when there is a noncustodial or joint custodial parent also functioning as a parent, the stepparent of the same sex must find ways to function as a parent while not usurping the role of the out-of-home biological parent.

Returning to the Spicer-Tyler-Henry binuclear family, let us take a look at how Craig and Nancy coped with their parenting roles in remarriage.

> *Craig*: When Nancy and I married we didn't expect it to be easy. All the kids seemed to get along pretty well while we were courting but we were concerned about how well they would be able to live in one household. I wanted to be very careful not to do anything that would make Jim feel like I was taking over as father of his kids. But I was also used to being a father and liked the idea of having a couple more kids. My relationship with Ellen was pretty good — I know how to father girls. But David was difficult for me. He seemed to resent my taking over the household. I tried being his friend but he just seemed to fight with me about everything. We're not at all alike and more and more we just try to avoid each other. It upsets Nancy a lot. And when Sally and Meg live with us things get even worse. David really resents them and withdraws to his room a lot when they're around. I find myself yelling at my own kids more now in my attempts to keep them from bothering David.

Craig was struggling to find a new role in his relationship with David but was not able in this early transition to befriend his new stepson. David had assumed many of the roles vacated by his father when his parents had divorced, and he was resentful of Craig's presence. David, who was 13 when Craig became his stepfather, had become accustomed to being in charge. This early adolescent stage of development, combined with the transition of moving from a one- to a two-parent household, has the potential for severe distress for both the child and the new stepfamily. In his relationship to Ellen, Craig was more successful in coping with his transition to stepparent, although his biological daughters experienced difficulty with the relationship.

At the same time as Craig was learning to be a stepparent, his relationship with his own children was undergoing a change. In his prior one-parent household he spent more time alone with his daughters and even felt he had developed a closer relationship with them than when he was married to their mother, Cynthia. But now, in his remarried household, he found himself often feeling anxious about whether his daughters felt "at home" there.

Nancy, too, was experiencing a major transition in her relationships with Ellen and David as she was trying to find new ways to stepparent Sally and Meg.

> *Nancy*: Sometimes I just don't feel like I have enough to go around. When Sally and Meg live with us I feel torn apart. I know it's hard on them but they seem to complain all the time. We gave them a bedroom of their own so they could feel like they really belong, but they are jealous of everything Ellen and David have. I sewed curtains for their room and they didn't even appreciate them. I really don't know how to act with them. When I try to please them they don't appreciate it and when I need to discipline them they run to Craig and complain. And it seems that whenever they are with us Ellen hangs all over me. The minute Craig and I go off into our bedroom we can count on a fight starting downstairs, usually between Ellen and Sally. Sometimes I think the only thing that will save our marriage is the one weekend each month when all the kids are gone!

For Nancy, the transition to stepparenting is a very stressful one. As the joint custodial stepparent of Sally and Meg she has a lot of responsibility for them but is confused about her role in their lives. She is not their mother, yet she is expected to perform many of the traditional mothering roles. At the same time she is having to cope with changes in her relationship with Sara, who is not used to sharing her with two "other" daughters. And she feels angry with David for not accepting Craig, while at the same time she understands the loss he feels.

The stepparent role is a highly ambiguous one in our society. But the role of stepmother is even less clearly defined than that of stepfather and is colored by the prevalent negative stereotypes of stepmothers. Some of the current research suggests that stepmothers experience more ambiguity and stress than do stepfathers (Ahrons & Wallisch, in press; Crosbie-Burnett, 1984). They are less likely to be called "mother" by their stepchildren, yet are expected to act like mothers in terms of providing nurturance and housekeeping tasks. When stepmothers were asked in the Binuclear Family Study to choose a term that described their relationship to their stepchildren, they chose such terms as "aunt," "acquaintance," and "adult friend," with some respondents adding such terms to our "other" category as "servant" and "rival." Stepfathers, when asked the same question, overwhelmingly chose "parent" and "friend." Stepmothers also reported less satisfaction with their role than stepfathers.

As custody arrangements are changed, the role of stepparent becomes even more ambiguous. Being a joint custodial stepmother with part-time parenting responsibility is quite different from the more usual role of noncustodial stepmother. Parenting children who arrive only on alternate weekends requires a different model from that for parenting children who live part-time in your home. The less usual role of full-time stepmother in father or split custody arrangements requires a still different role. Even though stepfathers, too, have differing levels of responsibility based on custody arrangements, the fathering role has fewer, more clear-cut expectations attendant to it.

The way one stepparents must, of necessity, change the biological parent-child relationship as well. Issues of conflicting loyalties and time allotment, both to the new spouse and his or her children—the stepchildren, require some changes in the relationship between parent and child, which had stabilized somewhat in the divorce reorganization.

Sibling Subsystems: Step and Half

The child development literature notes the stresses of adding children to the family with its normalizing of "sibling rivalry." In the remarriage family with children of both partners, the joining of the new sibling subsystems is a difficult transition for the children—acquiring an "instant sibling" can pose a threat to even the most secure child. The new remarriage partners have their marriage at stake and, therefore, need their respective children to like each other. Given a host of factors, such as the age and temperament of the children, the blending of two households of unrelated children requires major adjustments. Few newly blended families resemble the "Brady Bunch," but many have this as their model for this transition!

The usual competitive struggles among siblings often become major battles in remarried families, as children must adapt to sharing household space and parental time with new siblings. In the Spicer-Tyler-Henry family, the remarriage of Ellen and David's father included a new "kid sister" for them. That was followed a year later by their mother's remarriage, which included two more "kid sisters" who shared their home with them for one-third of every month. And, a few years down the line, they had to incorporate two half siblings when their father and stepmother had a son and a daughter. For Ellen, her stepsister, Jamie, was more difficult than Sally and Meg for her to accept.

> *Ellen*: It just doesn't seem fair. Every time I go to see Dad Jamie is there. And she always wants to hold his hand and sit on his lap and wants him to take her every place we go. I used to be able to sit in the front seat of the car with Dad whenever we went out, but now Jamie and I have to share the back seat. And sometimes she even calls him "Daddy." I can't stand it! She gets to live with him all the time. It's not so bad with Sally and Meg. Meg and I get to have some fun when we're together. Sometimes we fight but we get to play together a lot. And Mom always does something special with me alone when they're in our house. I don't have to share my things with them because Craig brought a lot of their stuff and they have their own room. Sometimes I get kind of upset when they get special privileges because they're not here all the time, but then sometimes we all get to do fun things together. Meg is a whiny brat sometimes and that's a pain.

For Ellen, sharing her father with Jamie posed a real threat. She had always felt like her father's "special little princess" and now Jamie, who was several years younger, seemed to have replaced her. The relationship between a child and her out-of-home parent is a difficult one, as the child adapts to seeing Daddy only occasionally instead of daily.[8] But as that relationship stabilizes, a child can begin to look forward to those times together as very special. To have to share her father with his new partner is difficult enough; to share him with another child is sometimes more loss than a child can bear. Ellen's jealousy and competition with Jamie are very understandable. Jamie had Daddy all the time, whereas she was with Daddy only on weekends, and even then he was not all hers. She dealt with Sally and Meg much better, at least in part because they came to *her* home. With Jamie, *she* was the "visitor" in the household.

David's experience, however, was quite different from his sister Ellen's.

> *David*: Jamie is all right. She tries to make us feel like Dad is all hers, but Dad and I still do things together that Jamie can't do. But Craig's brats drive me crazy. They move into the house and just take over. Meg sneaks into my room and messes up my models and Craig just excuses her because she's a little kid. Mom bends over backward to please them and all they do is complain.
>
> For the part of the month they live with us the whole place is topsy-turvy. Whenever my friends come over, Sally badgers us all the time. She acts like she thinks she's old enough to be with us. I'm supposed to be "understanding" — so Mom says — but I get to a point where I feel like I'd rather just go live with Dad. I liked things much better before Mom married Craig.

David's age and gender eased the transition of his father's remarriage. Jamie, being considerably younger, did not pose a serious threat for him in his relationship to his father. There was little role or relationship change for him in that transition. But his mother's remarriage required him to make considerable changes — changes that initially he was unwilling to make. He had to give up the many aspects of the role he had taken on after his parents divorced when he lived with just his mother and Ellen. And with the addition of two stepsiblings who now occupied "his" home, he had to share his territory with younger children, whom he identified as "nuisances." Sally, age 11, may have aroused some sexual feelings in David, now age 14, which he was not yet able to identify. He also felt protective of his mother and identified with her problems in relating to her stepdaughters.

Empirical research on the effects of remarriage on children is not as easily summarized as the literature on the effects of divorce. Although research is steadily increasing, we still lack major longitudinal studies identifying the stresses and developmental phases of adding new members to the binuclear family.[9] And sibling relationships in binuclear families have been a sadly neglected area of study. But it is our guess that for many children the transition to remarriage is more stressful than the transition to divorce. The addition of new family members can also mean more loss than gain for many children — if not permanent losses, then at least temporary relationship loss in the transition period. The changes children need to make when a parent inherits new children as part of his or her remarriage are numerous and difficult. And the newly remarried parent, who so frequently feels overwhelmed, may have her or his energies absorbed more in the new mate than in facilitating the child's transition.

Mother/Stepmother — Father/Stepfather Subsystems

Now we are faced with describing baffling relationships with a wordiness created by our current language deficits. We are hampered further in our efforts by the lack of clinical or empirical research on these relationships. Nevertheless, we will attempt here to describe some of the stressful aspects of these relationships, which form such an integral part of the remarriage transition.

In fact, these first and second spouses do have some bearing on each other's lives. For some second spouses, the "ghost" of the first spouse is ever present. For many, the first spouse can be an unwanted interloper, creating conflict between the remarriage pair. In other remarriage couples the first spouse is a uniting force on whom the new spouses place blame for all the problems of a dysfunctional family. This type of scapegoating is the subject of much humor and provides the basis for many of the prevalent negative stereotypes of this relationship.

Let us look once again at the Spicer-Henry-Tyler family. There are a number of first and second spouse relationships that must be accounted for in this family system. Nancy has both Cynthia, her husband's former wife, and Elaine, her former spouse's current wife, to deal with. Jim, too, has two such relationships. In this particular family constellation, Elaine also has two of these relationships, but Craig has only one, since his first wife, Cynthia, has not remarried. For the purposes of simplifying this highly complex cast of characters, we will use Nancy's relationships with both Cynthia and Elaine to illustrate some of the issues that define these relationships.

Nancy: I had to talk with Elaine on the phone yesterday because Jim wasn't home and we had to finalize some plans for the kids. It was the first time we really had to deal directly with each other. I've seen Elaine a couple of times when Jim was picking up the kids but we haven't talked. We were cordial on the phone but it is clear she doesn't like me. It seemed that everything I suggested she needed to alter in some way. And I was really feeling angry but didn't say anything when she made some comment about Ellen being a hard child to please.

Elaine: Nancy really bugs me. She calls and doesn't even acknowledge who I am, but yesterday we had to talk because Jim was out of town for a couple of days. She acted like I was not really involved with the kids and just sort of wanted to give me messages to give to Jim. I wouldn't mind dealing with her if she would treat me with some respect.

It is clear that Nancy and Elaine have feelings about each other, but thus far they have established a relationship which maintains a lot of distance. For both Nancy and Elaine the children's needs are the only reason for relating. Each feels the other interferes in some way in her relationship with Jim. Nancy feels Elaine intrudes upon her coparenting relationship with Jim and Elaine feels Nancy has too much presence in her marriage. But, unless Elaine and Jim's relationship ends in divorce, these two women will continue to interact over the years.

Now let us move to Nancy's relationship with Cynthia, which takes on a different style.

Nancy: I really think that Cynthia is a good mother and I can respect her for that. It was hard for me at first because Cynthia and Craig talk quite often and used to spend some holidays together before Craig and I married. Cynthia has come into the house several times when bringing Sally and Meg over and we've had coffee and chatted briefly. It feels kind of strange and Craig said he really felt uncomfortable. But Craig and I talked about plans for Thanksgiving and he asked me how I would feel about inviting Cynthia to join us. At first I reacted with a re-sounding "No," not wanting to spoil our first Thanksgiving as a family, but then I thought "Why not?" She was entitled to be with her kids too. My parents are going to come, too. They might feel uncomfortable but maybe it's worth a try this year.

Cynthia: When I first met Nancy I was sort of surprised. She's nothing like I expected after the kids' stories about her. But she was very nice, invited me to sit down and have a cup of coffee. It's hard — Craig and I did a lot of things together around the kids and now, with Nancy in the picture, I was scared that we would not be able to at all. But actually it's working out all right. Craig and I do less together with the kids, but I think we'll still be able to deal with the holidays and birthdays in some joint way. Actually, I kind of like Nancy.

Obviously, even in one family system, the relationships between current and former spouses can be quite different, depending on the type of relationship between the former spouse pairs and all the individual personalities. Nancy and Elaine may never develop much of a "coparenting" relationship, but she and Cynthia are likely to develop a cooperative relationship and feel a kinship over the coming years.

The possibilities and complexities in these types of relationships are vast, and our knowledge of them is almost nonexistent. But clearly the type of relationship style adopted by the former spouses is a major factor determining the relationship between first and second spouses. In many remarried binuclear systems the former spouse relationship is likely to diminish in importance over time, especially when there are no minor children to bind the parents together. As this happens, the need for first and second spouses to relate also diminishes.

In the Binuclear Family Study about half of the remarried spouses reported having some contact with their former partner's new spouse. The contact ranged from brief interactions at a family event to more frequent interaction centered on the children. Most said they felt somewhat detached and like "acquaintances," with about 25 percent reporting feelings that were sometimes competitive or jealous and another 25 percent saying that they liked the second spouse as a person. These remarriages were in their early stages, ranging from just remarried to four years of remarriage, and the numbers in each category were too small to calculate differences that might be attributed more to length of remarriage than to other factors (Ahrons & Wallisch, in press).

We are left with many more questions than answers about the nature of relationships in this subsystem, but, as with the stepparenting role, the relationship between mothers and stepmothers appears to be a more difficult one than that between fathers and stepfathers. In the Binuclear Family Study mothers and stepmothers reported less satisfaction in their relationship, but also, on the whole, reported more positive feelings as well. Ahrons and Wallisch conclude, "Rather than being contradictory, these findings might suggest that women parents are more involved, both negatively and positively, with each other than are men" (in press).

A related subsystem that we have not addressed requires a brief note here—the stepparent/stepparent subsystem. When both former spouses remarry, do their new spouses—stepmother and stepfather—form any kind of relationship as they parent the same children? In the Binuclear Family Study about one-fifth reported having some limited contact (Ahrons & Wallisch, in press). Again, we would venture to guess that the nature of these relationships is dependent on the style of the former spouse relationships. If former spouses have a somewhat cooperative relationship that involves considerable child-sharing, it might of necessity involve both stepparents to some degree. As is the case with first and second spouses, when there are children present, stepparents are likely to have knowledge about each other, albeit gained secondhand, and to develop feelings about each other based on this knowledge. Nevertheless, as the years pass and family events and crises become part of the binuclear family picture, these stepparents might, by virtue of shared children, feel like distant kin.

The Grandparent Generation

We will not discuss in detail the changes that may occur within and across generations in terms of subsystems, but, rather, just note briefly some of the potential impact that remarriage may have on grandparents in the binuclear family. There is some literature to suggest that paternal grandparents may suffer relationship losses after divorce when custody is with the mother (Ahrons & Bowman, 1982; Anspach, 1976; Furstenberg & Nord, 1985), but we have no empirical information about the subsequent effects of remarriage. Questions which need to be addressed are related to the changes in the roles and relationships of grandparents when stepgrandparents are added to the family.

Extended family relationships in nuclear families are highly varied in terms of the intensity of relationship between grandparents and grandchildren. One major research finding is that the grandparent relationship is highly dependent on the relationship between the first and second generations, the parent and grandparent (Wood & Robertson, 1976). We can only assume that this holds true for both grandparents and stepgrandparents: Their relationships with their grandchildren are dependent on their relationships with the adults in the middle generation of the binuclear family. In remarriage, if the second spouse has a close relationship with his or her parents, we can assume that the stepchildren will develop some relationship with their stepgrandparents. Whether this causes some loss to the biological maternal and/or paternal grandparents is probably again related to the relationship with the second generation.

Competition between maternal and paternal grandparents is not uncommon in nuclear families, and we can assume that in binuclear families additional competition may arise between grandparents and stepgrandparents. Again, the factors are so numerous that we cannot even begin to unravel the many possibilities. Recent court cases in which grandparents have petitioned the court for visitation of their grandchildren probably attest to the fact that divorce and remarriage disrupt some kinship relationships in the extended family.

Functional and Dysfunctional
Remarriage Relationships

Our definition of functional and dysfunctional systems in remarriage is very similar to that of functional and dysfunctional divorces posited in Chapter 5. Developing new roles and relationships in remarriage which take into account the existence and losses of divorced family relationships is critical to enhancing remarried family functioning. The addition of new family members can result in dysfunctional binuclear family systems if prior kin relationships are severed. If remarriage subsystems try to model nuclear families—that is, if they insist upon "instant" family and try to establish traditional parenting roles—they will experience resistance and distress. A functional binuclear family system needs to have permeable boundaries which permit children and adults to continue prior family relationships while slowly integrating the new remarried subsystem. This, of necessity, causes transitory stresses and strains created by the conflict between new and old alliances. Remarriage is still another transition, with even more possibilities for stress than divorce.

As we emphasized in the divorce transition, the clear delineation of boundaries is critical to successful functioning. The remarried husband coparent, for example, must clarify his role vis-à-vis his biological and stepchildren, and his first and second spouses. He and his ex-spouse need to renegotiate what is appropriate and inappropriate in his continuing role as coparent. Coparenting agreements that may have been satisfactory prior to his remarriage are likely to have implications for his current spouse. For example, if it has been agreed that he needs to spend more time with his eight-year-old son, who wants and needs his father's attention, this takes time away from his marriage. His responsibilities as a parent and his spousal responsibilities come into conflict. This can be exacerbated by opinions expressed by his current partner that the "boy is spoiled and demanding and needs to learn that his father can't always be there." Or she may feel that the former spouse is using the child as a way of hanging on to her ex-husband. And, of course, she may also be concerned about the time taken away from her and the children she has brought to this new marriage. But the new partner must also be sensitive to the degree that expression of such thoughts violates important boundaries between the new marriage and the old.

While he will be wise not to pass these opinions of his new partner on to the former spouse (these are clearly outside the boundaries of the former spouse relationship), unless the husband coparent is able to deal effectively with his ex-spouse around these conflicting pressures, crisis may result. His former wife may see him as withdrawing from the coparental relationship they have agreed upon. And she, not having remarried, may have a renewed sense of abandonment resulting from the remarriage of her former spouse. Given their agreements concerning coparenting, she has legitimate call upon her former spouse. At the same time, the remarried spouse has equally legitimate expectations related to their marriage. Without explicit negotiation of arrangements and reasonable expectations from both sides, thus establishing clear boundaries for his actions in both subsystems, he is destined to fall short in both.

The single former spouse also may experience considerable distress in adjusting to the expanded system. Noncustodial parents will feel some resentment at losing some of their former responsibilities in both division of labor and decision-making. They may also feel that the new spouse interferes in their relationship with the former spouse and their children. A custodial parent, usually the mother, will often experience a loss of services when her former spouse remarries. She may no longer be able to call on him for help, as many of her demands—except as they are related to the coparenting relationship—begin to fall outside the legitimate boundaries of the former spouse relationship. Clearly, agreements and court orders with respect to financial child support are legitimate. However, expectations that the former husband will perform repairs or maintenance on the home of the former spouse may have to be rejected. This may be difficult, since that home is likely be his former home, in which he may feel some residual investment, and in some cases may still retain some financial investment. However, resistance from the new partner to continuing such tasks is likely to severely restrict any such activity. All of this may be softened or made more difficult, depending upon the kind of postdivorce relationship style which has developed.

Remarriage restructures the division of labor developed in the postdivorce reorganization. New spouses of custodial parents take on many of the day-to-day responsibilities for care of children and household tasks formerly handled alone by the custodial parent or carried out by one of the children from time to time. As we have seen, this may lead to some genuine friction, as children resent the new stepparent's "taking over" or displacing them in some valued responsibility. If the new spouse attempts to assume responsibilities which the noncustodial parent may have continued, this is another source of potential stress. The former spouse may resent it, the stepchildren may resent it, and even the new spouse may have difficulty in accepting it.

Decision-making and the power structure implications carry similar potential stress. This will be especially true around decisions concerning the stepchildren, but may be true in other areas as well. If a new spouse has been used to having his or her former spouse participate and be involved in decisions concerning the children, the new spouse can easily be seen as "interfering," both by the other biological parent and the child. For example, as we have seen in the case presented in this chapter, Nancy resented Elaine's parenting involvement.

The style of the postdivorce ex-spouse relationship may either ease these adjustments, as with the perfect pals and cooperative colleagues, or make them more difficult, as with angry associates or fiery foes. If former spouses are insecure and competitive about their parenting relationships with their children, as is common between angry associates and fiery foes, the addition of a new parent figure will intensify those feelings during the transition. An ex-spouse may feel threatened by the "new family" of the remarried spouse, anticipating that the children will prefer this new household to the one-parent household where they currently live.

When parents — both biological and step — are unclear about their roles, children are likely to use the ambiguity to manipulate the new stepparent, their custodial parent, and the noncustodial parent. During the early stages of the remarriage transition it is not unusual for children to play one parent off against another for some personal gain. For example, in the Spicer-Tyler-Henry family, Ellen, after spending a weekend at her father's house, might very well tell her mother that Elaine, her new stepmother, "lets me watch TV until 10 p.m." Ellen's hope, of course, is that her mother will respond by permitting her to stay up later than her usual bedtime. Sometimes, new stepparents will be more lenient with their stepchildren in the hopes of being liked and accepted by them. Consciously, or perhaps unconsciously, the new stepparent is competing with the other biological parent for the child's affections.

Although former spouses may have worked out consistent rules for discipline, etc., during the divorce transition, these are likely to need renegotiation when a new parent enters the family. Only now, the renegotiation is more complicated, as three parents become part of the process instead of the original two. And if the other ex-spouse remarries, there may be a replay of some of the issues as the system accommodates to a fourth parent. As we noted earlier, however, this may be an easier transition. Not only are the parents familiar now with many of the problems of adjustment but the system itself is in better balance. There are now two stepfamily households, with each biological parent having an ally.

The remarried binuclear family faces a unique problem in controlling intimacy in the family. Incest taboos, which are assumed between blood kin in first marriage nuclear families (though, as is now being revealed, more often violated than many have known), become an important issue. The function of such taboos, of course, is to maintain unambiguous and appropriate intimate relationships in families. The potential for sexual feelings and possible abuse between non-blood parents and children, as well as between adolescent stepsiblings, is high. Therefore, establishment of clearly defined boundaries in this highly charged emotional area is essential.

A situation observed by one of the authors in family therapy illustrates how dysfunctional failure to establish such boundaries can be. In the course of the session, an adolescent stepdaughter revealed that she had been sexually involved with the son of her stepfather, i.e., her stepbrother. There were indications that this involvement was involuntary on her part. The mother of the young woman became very angry. At this point, the two biological daughters of the stepfather, who no longer lived in the household, confronted their stepmother with their sexual experiences some years before with her son — their stepbrother. They were extremely angry with the stepmother for not having the same reactions to their experiences, of which they believed the stepmother to be aware. These revelations, of course, provided some understanding of the kinds of conflicts in this stepfamily that had prompted the request for therapeutic treatment. The issues extended far beyond the matter of sexual abuse to include the entire range of emotional relationships which had developed in this remarried family over several prior years. Failure to have defined appropriate intimacy boundaries in the reorganization of this binuclear family had contributed to an extremely dysfunctional situation.

Relationships with extended kin find new stresses facing them upon the remarriage of one or both ex-spouses. Children may be particularly puzzled by suddenly finding their access to one set of grandparents or a favored aunt or uncle severely restricted or cut off. The nature of those relationships may also be changed, even if they are continued, by the inability of the extended kin to keep their feelings about the ex-spouse from contaminating their interactions with the children. Further, the introduction of new extended kin can also be confusing and stress-producing for children.

The new relationships with the spouse's extended family are not of the same character as those of first married couples. They often carry residual elements from the former marriage, particularly since these are not just in-laws, but also grandparents, uncles, and aunts. In addition, in many cases there are also associations to be worked out with the former spouse of the new partner. Until new relationships with extended family are established, they tend to be mediated through the new marital relationship.

CONCLUSION

The complexity of remarried binuclear systems has made this chapter a difficult one to write. The study of even one remarried subsystem alone presents sufficient complexities to cause many social scientists to return to studying individuals rather than family systems. Our lack of both language and analytic tools, as well as the difficulties in conceptualizing the totality of these complex systems, creates frustration in both the writer and the reader.

All of this brings into sharp relief the importance of developing a new set of meanings for the relationships between former spouses, with the new spouse, between former and current spouses, between stepparents and stepchildren, between step and half siblings, and with extended kin. If the expanded binuclear family structure is to survive and function in an effective manner, then all parties must develop clear understandings of what these meanings are in the new remarriage situation. These meanings are most likely to center on the coparenting responsibilities that the ex-spouses share, but they go well beyond this.

Clearly delineating a precise definition of functional and dysfunctional remarriage binuclear families is not possible, given our current lack of knowledge. Although we can comfortably conclude that remarriage subsystems must be open systems with permeable boundaries, we cannot say what degree of openness is optimal. Remarriage subsystems need to be able to develop their own sense of connectedness and independence, while simultaneously functioning as interdependent units.[10] Stepparents have a confusing and difficult role. In most families they need to develop new parenting type roles that supplement, rather than replace, biological parents. And they need to do so expecting resistance and a long developmental process of integration. What is required is a new model of familying that encompasses an expanded network of extended and quasi-kin relationships.

EIGHT

Family Career Implications of the Remarriage Transition

The further branching of the binuclear family tree through remarriage sets in motion a complicated set of "mutually contingent careers"—both of an individual and familial kind. As we analyze this complex system, we see how the expanded binuclear family subsystems may experience remarriage differently in the various family career periods. The system is so potentially complex and widespread that we cannot hope to cover it all. Rather, we will focus on some of the most salient family career aspects of each subsystem in the expanded binuclear family, focusing the major portion of our discussion on midlife remarriage.

CHILDLESS COUPLES

Remarriage of a former spouse may have the least impact in this career period. However, there is often a high salience in the meaning attached to the "first love" in one's life. Many of these marriages carry that meaning. Beyond this, genuine friendships in childless former marriage relationships are more possible because the divorces are less complicated—there are fewer remnants of the marriage with which to deal. The issues around child custody and child support are absent. It is also less likely that issues of property settlement and spousal support are as complicated, Thus, there is likely to be less anger generated by the legal divorce process. The remarrying individual may want to continue a genuine friendship with the former spouse, while not threatening the new marriage relationship significantly.

Others in this stage may tend to treat the remarriage as their first marriage. Some do not really "count" this as a remarriage, especially if their first marriage was very brief. Some women and men in this category seek in their second marriage a spouse with children, thus producing an "instant" family. The degree of salience of the first marriage in such circumstances, if it existed to any extent, probably falls off rather rapidly.

Perhaps, then, it is only the perfect pals and fiery foes who will face any significant pressure for reorganization of their former spouse relationship. The threat to the new spouse which the perfect pal former spouse relationship can represent will undoubtedly call for some restructuring of that relationship. If there has been some continuing relationship around division of labor and decision-making, as we posited in Chapter 6, this is quite likely to be reduced after remarriage. Aside from the jealousy a new spouse may feel, the time and energy demands of continuing to be a perfect pal to a former spouse while simultaneously developing the new remarriage relationship may be too much. Indeed, some modification may have already taken place during the remarriage courtship period.

One possible style would be to incorporate the former spouse into a friendship relationship with the new couple. The degree to which the new spouse finds the former spouse a threat, however, will probably determine the future course of the former spouse relationship. The general norms about carrying on relationships with former lovers after marriage are likely to operate in this situation. All in all, we can expect a reduction in the frequency and a change in the quality of the perfect pal former spouse relationship in the face of remarriage. Certainly, if the unattached former spouse also enters a new relationship, the former spouse ties will be less significant for both.

The fiery foe relationship carries a different implication. To the extent that the remarriage reduces the need for the remarried former spouse to carry on the warfare, the relationship may resolve itself into an uneasy truce and finally fade away. However, the single former spouse may find the new relationship one more target for continued hostility. If this is the case, or if the remarried ex-spouse cannot let go of the old relationship, the new spouse may find her/himself drawn into the battle as an active participant. Needless to say — and this certainly will apply to all of the other family career periods — individuals considering marrying a member of a fiery foe former spouse relationship need to work out some of these issues prior to the remarriage.

The often fatal approach of many prospective marital partners that this "will work out after the marriage" seems particularly dangerous here. Finally, the remarriage of the unattached former spouse could bring a final halt to the conflict, as both former spouses concentrate on new spouse relationships and relinquish the old ones.

Remarriage for childless couples will most probably result in the dwindling away of cooperative colleague and angry associate relationships. Neither the need to collaborate nor the lure of conflict is so strong in these two types as to overcome the pull of the new remarriage relationship. Single spouses may experience some pangs at first, but these are not likely to linger. Their remarriage would certainly sever any remaining ties.

Finally, dissolved duos are unlikely to be affected by remarriage. Indeed, the former spouse may learn about the recoupling by chance or maybe not at all.

Current stereotypes about former spouse relationships among childless couples would suggest the lack of any continuing relationship with extended kin. But meaningful relationships with extended in-law kin during the marriage may continue after the divorce. Some of these relationships carry great importance for the individuals. Where genuine friendship between the former spouses exists, as in the perfect pals, or develops, as is likely in the cooperative colleagues, these in-law relationships may continue after remarriage in an almost unchanged fashion. Many young women and men develop relationships with mothers- and fathers-in-law that survive the severed marriage. Even angry associate former spouses will continue to hold on to these friendships — though it is less likely among the fiery foes and dissolved duos. Similar patterns take place in relationships established with siblings-in-law or even with a special uncle, aunt, or grandparent of the former spouse.

MIDLIFE COUPLES

Great diversity characterizes the midlife period of the family career. Some midlife couples in their forties have young adult children, some of whom are in the early stages of their own marriages. There may be one or more children in late adolescence who still live at home or, at least, return home during college vacation periods or between jobs. Other midlife couples have children who are well into the child-rearing period of their own marriages, so that the grandparent role is a significant aspect of life for the remarried spouses. Many are nearing retirement from full-time employment for the husband and, less often, the wife. The lives of these couples may be dominated by the anticipation involved in finally reaping the fruits of their years of bearing responsibilities. And, of course, a large portion of midlife couples will have aging parents for whom they carry continuing responsibilities.

Thus, midlife marriage is not the homogeneous period that the label might imply. Consequently, remarriage in midlife carries the potential for a wide variety of patterns. We are aware of no empirical studies on midlife remarriages. We must depend, then, upon our theoretical model and on material gleaned from case experience and anecdotal accounts for much of our discussion.

Remarriage for midlife divorced couples has two immediate implications, which carry some important interrelated consequences. First, the probabilities are considerably lower that the former wife will remarry. The data on remarriage make it very clear that women in this period of life remain single considerably more often than their male counterparts.[1] Second, the focus on restructuring of the coparenting relationship which we saw in childbearing couples shifts to a focus on reorganizing the more individual parenting relationships with adult children. That is, without the need for major relating around dependent children's needs, divorced midlife parents may work out their parent-child relationships with less interdependency. Remarriage reduces this interdependency even more.

Divorced women in midlife whose former spouses remarry are especially likely to encounter a confirmation of the feeling of being abandoned—a feeling which may be quite in tune with the facts. While the character of the divorced relationship may have varied from the easy perfect pal to the warring fiery foe type, the redirection of the former husband's attention to a new partner, with the inevitable reduction in contact, intensifies the displaced homemaker status which the former wife often holds.

With the exception of the fiery foes, where continuation of any mutual service to the former spouse probably terminated at the divorce, there are probably some inevitable losses both in the area of division of labor and in decision-making. As we have seen, women in this age group are less likely to have developed the full range of skills necessary to function as single persons. Similar limitations exist in men of this age. Men fill this deficit with new spouses, but women may find themselves lacking in necessary resources. Remarriage thus represents possible major stress and potential crisis for women unless they are able to develop new resources. One major possibility, of course, is to call on adult children.

Remarriage in midlife underscores some of the financial issues which first appeared in separation. Perhaps with the exception of fiery foes, matters of child support, spousal support payments, property distribution, and other such matters tend to become routine, once settled. (For midlife couples, child support may appear not to be an issue. In discussing the parent-child subsystem we will see that there may still be some significance to it.) Some issues, such as changing the names of beneficiaries on insurance policies or employment death benefits, may have been ignored, since they did not appear to have any immediate significance. These are often viewed as providing additional security for women in providing for dependent children in the event of the husband's death. In midlife, they may have lost some of their immediate salience.

The introduction of a new spouse can precipitate new attention to these issues. The new spouse will have some feelings about the financial obligations of her husband to the former spouse and to his children. This will be especially so if she has dependent children of her own. (This is a real possibility, given the tendency of men to remarry younger women.) While she may have been somewhat aware of what his principal obligations were, the significance may not have been completely clear prior to the marriage, or she may have hesitated to make too much of an issue of them before the marital commitment was in place. After the marriage, she may find that a large spousal support payment to the former spouse restricts the anticipated financial resources. She may press her new husband to return to court to renegotiate financial obligations. Or, she may suggest to her new husband that it is important for her financial security and that of her children for him to designate her as beneficiary of his various death benefits.

The remarried husband is placed in a difficult position. Whether out of guilt or as a result of his concern for reaching a just settlement, he may have agreed to arrangements which now take on a different significance. He has taken on new obligations, which are strained by the old obligations. His former spouse is not likely to view any change in the spousal support arrangements as desirable, especially if she has not managed to develop new resources of her own. Removing her claim to death benefits or to endowment-type insurance policies may represent a violation of what she sees as an unwritten agreement that these were part of her security in later life, a means for providing for children's college educations, or other later life benefits.

These circumstances highlight the need for some interrelated kinds of agreements. The prenuptial agreement is one example. It is unlikely in this age group that the first marriage had any such document. Nor is it likely that many of these matters were explicitly written down during the marriage. Marriages in this era were filled with many suppositions, based upon the primary assumption that the marriage was permanent. For the remarriage, however, couples would be wise to consider a prenuptial agreement — even though it is lacking in romance and carries the aura of a business transaction. The reality is that marriage is very much a business relationship. By failing to confront the financial issues that remarriage involves, couples are only temporarily avoiding the inevitable.

Another agreement, that contained in the divorce decree, may be incomplete. Divorce settlements often do not take account of the implications of remarriage. But the high probability of remarriage, especially for men, requires that they do so. Making explicit some of those implicit or unwritten contracts of the original marriage can avoid the kind of stress and potential crisis in the financial arena which remarriage may produce.

This situation is most salient for divorced midlife women whose former spouses are likely to remarry. Clearly essential is a divorce agreement that, regardless of the ex-husband's remarriage, provides for some assistance in gaining or refreshing wage-earning skills or for maintaining a central level of economic security. Even if the ex-wife is able to return to the labor force, she is likely to have lost a considerable portion of her competitive edge if she has been absent for any length of time. If she has not been gainfully employed, she is even more likely to be at a disadvantage. For women of this age group the status of displaced homemaker is not wholly of their own making. There may have been an implicit understanding that taking care of the house and children was her major contribution to the family. Part of this implicit agreement probably involved an assumption that she was a full partner in the economic assets of the marriage even though these were being brought in by the husband.

Some midlife women do manage to become involved in educational or other kinds of experiences which allow them to escape the displaced homemaker status. Many enter an entirely new arena, which they find stimulating and personally fulfilling. Reality requires, however, that they be viewed as the fortunate minority. Being aware of this reality at the time of divorce and anticipating the probable remarriage of their former spouse may be critical.

It would be a mistake to assume that only women former spouses would benefit from more conscious attention to these issues. It is clearly in the former husband's best interests to have a clear statement of his, and his former spouse's, obligations in the event of remarriage. An agreement, especially an unwritten one, which assumes no change in his obligation in the event of his former wife's remarriage is clearly not in his best interests. And, even if she does not remarry, the sense of meeting clearly stated expectations provides a more positive personal self-image. In the kinds of long-term marriages represented by midlife divorce and remarriage, this can be of major significance for both former spouses.

The long history of marriage for the midlife divorced makes remarriage a particularly crisis-prone event. There is likely to be a high degree of attachment to the lifestyle which had been built up over the marriage. This has two implications. First, for the remarrying individual, it may mean a considerable adjustment in attempting to adopt a new pattern with the new spouse. In the flush of courtship and early marriage, there may be a number of major changes in behavior. However, as the remarriage becomes more routinized, there is some likelihood of reverting to old comfortable patterns. The remarrying midlife man may have found the new love exciting and energizing. A highly active social life, trying new things, and all that goes with a new relationship are very stimulating. Such a pace is difficult to maintain in the face of ongoing work and day-to-day responsibilities, especially in a period of life when he is beginning to lose some of his youthful physical energy. Returning to his former pattern of coming home from work to read the newspaper, eat dinner, and settle down for a quiet evening of watching television may begin to seem very inviting.

Women, especially those who are gainfully employed, may have similar experiences. As in any marriage, the maintenance of the vitality of the relationship is tested in this period of return to "normality." Finding that this marriage isn't really very much different from the first one may bring disillusionment and may account for some of the higher rate of redivorce we have noted.

Another factor related to the long-term first marriage is the stress introduced by seeing another person enjoying some of the "fruits" of the first marriage. An ex-husband may find it difficult to contend with the knowledge that his former spouse's new husband is living in the home (awarded to the wife in the divorce settlement) which was such a central focus of effort in that first marriage. Former wives will similarly have to deal with knowing that the new partner is enjoying the vacation cottage or motor-home which represented a long anticipated source of pleasure in their later years. Both of these possibilities represent an invasion of "their space," to which they are likely to still hold a good deal of attachment. These factors will not facilitate the development of good relationships between former spouse and current spouse. It is easy to understand, therefore, why many such relationships in midlife are acrimonious.

This is likely to be a time, also, when there are a high number of important family occasions which call for celebration. Graduations and marriages of children, bar/bas mitzvahs and christenings of grandchildren come readily to mind. Including the new spouse in these events often calls for some creative planning. In the film "Four Seasons," the daughter's graduation from college was an excellent illustration of some of the problems which may arise.

We are familiar with a wedding which took place between two young adults, both the children of divorced and remarried parents. The wedding events were crowded with kin and quasi-kin, since each young person had two biological parents and two stepparents. Several siblings, half-siblings, stepsiblings, and sets of grandparents were also involved. Seating arrangements at the reception dinner provided a major challenge, since not all of the former spouse relationships were of the perfect pal, or even cooperative colleague, variety. And, of course, the wedding photographer was soon plunged into total confusion as he attempted to set up appropriate photographs with the "parents" of the bride and groom. He was rescued by the sister of the bride who, of course, had a very clear understanding of the relationships involved.

It is probably most critical for the unremarried former spouse — usually the wife — to ensure that her relationships with her adult children are not disrupted or weakened. The center of her concern is likely to be the possibility that the new partner will interfere with the patterns of interaction with their children which have been worked out with her ex-spouse. It can be expected that the former husband will want to have his new partner accepted and included in his contacts with his children and grandchildren. How will this affect the biological mother's access and relationships with them? Will there be attempts to gain more time and, more importantly, attempts to shift loyalty and affection away from her? This seems more likely in angry associates and fiery foes than in the other two types. If it does occur, the ex-wife has good reason to feel "cut off." She is likely, therefore, to engage her former spouse in direct negotiations over a confirmation of patterns set up — or she may attempt to gain a new advantage, giving as a justification that he now has someone to whom he can feel close, while she is more alone than ever.

Meanwhile, the adult children are not simply bystanders in this experience. They will undoubtedly be subjected to appeals from their mother designed to maintain, if not intensify, their commitment to her. And their father will certainly be developing expectations about their relationship with their new stepmother. As in the initial divorce reorganization transition, these adult children are going to find themselves in the middle to a considerable extent. They are likely to attempt to reassure their mother that "nothing has changed," while at the same time attempting to convince their father that they will bring his new wife into their lives in the way he would like.

Of special sensitivity, one would expect, is the place of grandparent-grandchild relationships in the event of the remarriage of one of the grandparents. The adult children are certainly "in the middle" in this situation. They will play a central role in interpreting to their children the meaning of the remarriage of one of their grandparents. Who is this new person that Grandpa or Grandma has brought into the family? Where should their loyalties lie? What can they say to one person, but not to another? How can they deal with all of the past history that they have with their grandparents as a pair? They will not be unaware of the changed way in which their grandparents relate to them, as well as to their parents. And it is unlikely that they can remain ignorant of some of the conflict which is a part of the restructuring of relationships precipitated by the remarriage. Especially as they experience holidays or special personal celebrations, this new set of circumstances is bound to present itself as an important factor.

Midlife men frequently marry younger women. This narrows the age difference between the stepmother and stepchildren. At the same time it is likely that the age difference between stepsiblings is widened. The issue here, then, is not one of the new stepmother "replacing" the biological mother. Rather, it is the inappropriateness of a mother-child relationship being established between two adults who are not very discrepant in age. Parent-child relationships do change when children reach maturity. They may become more peer-like, but they rarely become completely so. Even when "children" reach midlife, they are likely to maintain a different kind of relationship with their aging parents than they do with others of a similar age. While it may be possible to develop a peer relationship with their father's new spouse, this is complicated by their continuing parent-child relationship with him. Without any clear role models, the development of these relationships is likely to be stressful.

New spouses require readjustment by children in relationships with their parent. Many daughters develop a close confidant relationship in adulthood with their fathers. The introduction of a new wife, perhaps not much older than the daughter, may disrupt this pattern. The new wife may view the father's close relationship with his daughter as competing with her own role as wife/confidant. Daughters will probably find their father less likely to share more intimate thoughts and may resent it. At the same time, daughters may feel some anger when they compare their father's situation to that of their mother. They may identify with the further isolation created for their mother by the father's remarriage. It would be surprising if some of this resentment did not affect their developing relationship with their father's new partner.

Sons encounter other kinds of difficulties. They may have grown used to having more time with their father in recreation or pursuing some common hobby. Remarriage will reduce the time available for this kind of activity. The narrow age difference may also introduce some emotional ambivalence for sons. They may find themselves with feelings of physical and sexual attraction to the father's new wife, which produce profound conflicts. Also, they too may feel some protectiveness for their mother in the light of their father's new romantic involvement.

Midlife remarriage, however, involves more complex parent-child aspects than ones related simply to access. These focus on the emotional nature of the relationships introduced by remarriage. In thinking about remarriage we often have in mind younger divorced persons. While it is recognized that children will have to make adjustments to the new stepparent and that biological parents and children will have to develop new styles of relating, these adjustments are often characterized as "blending" or "reconstituting" stepfamilies. This is especially true where both new partners have children. Adult children of a remarrying parent are less likely to develop the kind of stepparent-stepchild relationship which is involved in these younger remarriages. Because of the systems properties of families, this also means that their relationships with their remarried biological parents are not likely to develop in the same way. Several factors are involved.

Another possible reaction of adult children to their father's new spouse is seeing her as the "other woman" who "broke up" their parents' marriage. It is another one of those peculiar double-standard cultural attitudes which places the responsibility on the new wife, but rarely on the new husband. In midlife remarriages, of course, the probability that the new wife is younger makes this attribution of blame even more likely. After all, Dad would never have looked at another woman mother's age — or older. He must have been seduced against his better judgment! At the same time, they may suspect — or even know — that their father and his new wife were involved before the divorce. Regardless of what other extenuating circumstances may have surrounded their father's behavior, many adult children are never able to rid themselves of the "once the other woman, always the other woman" feeling towards their father's new spouse. Especially if their mother has expressed little interest in other men since the divorce, adult children often have great difficulty in accepting this intrusion into what they preferred to view as a happy and permanent relationship between their parents.

The film "Twice in a Lifetime" provides an excellent portrayal of several of these issues in a midlife divorce. The husband, attracted to a younger and more attractive woman, is faced with the rage of one of his daughters, with whom he had an especially close relationship. The other daughter, while somewhat more understanding of her father, nevertheless experiences considerable stress around the planning of her own wedding. Both daughters place pressure on their mother to "get on with her life," to which the mother reacts with considerable anger. The adult son in this family finds himself caught between supporting his mother in her period of distress and attempting to maintain his newfound "man-to-man" relationship with his father. The final scene takes place outside the church after the wedding of the daughter. It dramatically summarizes the pressures. The son moves back and forth between his father and his mother and two sisters, attempting to arrange an invitation for his father back to the family home for the post-wedding party. He is faced with the failure of his attempt and has to explain to his father that it is probably "best" if he doesn't attend. The film closes as the father walks down the street alone to return to his new partner who, of course, was not invited to the wedding.

We must also observe that a source of stress for adult children and their parents in midlife divorce and remarriage is that one or the other parent may not be invited to important events in the lives of their children. "Twice in a Lifetime" showed how peripheral the father's participation in his daughter's wedding was. This can occur either as a result of explicit pressure placed by one of the parents, or even another family member, or as a result of feelings of anger or fear of conflict erupting. Whatever the reason, adult children may just feel that one of the parents should not be at their graduation, wedding, the christening or bar/bas mitzvah of a grandchild, or some other important ceremony. This will probably be very hurtful to the excluded parent, though he or she may not reveal it — preferring to maintain the quality of the relationship with the child involved. On the other hand, it can be the source of further conflict between the former spouses, or with the child. This, of course, is most likely in the fiery foes pattern. Some children of angry associates, or even collaborative colleagues, may also find these special ceremonial occasions just too much to cope with if both parents are present.

It is difficult for adolescent and young adult children to accept change in their parents. There are often comments from them, such as, "If he had been this way with Mom, there would never have been a divorce," or "It makes me angry to see my Dad bringing flowers to her and taking vacations. He didn't do that with Mom." Mothers are not free from these reactions, either. "If Mom had taken better care of herself like she is doing now, Dad would have never lost interest," or "If only Mom had spent the time doing the things Dad wanted to do the way she does with Bill, everything would have been all right."

Of course, children don't know everything about the development of their parents' marital relationship over the years, especially after they left home. They have little awareness of the critical events which may have occurred in the marriage. Unless the parents have carried on many fights in their presence, they are likely to be unaware of many of the tensions that were a part of that relationship. The period of childrearing carries with it a number of demands on both parents and these tend to affect the marriage. Child-care demands on the wife and work demands on the husband arc, of course, especially heavy during this time. The deterioration in the spousal relationship may be quite gradual. When the couple reaches the time when their children are grown and there is opportunity once again to focus on their marriage, they may not know how to revitalize it. Cuber and Harroff (1965) identified several marriage types in their classic study of longer-term upper-middle-class marriages. One of the major categories was the "devitalized" marriage.[2] We suspect that many midlife divorces are the consequence of such devitalization. And, of course, the prospect of a new love provides great motivation for more vitality in their behavior.

Midlife divorce is often accompanied by profound personal developmental changes. The focus has often been placed on the so-called "midlife crisis" of men and its relationship to marital disruption. Regardless of the validity of that characterization, it is certain that midlife does contain important individual developmental changes for both men and women. These changes are often masked in midlife by the apparent continuity provided by the marriage. Divorce in midlife provides the opportunity to make more explicit some of these changes in conjunction with the restructuring of life that is required by the divorce. Of course, some kin and friends may be more conscious of them, since they are already watching and being affected by the changes resulting from the divorce. In the overall context of adjusting to their parents' divorce, adult children may find some of the behavioral expressions of these developmental changes difficult to understand and they may be confused about how they are to react to them.

When their divorced father begins to express interest in other women, it is often their first experience of this kind with him. After all, they were not around when he was courting their mother! It can be deeply disturbing to see their parent behaving with such open sexuality and expressing interests in ways that they may have come to believe were reserved for the young — or, at least, are wholly new in their lifetime experience with him. These need not be of the kind represented by the bizarre stereotype of the midlife man who adopts a "mod" hair style and wears shirts open to the navel, gold pendants, and other rakish jewelry. He may only be expressing interests in activities and personal relationships — interests which are quite conventional but in striking contrast to his past behavior. Even if he might have been characterized before the divorce as something of a "ladies' man," it is likely that this was seen more as a harmless, humorous, and even lovable aspect of his personality. A serious and obviously sexual interest in a woman, especially a younger one, may be very difficult to handle. And, when this interest results in remarriage, the children must handle it.

The midlife changes of their divorced mother may be less difficult for them. As we have seen, she is less likely to become involved with a younger man, although, if she does, it is quite likely that this will produce some of the same kinds of stresses encountered for fathers. More probable is a relationship with someone of similar age or even older than she. If the new partner is considerably older, this may also produce some problems of relationship resulting from the large age discrepancy between the children and the new stepparent. The courtship in such cases is likely to be more conventional, probably with less revelation of the sexual and romantic aspects of the new relationship — though they almost certainly exist. The emphasis, however, may be on the stability, dependability, and security which this new relationship promises for their mother.

Midlife women often express new directions of interest in more conventional and thus more easily accepted activities — a new hobby, a new sport, or a new career interest. There is good reason for much of this. Midlife women are realistically more vulnerable to insecurity, especially of a financial kind. Midlife men tend to be financially and occupationally secure. Indeed, one aspect of the "midlife crisis" view of men is their abandoning this secure existence for more risky pursuits. Many midlife women do not have that luxury. On the other hand, some women, recognizing their lower probability for remarriage, engage in quite radical and high-risk (though usually still conventional) changes in direction. It must be said, however, that there is often little to lose in taking such risks, except the very serious damage to self-image and self-confidence should they fail. The gains, on the other hand, involve a new sense of self-worth and control over their lives. Many women have found the risk worth taking.

We are conscious of the danger of overstating the situation for both men and women, thus perpetuating the common gender stereotypes. However, it is important to recognize that these gender stereotypes have their foundation in societal attitudes about gender appropriate behavior. Middle-aged men are often seen as becoming more attractive as they age. It is seen as quite appropriate that they choose as partners women who are younger than they. Women are most frequently seen as losing their physical attractiveness and, thus, their remarriage possibilities in midlife. Only recently has there been much attention paid to the possibility that older women might select younger men as spouses. Much of this attention results from the cultural pattern of publicizing the experiences of a few highly visible and, usually, physically attractive women. There is often the implication that this is not something that could happen to the ordinary woman. The children of midlife divorced parents are not likely to be free of these cultural views. They are more able, nevertheless, to adjust to the behavior of their mothers than of their fathers, since it usually has more continuity with their long-term experience.

There may be a tendency to view the fate of the midlife divorced woman as less advantageous than that of the midlife divorced man, because she is less likely to remarry. To some extent this arises from the promarriage attitudes of our society. While it is true that some women are never able to escape the displaced homemaker syndrome, it must also be observed that they tend to have more resources available to them which make remarriages less critical for their personal adjustment.

Lillian Rubin (1983) has observed that women develop friendships in a much different way from men. Whether single or married, they use other women as major resources in their lives. Thus, many women find that they can develop a strong support group of other women like themselves, widows and divorcées, who have been through the experience. They have much in common and are able to learn a great deal from one another. On the other hand, Rubin observes, men do not form these kinds of same-sex friendships. Rather, they look to other women, often one particular woman, for support. It is possible, therefore, to interpret the more rapid remarriage of men as the primary means for coping with the fact of their divorce. Midlife women, on the other hand, may have more options available to them, thus reducing the pressure for remarriage.

Once again, "Twice in a Lifetime" provides some excellent illustrations of these divergent experiences of two midlife former spouses. While the divorced wife initially had difficulty in redirecting her life, she eventually did so, with a good deal of help from her women friends. The divorced husband, on the other hand, found his closest male friend and other of his workmates reacting very negatively to his behavior. A little harmless flirtation with the new waitress at the neighborhood bar was one thing. Developing a serious relationship with this woman was quite another matter. His resource, of course, was his new love.

Both sons and daughters often face another experience. They find that their remarried father, having taken on the dependent children of his younger wife, devotes much time and effort to these new stepchildren. Once again, because of the age differential, the stepsibling relationship is not the one usually envisioned in "blended" families. While they may not be old enough to be the parents of these stepsiblings, they are not young enough to develop a more typical sibling relationship. The problems of conflict between younger stepsiblings related to competition for space and daily attention are not usually the primary ones in midlife remarriage. Rather, the adult children often face a loss of relationship with their father on the very legitimate basis that the younger stepchildren require more of his attention. So, not only must they develop some style of relating to these new people in their lives, but their presence also requires restyling the relationship they have developed with their father in their more mature years.

Another factor making positive relationships with these young stepsiblings difficult is the threat that they may pose to the adult children's expectations for certain material benefits from their father. Aside from any inheritance concerns that they might have, children may have grown up expecting that college educations, first automobiles, or assistance in getting started in a new career or marriage would be funded by their father. His new obligations to his stepchildren may cause some revisions in his ability to meet these expectations of his own children. Adult children will probably resent this change in their father's ability to assist them. A recent newspaper article reported a suit filed by an adult child against his remarried father to obtain the funds for university educational expenses. Litigation in divorce does not take place only between the spouses!

Still another aspect of this, of course, involves the expectations of the new spouse concerning her husband's financial activity. She may expect certain benefits for her children based upon her assessment of her new husband's financial status. Indeed, one possible reason that younger divorced women with children find older men attractive potential mates is the promise of financial security. There may or may not have been any explicit agreements reached on these matters prior to the marriage. And, as the new wife observes the money which her husband spends on his own children, she may begin to see this as a threat to her own expectations.

One remarried couple with whom we are familiar consulted a therapist over just such issues. The wife had major concerns about the way her husband "spoiled" his children by giving them what she considered to be excessive allowances and by purchasing automobiles and other items for them. He was disturbed by the pressure which she brought to bear and felt that she did not understand the commitments he had to his own children. Former spouses may also become embroiled in these situations, placing pressure on the ex-spouse to meet the unwritten agreements they may have had with respect to their children's early adult years. These kinds of situations do little to improve the relationships between the new partner and her husband's children and former spouse.

Remarriage in midlife involves more than the immediate families of the individuals involved. There is a large extended kin network in which each party is involved. In this period of the family career these networks may be much larger than in other periods, and they also have a long history. Integrating a new spouse into these networks is a major task. Women, more frequently than men, are the kin-keepers in many families. This usually means that the wife has maintained the contacts not only with her own blood kin, but also with her husband's relatives. In divorce, she may still maintain some of these contacts. If she remarries, however, it is unlikely that she will continue to do so. This is not only because of the animosities which may be involved, but because of the increased load of kin taken on with her new spouse. Remarrying husbands may find that not only do they take on the new extended kin of their new partner, but they must also reestablish relationships with their own kin which were maintained by their former spouse.

The integration of new spouses into these extended kin networks is not simple. There is so much history of which the new spouse was not a part. Family gatherings inevitably will involve assumptions, as well as discussions, about established patterns and about knowledge of this history. Some families traditionally gather at a family vacation cottage for Independence Day or Labor Day celebrations. Or, there may be long-established patterns of spending a period of the summer at such a place by one or more branches of the extended family. A new wife may find herself very much a "fifth wheel" as her sisters-in-law carry out certain expected duties in these family get-togethers. A new husband may have similar difficulties in meeting the assumed expectations for helping winterize the sailboat or carry out needed maintenance on the cottage.

Attempts by the new wife to take on some of the kin-keeping with her husband's family may be frustrated simply because she does not have the knowledge to do it effectively. This all may be more than the remarried couple can handle. Given that they have major adjustments to make in establishing their own relationship and, often, relationships with stepchildren, they may choose to distance themselves from extended kin. In such circumstances it is often the adult children of remarried parents who take on some of these kin-keeping roles. They may find themselves becoming a major link in communicating the important events which occur in the lives of extended kin.

Adult children also may take on organizing some of the family ceremonial occasions which before were handled by one or the other of their parents. Thus, for example, an adult daughter may become the person who arranges for the celebration of her paternal grandparents' 50th wedding anniversary—a role which her mother might have performed, but for which her new stepmother is ill-prepared. Or she may take over organizing the family Thanksgiving dinner. Here, of course, the invitation list becomes very difficult. Not only does this involve the question of whether former spouses will both attend, but the question of half-siblings and step-siblings being included is also raised. The degree to which these quasi-kin have been integrated into the new kin network will be an important determinant in such decisions.

Midlife Remarriage—Summary

How all of this is worked out, of course, depends upon a number of other factors, e.g., how all parties dealt with the separation and divorce, the experiences that they may have had in the earlier negotiations around their place in the former spouse relationship, and their personal feelings about the new spouse. It also depends upon whether the former spouses are perfect pals, cooperative colleagues, angry associates, or fiery foes. Remarriage will almost inevitably reopen issues that all may have thought were settled in the postdivorce reorganization process.

Once again, the maintenance of meaning of the former spouse relationship appears as a critical factor. Without the central requirement to continue to relate as coparents of minor children and with the confirmation that the former spouse relationship carries less significance for the remarried partner, the primary reason for continuing to relate in any intensive manner is removed. However, their long relationship as married partners has set in motion a whole set of other relationships which will have to be dealt with in a new definition of the meanings. If acceptable patterns for routine contacts with children and grandchildren and meaningful participation in the important ceremonial family events can be worked out, then a satisfactory meaning for the former spouse relationship after remarriage can probably be established. If the boundaries are clarified so that the remarriage does not threaten their association with their adult children and with their grandchildren, the former spouse relationship probably loses a great deal of its significance.

Meanwhile a whole new set of meanings surrounding the remarriage relationship comes into play. The degree to which these meanings may be made compatible with those which survive from their former family experience will be very significant. We could expect that, where there is incompatibility, the new meanings will take precedence. However, such choices will not be without their stresses and the potential for crisis in the remarriage reorganization process.

AGING COUPLES

We are not dealing with a significant number of couples at this period of the family career. If divorce in this period is relatively unusual, remarriage is even less frequent. And, although we have no significant data upon which to base this evaluation, we would expect that the redefinition of the former spouse relationship would carry similar characteristics to those of the midlife group. The significant aspects of the content of the relationship with adult children may center more on the continuity of help and assistance, especially for the ex-spouse who remains unmarried, but the general nature of the issues is likely to be very similar. Until we have more research on this aspect of divorce and remarriage, we must necessarily remain ignorant of the factors which may make it unique.

CONCLUSION

Well-known humorist Erma Bombeck attests to the viability of surviving the complexities of a remarried family in a newspaper column titled "Here Come the Stepfamilies":

> I had a whole brother and a half sister. She in turn had a half brother, a half sister, a stepsister, and a full sister. We always prefaced every meeting with, "Who's your father?" and went from there. We had half aunts, uncles by divorce, and a few dozen cousins by association. We racked up stepchildren three years younger than their stepmothers, brothers who couldn't begin to spell their sister's last name, and grandfathers who were never too sure who you were.

Although we are unable to provide any comfortable answers for the families created in this era of serial monogamy, Bombeck again gives us some direction:

> The computer would not only keep pace with how many tickets are needed for graduation and seats for the wedding, but whether the separation would allow for three mothers and three fathers to sit in peace and love or be scattered throughout the crowd. (Wisconsin State Journal, March 25, 1984)

Our knowledge about these families to date is woefully inadequate. We are desperately in the need of longitudinal information, especially on those new extended families that are functioning adequately, to begin to understand how they cope with the many transitions of reorganization and redefinition.

NINE

Strengthening Binuclear Families

Current projections based on the divorce rate indicate that by 1990 there will be more binuclear families than nuclear families in North American society. How they cope with the life course transitions of changing family membership will, in large part, be dependent on societal reactions. Social institutions have been slow to respond to the needs of binuclear families. As society clings to the belief that the traditional nuclear family model is the ideal family form, binuclear families have had to settle for being considered alternative and, hence, deviant family forms.

Our focus in this book has been to provide a new model based on the normal developmental changes in families during and after divorce. We have held to the premise that the function of the family remains unchanged, although the structure changes dramatically as the family moves through the developmental transitions of the divorce process. As we have noted throughout, divorced families have few role models or societal supports to assist them in the difficult and often tumultuous structural and emotional changes they experience in this lengthy process.

In this concluding chapter we move beyond the experiences of the families themselves and address the kind of societal changes that we think are needed to assist families in reducing the stresses that accompany the transitions of the divorce process over their life course — and, hopefully, to enable them to encounter less crisis in that process.

FROM DEVIANCE TO NORMALITY

To change our thinking about divorced families — to remove from them the label of deviance or pathology — does not mean merely to give lip service to accepting them as alternative forms of familying. We must unambiguously acknowledge and support them as normal, prevalent family types that have resulted from major societal trends and changes.

Rapidly increased divorce rates have created what Paul Bohannan has called the "divorce industry." He notes that it " . . . is an amalgam of other industries and professions, and certainly it is one of the most important developments of the social history of the 20th century. It lacks a vast network of factories and sales rooms and fueling stations, but hundreds of thousands of people are involved in the divorce industry at thousands of sites" (1984, p. 16). Divorce is big business in our society. Two of the professions that are undergoing change and expansion in the divorce industry are lawyers and mental health professionals.

No-fault Legislation and the Adversarial Process

The emergence of no-fault legislation acknowledges that marriages may terminate without a presumption of fault by either party. This can be interpreted as an encouraging move toward normalizing divorce in our society. Although no-fault legislation has as its intent removing the issue of fault from the legal divorce, the actual process still maintains an adversarial stance. The objective of the adversarial process, with its two opposing forces, is to protect the rights of each individual. However, this process, though well intentioned, is not aimed at preserving the functions of the family.

When the two spouses approach divorce as adversaries, the end product is frequently an escalation of anger between the spouses. The issues of property, support, custody, and visitation become enmeshed in a power struggle for equity — and often, advantage. Although compromise is inevitable, the road traveled on the way to compromise is often fraught with accusations and increasing distrust between the spouses. It is not uncommon for spouses to cease talking with each other as they use their lawyers to negotiate the issues of their settlement. This process often runs counter to efforts by mental health professionals, who may be simultaneously attempting to assist the spouses to work through some of their anger and the pain of their failed relationship. The therapeutic process is apt to dissolve as the adversarial process gains momentum.

Divorce Mediation

Divorce mediation has emerged in the past ten years as an alternative to the traditional adversarial approach in the legal process. O. J. Coogler, an attorney who experienced personally the negative effects of his own adversarial divorce process, introduced the concept of divorce mediation. Basically the approach assumes that divorcing couples can resolve the issues of support, property, and custody through a negotiation process facilitated by a trained mediator (Coogler, 1978). Its purpose is to put the power for settling these issues back in the hands of those who created them — the marital partners. And, the stated goal is that, when marital partners resolve their issues through negotiation and compromise, they will be able to abide by their decisions without continued acrimony.

Mediation for divorce is an early intervention strategy that is aimed at normalizing the process of negotiation of differences and reducing continuing conflict. We know enough at the present time to state that certain types of conflicts in divorce are sufficiently common to be called normal. We can anticipate that most people who divorce will have some conflict over the division of property, over child-care arrangements, and over continuing support of both children and disadvantaged spouses. These same types of conflicts have been identified as common in marriage as well. However, in marriage it is not necessary legally to clarify these differences; what has been unwritten in marriage must become written in divorce. The need to separate the household brings all these unresolved issues out into the public arena. Divorce adds the additional expenses of operating two households and requires more clarity about child-care responsibilities.

Although divorce mediation is only ten years old, it has now become part of the divorce industry. There are now several professional organizations, an increasing number of books by lawyers and mental health professionals describing their brand of mediation, a professional journal of mediation, and a variety of programs aimed at training professionals to become mediators. As this specialty develops, there are also the usual professional territorial and turf issues. Who is qualified to practice mediation? Does it take special training? Should mediators be licensed? Is it the domain of lawyers or mental health professionals?

The mediation movement is too much in its infancy to state with any certainty for whom and in what dimensions it will reach its desired outcomes. As the field develops, the research comparing mediation with the traditional adversarial process will provide the necessary evaluation of the effectiveness of this new intervention strategy. However, its premises are well founded and hold the promise for assisting couples through the difficult process of divorce without creating more issues for anger to carry on into the divorced family. At the time of this writing mediation appears to have the potential of providing a healthy arena for aiding the functional reorganization of the family.[1] Hopefully, as this divorce industry grows, lawyers, mediators and therapists will need less to define and preserve their territory and will work better together to devise combinations of professional help to address the needs of divorcing and divorced family systems.

Divorce Therapy

Another professional specialty recently introduced is divorce therapy or counseling. In the past helping professionals have dealt with divorce under the guise of marital counseling or therapy, which resulted in viewing divorce as a failure of marital interventions. With the development of theoretical frameworks concerned with divorce, the emerging field of divorce therapy will expand its techniques and strategies to assist families through the process of divorce.[2]

Although divorce therapy is a separate modality of treatment that seems to be on the rise around the country, it appears more fruitful to us to include the treatment of divorced families as part of the domain of all those in the helping professions. But what is it that makes the treatment of divorced families different from that of first married families? First, divorced families tend to be more complex systems than most first married systems. Second, the developmental transitions are different from those of first married families. Third, there is no clear set of role models for divorced families.

Mental health professionals who are to support and strengthen binuclear families must have a clear understanding of the normal processes of family change. Not only is it important to help reduce the pain of the process, but it is also important to provide options for the family's functional reorganization and redefinition. Clinicians need to examine their own stereotypes and biases about divorce so that they can truly value their clients' choice to change the structure of the family.

Only then can they assist families in developing relationships which facilitate continued interactions.

Family therapists have written extensively about the importance of the family of origin to the individual developmental process. This same theory extends to the binuclear family: The kin and quasi-kin relationships formed by a marital union have salience for the individual's functioning in future divorced family relationships. Anger, for many divorced spouses, merely provides a more comfortable defense against depression over the loss of not only the person, but also the traditional nuclear family and all of its dreams. For many it is an effective individual coping mechanism during a stressful transition, but in the longrun it may destroy the possibility of enjoying the later developmental roles of family life. It is important that the emphasis be not on "writing off" the failed marriage and its participants, but rather on creating options for new ways of integrating these relationships.

Treatment strategies for divorced families need not take on a whole new character, if one assumes that the relationships of former marriages have similar characteristics to other extended family relationships. Much of individual therapy is based on understanding one's past and how it affects one's present, on understanding and accepting the limitations of one's parents, on gaining insight into one's unrealistic expectations and faulty beliefs. These same principles may be applied equally as well to relationships that were formed as part of a marriage.

If we are truly to accept binuclear families as normal, clinicians will have to view the family through a wide angle lens. This will mean thinking in terms of families, not households. The stepfamily household consists of a number of subsystems which are part of the larger binuclear family system. Most "single-parent families" are one-parent households that are connected systemically to another one-parent household. Criteria for deciding when to treat the whole family system and when to treat subsystems or individuals separately will depend upon the theoretical orientation of the therapist. These same orientations should determine the mode of treatment with binuclear families. For some therapists, the thought of conducting an interview with mother, stepmother, father, stepfather, and an entourage of children from the various unions will be overwhelming. For other therapists, comfortable working with large systems, this family constellation is the preferred mode of treatment.

Normalizing Marital Termination

We referred to the research of Hagestad (1981; Hagestad & Smyer, 1982; Hagestad et al., 1984) and to her assessment that divorce is seen as an unscheduled event in the social structure. It is clear that a revision of this orientation is called for in respect to both parts of that conceptualization. Beyond the problem with the "event" aspect of that view, which we will discuss in the next section, we also need to redefine divorce as a possible, if not *probable*, process in the lives of people. Even if they do not experience divorce in their own marriages, they are unlikely to escape it in the lives of their extended family, their children, or their friends.

If we are to genuinely accept the pervasiveness of divorce documented by the divorce statistics, we need to plan in marriage for the possibility of its termination. No one wants to have a debilitating illness, accident or premature death, yet most families plan for the possibility of those events. Health, automobile, and life insurance are commonly accepted as necessary provisions for unfortunate unscheduled events. Why not divorce insurance? We are not suggesting that this be insurance in the same sense as that taken out for deaths, illnesses, and accidents — though it is somewhat surprising that the "divorce industry" has not spawned such plans by insurance companies. Rather, we are suggesting that couples need to insure that they have adequately taken into account their vulnerability to the experience of divorce. Given the 50/50 risk of a marriage terminating in divorce, marriage partners would be wise to plan ahead for the known conflicts.

In addition, the divorce possibility also infers that other issues should be specified by the marital partners. The economic consequences for women and children who experience divorce are a disturbing fact of our times. But all the inequities of marriage cannot be righted by the divorce decree. Many women are disadvantaged because they were not paid for home care, child-care, and other supportive services in marriage. It is too late to right these wrongs at the termination of the marriage; they must be accounted for within the marriage. If all the debts are left to accumulate until the divorce, as is so often the case, women will continue to suffer from underpayment, default of payments, and debtor's bankruptcy.

If binuclear families are to have the same status as nuclear families, we will need to invent new relationship terms. For example, we need to have a kinship term for the relationship between a mother and a stepmother who are involved in parenting the same child. Many mothers and stepmothers share childrearing and yet we have no term which gives that relationship credibility. We need new terms that connote the present relationships of in-laws of the first marriage. "My former mother-in-law, the grandmother of my child," is insufficient to acknowledge the continuing kin relationships. As Margaret Mead (1971, p. 125) stated it: "No institution is fully viable unless it has verbal as well as legal commitments. . . . At present, the vulgar 'my ex' is all that we have to deal with the relationship which may involve twenty years and five children. We should be able to do better—and soon."

The movement toward normalizing the binuclear family requires changes in most social institutions with which families interact. School systems, religious groups, and health care providers tend to be structured to deal with the traditional nuclear family and become confused when families do not fit this model. For example, most school systems still use demographic information forms with places for information only about the traditional biological parents. Who gets sent report cards, who gets invited to parent-teacher conferences, and who gets called in case of emergency are all questions which school personnel must address about each child. It cannot be assumed that the answers will be the same for all children in the same binuclear family.

Textbooks in the primary schools still use models of the nuclear family in teaching children about family life. This leaves many children, if not the majority, feeling as if their families are peculiar. There is no educational reason for continuing to ignore the fact that many readers of these texts are having a different kind of family experience. Introduction of binuclear families into the school text literature would do much to normalize the divorced family.

Religious groups also participate in the subtle stigmatization of binuclear families. While many of these groups have recognized the level of divorce in the society—and in their membership—and have developed programs for those affected by it, the general nuclear family bias is still prominent in the religious setting. This, of course, involves difficult issues of theology for many of these groups. Some have faced these issues head-on and have developed new theological statements concerning their view of marital breakup. Others have steadfastly maintained their basic commitment to marriage as a permanent relationship ordained by God. We are not theologians and tread in this area with some trepidation. We only observe that such theological stances do little to assist contemporary binuclear families to incorporate their religious beliefs into the reality of their experience.

Finally, much of the current social welfare legislation, policy, and programming supports a nuclear family bias. There is some hope here as more laws are passed which recognize: the needs of both parents for access to their children and of the children to both parents; the rightful claim of wives to the economic benefits gained in a marriage beyond minimal child support payments; the right of access to credit and other financial services as an individual, not because of spousal status; and other sorts of legislation. However, many policies and programs are designed to deal with problems only after they arise. We would advocate attention to preventative approaches which keep these problems from arising in the first place. We would also argue for a change in philosophical approach from one which seems primarily concerned with removing the "burden" of these families on the society to one which recognizes their right to the same sort of supportive environment accorded the nuclear family.

The sociological basis for many of the issues we have discussed is clear. A society committed to a particular family form will be slow to add elements to its normative structure which would allow its members to practice other patterns. If we believe that "a woman's place is in the home," we are not likely to develop structures which allow her ease of absence from the home, such as affordable and effective child-care or equitable compensation for gainful employment. At the same time, other values of the society, discussed in detail in Chapter 1, are at the root of these familial changes. All societies contain value conflicts which are played out in their normative structures. The conflicts we have identified are of critical significance to the continued strength of the society. Therefore, although the complexities of family life in the latter part of the 20th century are confusing, it is important that social institutions revise their policies, procedures, and programs to include these changes.

FROM EVENT TO PROCESS

Although there is increasing awareness that divorce is a process, the prevailing tendency is to view it merely as an event that disrupts normal family patterns. The focus on process has come out of clinical work, based on the knowledge that adjustment to divorce is a more extended experience than originally had been assumed. Attention has been centered on the emotional divorce, noting an extended grieving process and the persistent attachment between former spouses. But it is only when we manifestly begin to view divorce as a long-range developmental process that we will be able to develop policies and programs that are effective in assisting families through the transitions of family change.

Although the research on divorce has been steadily increasing over the past decade, there are still large gaps in our knowledge about divorced families. As is often the case with any new area of research, the findings are often contradictory and fragmented. Because of the paucity of longitudinal studies and the focus on individuals rather than on family systems, there are as yet few empirically supported conclusions about the developmental processes of divorced families. And because the last decade has been one of major attitudinal, legal, and social change in relation to divorce, much of the research conducted in the earlier decades has lost its validity for understanding divorcing families in the 1980s.

In 1965, for example, a ten-year-old child whose parents divorced might be one of a small handful of children in a classroom dealing with a changing family structure. In 1980, that same child would be more likely to have had many peers dealing with similar life changes. And in 1990, we can anticipate that a ten-year-old experiencing a parental divorce would find at least half of his or her classmates living in new family structures created by divorce. Being a minority in any social situation produces responses different from those of the majority. The current social context surrounding divorce is sufficiently changed to warrant questioning the application of earlier research findings to families in the latter part of the 20th century. It is not that we need to totally disregard earlier research; rather, we need to regard those earlier findings more as heuristic hypotheses to be tested in light of the many societal changes of the last decades.

Most of the current research on the effects of divorce is premised on divorce as a disruptive, crisis-potentiating event. This premise has produced research which seeks to discover the consequences of the precipitating event of divorce on individuals. Much of the investigation is concerned with individuals rather than families and has focused on examining the negative consequences for both children and adults.

Furthermore, it has been concerned more with immediate consequences than with long-range processes. Hence, most of our current knowledge is about individuals in the separation transition. For example, we know that the transition of separation is likely to result in temporary distress for one or more of the family members. For adults, the extent and duration of distress have been associated with age, gender, and control over the decision. For children, high conflict between parents and the attenuation of the father-child relationship appear to result in a range of dysfunctional reactions, from depression and withdrawal to low self-esteem and an increase in behavioral problems.

But we are lacking answers to questions about differential factors affecting the process. For example, what family patterns and individual personalities are predisposed to more distress and dysfunction upon marital separation? Does a slow process of separation result in less distress for family members? What extended family patterns aid in the reduction of distress? How are sibling relationships associated with level of distress?

What about the effects of midlife divorce on young adults? We have almost no information on this family career phase for both parents and children. Do young adult children, who are struggling with individuation and independence, as is characteristic of their developmental stage in life, experience more difficulty in leaving home in the midst of their family disorganizing? Many parents are known to say, "We waited until the children were grown before we separated." Might the children have been better off if their parents had terminated their marriage during an earlier stage of their development?

Similarly, we know little about the impact of midlife and older divorces on the former spouses themselves. Yet, the trends are clear that more married couples will end their marriages in these periods or will have divorced earlier and not remarried, thus entering this period of life as members of binuclear families. What are the requirements of such people? Are there special aspects of legal and social policies which need to be addressed if they are to live satisfying and productive lives? Given the life expectancy of individuals in the society, the situation of the midlife and aging divorced must be illuminated by research revealing the process beyond the immediate event and the limited period following it.

Once again we need to refer to the social institutions established to help and protect families. By treating divorce as an event, their programs may in fact be limiting binuclear families in their reorganization. As we have seen, coping with the initial experience of separation and divorce is only the first stage in the transitional process. By focusing on the adjustment phase of the process and failing to assist in the restructuring and consolidation phases (McCubbin & Patterson, 1983), these organizations may encourage families to truncate their reorganization at a less than optimal level of functioning. Effective programs for assisting binuclear families should assist them to prepare for the transitions which lie ahead.

For example, some churches and synagogues have programs that help separating families by insuring that adequate child-care is available, aiding separated wives in finding suitable employment, and providing immediate financial assistance. They are certainly performing a valuable service. However, such programs need to incorporate a longer-term perspective, in order to assist families beyond the immediate requirements. While the religious organization itself may not be equipped to provide the full range of follow-up services called for, it can be an effective agent for referral to other resources. And it certainly is a potentially effective setting for support groups for family members as they move through the process.

Many school systems have set up support groups to assist students experiencing separation and divorce. Once again, if these groups are conceptualized only as dealing with the initial stress of early separation, they fail in the long run. Such groups could be structured to include students who have experienced the later transitions and can provide a kind of anticipatory socialization for those in the earlier phases of divorce. Again, the school provides a potentially effective support group setting and an important referral agent.

Therapists and other helping professionals may play a crucial role in assisting families with the long-term process. Using the two-tiered developmental process we have posited, the therapist can both determine the transition in which the family is involved and interpret that in light of the family career period. Intervention strategies for a family in midlife experiencing divorce will certainly differ from those for a family in the childrearing period embarking upon remarriage.

In the early transitions, parents need to be helped to understand the long-range implications of their decisions. The client who says, "I never want to see him or her again," needs to understand the negative consequences of that behavior, and in many cases, the improbabilities.

While such emotional responses to the immediate stress are to be expected, they cannot be seen as final. It is not likely that very much that occurs in the early adjustment phase of any of the transitions of separation, divorce, or remarriage will stand the test of time. This is, after all, a time when the participants are simply trying to cope with the immediate stress of the process.

Therapists may find that clients will work through one phase of the transition and then need to return to therapy during another transition. Helping a client prepare for the next transition can ease the stresses which accompany it. Providing realistic expectations will assist the client to develop functional coping mechanisms and facilitate the transition.

In the early stages, it might be wise to bring in extended family members when they appear to be very much involved in the process. Many an angry mother-in-law can be turned into an ally with some sensitive counseling. Involving both former spouses in therapy may have important benefits throughout the process of reorganization. It is insufficient to merely facilitate working-through the anger; the former spouse clients need to learn new modes of communicating in order to deal effectively with the many issues that will continue to arise throughout the long-range developmental process. When the family expands in remarriage, the inclusion of the whole binuclear family for a few sessions can circumvent the usual scapegoating of the "other" parent. It can also help reduce the threat posed by adding new family members and aid in the development of communication across households. At the very minimum it will provide the family with a new image of itself as an interdependent binuclear family system.

Finally, more socially responsible lawyers should join some of their colleagues in seeing their role in the divorce process as extending beyond the court hearing, the final decree, and other litigation issues. Since many of the difficult cases involve a return to the lawyer for possible further court action, attorneys are in a particularly crucial position to suggest alternatives to litigation. Just as effective physicians keep a list of referral resources for their patients, lawyers should have readily available the names of therapists, counselors, mediators, and social agencies who may assist their clients.[3] Some law firms have followed the medical model by having on their staff a therapist or other mental health professional to help clients with the nonlegal elements of the divorce process.

It becomes clear that approaching divorce as a process, rather than an event, requires an orientation which is much closer to a maintenance strategy than to a repair operation. It also calls for more networking among the various community groups which have direct experience with divorced families.

FROM MARRIAGE TO PARENTING

Redefining Parenting

"Family" is an elusive term which has different meanings for different people. Until someone marries it usually refers to his or her parents and siblings. After marriage it may include a spouse. However, the tendency is not to think of a married couple as a family unless they have children. Childless couples are often faced with the question, "When are you going to start a family?" In this case "family" requires the presence of children.

Whatever definition of family we use, one major function of families is to provide for the rearing and socialization of children. Society's major concern about divorce is not that marriages break up. It is that parents break up. The common term "broken home" has become a synonym for divorced families and implies that children lose their families through divorce. In practice this usually means that children lose their fathers, and without a father and a mother in one household a child is labeled as coming from a broken home. What is really conveyed, however, is that divorce severs parenting.

Not only do we have to rid ourselves of the myth of the predominance of the traditional nuclear family, but we also have to rid ourselves of the myth that it is exclusively the best way to rear children. Children have needs and rights to adequate nurturing and child-care, and parents have obligations to fulfill them. These parental obligations come with the role and are not restricted to one gender or confined to marital status.

A slight shift in our thinking—and one much more in touch with the reality rather than the mythology of nuclear families—would permit us to expand our definitions of parenting. First, we need to separate marriage from parenting. Biological parenting can and does occur irrespective of marriage. Second, we need to expand our definition of parenting. Sociological parenting does occur whenever an adult assumes responsibility for childrearing. This expanded definition of parenting would allow us to hold a view of families in which children may be reared successfully in one- or two-parent households, in families which span more than one household, and in families which may include more than two parents. Children then may have one, two, three, or more parents, sociological and biological parents, and parents of one or both genders. If we were to really accept this broader definition of the functions and responsibilities of parenting, divorce would not need to deprive children of adequate parenting. The question of custody would then become *how* parents will continue their parenting — not *which* parent will become the responsible parent.

Custody and Parenting

The movement toward joint custody is a powerful new trend reflective of the current social changes. The increased prevalence of dual — career marriages and a new interest in the father's role make this a ripe time for challenging the prevailing practice of awarding custody to mothers. Joint custody does not denote "equal" parenting. It merely means that both parents continue to be responsible parents, at least to the degree that they were responsible up to the time of divorce. If they were joint custody parents in the marriage, why should they not continue that contract in divorce? Unless they choose to change their parental contract when they terminate their marital contract, or unless it is not in the best interests of the child, there appears to be no reason for them not to continue as joint custody parents. Certainly, not all parents share childrearing equally in marriage, nor are they always cooperative. To expect parents to radically change their parenting styles in divorce would be unrealistic. Relabeling the divorced father as joint custodial rather than noncustodial has the potential of changing the expectation for the role of divorced fathers — it would accentuate the message that parenting rights and responsibilities are not based on marital status.

The confusion and ambiguity surrounding joint custody are not in its philosophical intent but in the practicalities and social politics of putting it into action. One problem is our gender-specific roles of mothering and fathering. Although we may be in the midst of change when it comes to concepts of parenting, most families still function as if parenting means mothering. As long as mothering — and not fathering — means parenting, women will suffer inequities with joint custody. Having the primary responsibility for child-care, with its severe economic repercussions, leaves women at a disadvantage in a joint custodial arrangement. These same inequities are present in marriage as well. Women, even in dual career marriages, carry the major burdens for home and child-care. This places them at a disadvantage in the labor market.

Custody often represents power and as such infuses the struggle and decision with all the emotional baggage of the unresolved conflicts between the spouses. The current joint custody controversy is saddled with this power issue. As states try to refine their statutes about joint custody, pressure groups such as NOW and Fathers United express their concerns about the outcomes of varying custody decisions. Philosophically one can support joint custody as a preferred custody arrangement for many families because it is in the best interests of children and continued effective parenting. However, it is impossible to totally eliminate the possibility that the desire for joint custody by one or both partners is part of a power play in the divorce. New intervention approaches in resolving custody conflicts inherent in many divorces aim to diagnose and intervene in the power issue. Yet, because of the current gender inequities in our society, it may be impossible to remove the issue of custody from the economic issues. Who gets the family home may be tied to the custody decision. Child support awards are tied to custodial care.

Joint custody is still too new for us to draw many conclusions. We will need longitudinal, large-scale research to provide answers to the many questions that it poses. Does joint custody result in lowered financial support for children? Mothers economically disadvantaged by a joint custodial arrangement still need to provide the usual necessities, such as a home and child-care for children; as custodial mothers they would have received more toward these costs. Do joint custody awards encourage fathers to be more active parents? The current research does not provide answers to these questions.

The history of custody shows us that custodial decisions reflect how society values gender and family roles. If we hold the view that families today exist in many forms, then we need to expand custody options. That means that we must avoid making any one type of custody award the *presumption* of the courts, as father custody was in earlier times, as mother custody has been more recently, and as joint custody has the potential of becoming. It is important that we keep custody options unmistakably open — without assuming that one type of custodial arrangement is superior. While it might be in the best interests of children and parents who develop perfect pal or cooperative colleague relationships to have joint custody, it might be disastrous for angry associates or fiery foes. Conflict-ridden parental relationships in which children become the battlefield are not healthy environments, regardless of marital status. It may be that joint custody between antagonists only perpetuates and, perhaps, even escalates the war. Now, with the increasing incidence of joint custodial parents, research can begin to address the many unanswered questions around which type of custodial arrangement is best suited to which type of former spouse relationship.

We will also need to address the added complexities of the relationships that are necessary if these child-sharing arrangements continue after the remarriage of one or both partners. What does it take for a remarriage subsystem to function adequately when both partners are joint custodial parents? How does the child in this situation master the transitions as he or she crosses from one remarried household to another with step — and half — siblings in both households? We have no answers to these questions, nor are we even able to make educated guesses.

Therapeutic Implications

Most married spouses have little preparation for parenthood. When problems arise they turn to current popular books to try to solve problems they are having in coping with their children at varying developmental stages. Again, many of these books are aimed at mothers and do not address the relationship between parents as they develop their individual styles of sharing parenting responsibilities.

Much of therapy with divorced spouses focuses on the spousal relationship, often ignoring the parenting relationship. In the transitions following separation, however, the parenting relationship is often fused with the spousal relationship and creates the stresses in reorganization. Divorced spouses, even those who still hold onto spousal anger, can learn skills of cooperative parenting. As a rule of thumb, the greater the anger the greater the need for more structure in the postdivorce parenting relationship. Perfect pals and cooperative colleagues will usually be able to handle and effectively negotiate a flexible coparenting relationship. However, angry associates and fiery foes will probably require clearly designated rules which they can follow without much interaction. They will probably need to return to therapists and mediators to renegotiate new rules as they move through the transitions of individual and family developmental change. And which form of helping system they choose to settle their issues (e.g., family therapist, mediator, lawyer, judge) may closely parallel the type of relationship developed (Beal, 1985).

The restructuring phase becomes a time for somewhat more careful testing of various solutions to shared parenting. Emotions may still color some of these situations, especially for angry associates and fiery foes, but there can be more consideration of alternative courses of action. Former spouses need to be helped to avoid premature consolidation into a given pattern, which may not be the best solution available.

It may also be necessary to offer some training for parenthood to stepparent families. This may involve not only teaching parents and stepparents certain parenting skills but also providing them with a fundamental redefinition of parenting. Being a stepmother or stepfather can never be the same as being the biological parent — especially when the biological father or mother is still active in the binuclear family. Thus, a unique definition of parenting for the stepparent will be essential.

Many stepparents feel guilty for not instantly loving their new stepchildren. Others expect a much shorter process of adjustment in the blended family than is realistic. David Mills (1984), a family therapist, has described the gradual phasing process which he uses in his own practice with stepfamilies. He proposes that the parent and stepparent first establish long-term goals that they wish to reach at some future time. He suggests that this might be done in terms of a "guided fantasy, set some years in the future" (p. 368).

At the outset of the establishment of the stepfamily, parents, and not stepparents, should set limits for their own children. Mills suggests that this process is very similar to that which parents go through in making arrangements with sitters they have engaged. And, he observes, it is quite appropriate in such situations for there to be different rules for different children, since they will have different histories. This, of course, is especially crucial in those families in which both spouses have custodial children. During the period in which this system prevails, Mills argues, the process of stepparent bonding can take place in much the same way that bonding, characterized by nurturance without limit-setting, takes place between parent and infant during the first year of life. Without a bond between stepparent and stepchild, it is unlikely that the relationship will develop in the hoped-for direction.

Finally, Mills suggests that after an extended period of time family rules may be blended. This takes place in his approach through a series of frequent parent-stepparent "executive negotiation meetings." He notes, "Couples should be cautioned at the beginning to be careful of premature or assumed agreements" (p. 369). He also points out that any agreement concerning rules which does not have the support of the biological parent is unlikely to be effective with the child, since the child is sure to be aware of his or her parent's lack of support for the rule.

Many couples may be surprised at the time scale which he suggests for reaching this final blending. His estimate is that it will take about as long as the chronological age of the child. That is, for a three-year-old it will take three years, and for a six-year-old, six years (p. 370). His reasoning is that it is likely to take as long for a stepparent to establish the kind of relationship with a child that the biological parent took with that child. If Mills is correct, couples attempting to establish blended families with teenagers should not be surprised if they fail to achieve the kind of family style that exists in the idealized traditional nuclear family! Mills' approach is one example of a therapeutic strategy which clearly takes into account the process nature of the divorce transition.

Mills' use of executive negotiation sessions recalls Minuchin's notion of the parental executive function. In our view this function can be spread over several parents, thus relieving the pressure placed on any one. Mills' system, by the way, would not rule out such an approach. His point would be that a stepparent, during the period prior to the blending of stepfamily rules, should be careful to make it clear that he or she is invoking a rule set by the biological parent. In truth, the stepparent is simply functioning as the executor of the rule, not the formulator of it.

Particular emphasis needs to be placed on increasing the role of the father or stepfather in parenting. We have observed the heavy responsibility for parenting placed upon mothers in the traditional nuclear family. This pressure is likely to be considerably increased in the remarried binuclear family. Fathers and stepfathers who have been used to leaving the parenting to their spouses need to recognize the risks that the continuation of such a pattern involves for a satisfactory restructuring of the remarried family. This point of view is founded on more than feminist ideology. The practical situation simply requires a greater involvement in parenting by all the parents—custodial and noncustodial biological parents *and* stepparents.

Bringing together the whole binuclear family for a few sessions can bring about more relief of tensions than family members usually anticipate. For many families, it is the first time they have been together in the same room. Mothers and stepmothers, fathers and stepfathers, all of whom have considerable secondhand knowledge about each other, can benefit greatly from direct interaction. Ghosts may be killed off. And as a result of therapeutic intervention some mother/stepmother and father/stepfather combinations can be helped to find methods of cooperating in the spirit of childrearing.

TOWARD A WELL FAMILY INDUSTRY

Bohannan (1984) has asserted that divorce is now as much of a societal institution as marriage and our efforts need to be geared toward a "well family industry."

The issues which we have addressed lead us to the assessment that there is still some distance to go before complete institutionalization can be claimed. It is easy to become discouraged about the changes in the social structure which would lead to a normalization of divorced family structures and encourage the development of greater efforts devoted to their wellness. It is said that a pessimist sees the cup half-empty and an optimist sees it half-full. So, whether we conclude that the cup is half-empty or half-full depends on the kind of bias we carry.

We prefer to see the societal changes that have already begun to take place as indications that progress has been made. Both the rapid legislative decisions toward joint custody and child-sharing and the new advances in mediation as an alternative to the adversarial approach to divorce indicate a societal shift. Of major significance to us is that the legal and societal thrust now and in the future needs to rest on the confidence that most divorced parents can be cooperative and continue parenting after divorce.

Divorce reform in this next decade will be focused on finding solutions to the many complexities of changing family structure and process. Certainly binuclear families will change the nature of family life as much as they will be affected by it. How support develops for these family changes, which may be seen by some as "undermining" the family, will be crucial. Professionals in the legal, therapeutic, religious, and educational fields will need to take leadership in demonstrating that it is far more destructive to allow such a large proportion of the population to be left without the socially supportive structures that they require for functional family life. There is, of course, a large and growing constituency in the general population who can be counted on for support in such a movement—the divorced families of the present and the future. Perhaps, if more of them can demonstrate the constructive and healthy functioning that is possible in binuclear families in their numerous forms, those who see these family forms as threatening to the society will change their views. If nothing else, such greater public knowledge of effective divorced family functioning can provide the much-needed role models for other divorced families.

The title of the opening chapter alluded to the traditional children's tale about Henny Penny, the somewhat hysterical chicken who concluded that the sky was falling because she had been struck on the head by an acorn. Being a socially responsible chicken, she concluded that she must tell the King. En route to the King's palace, she managed to get a large portion of the animal population involved in her belief and committed to the movement of delivering the message. In the story, they never reached the King because they were tricked by a clever fox and lured to his den where, presumably, they were eaten. Thus, the story concludes, the King never got the message.

Unfortunately, the Henny Penny message on divorced families is still being spread. Equally unfortunate, the King has received the message. We think the impact of the "acorn" of a changed divorce and marriage situation has been misinterpreted. As a consequence, a large portion of the population, as well as many professionals and policymakers, have been acting on these misinterpretations with behaviors, legislation, policies, and programs. The results have not helped binuclear families to achieve a functional family reorganization in many instances.

While we would reject being cast in the violent and deceptive role of the fox (all analogies break down at some point), we do think that the spread of the false message should be stopped, and a new message conveyed to the population—and to the King!

Appendix

Appendix Table 1: Marital Status of the Population, By Sex and Age, 1920–1985.

Year, Sex, & Age	Total	NUMBER (1,000)				PERCENT			
		Single	Married	Widowed	Divorced	Single	Married	Widowed	Divorced
1985									
MALE	81,452	20,453	55,206	2,109	5,264	25.1	67.8	2.6	6.5
18–19	3,640	3,534	109	0	0	97.1	3.0	0.0	0.0
20–24	10,055	7,605	2,406	3	138	75.6	23.9	0.0	1.4
25–29	10,420	4,037	5,958	3	629	38.7	57.2	0.0	6.0
30–34	9,764	2,027	7,042	7	926	20.8	72.1	.1	9.5
35–44	15,333	1,444	12,687	54	1,581	9.4	82.7	.4	10.3
45–54	10,848	682	9,424	131	939	6.3	86.9	1.2	8.7
55–64	10,377	633	8,921	388	644	6.1	86.0	3.7	6.2
65–74	7,259	380	6,027	672	307	5.2	83.0	9.3	4.2
75+	3,755	200	2,632	851	100	5.3	70.1	22.7	2.7
FEMALE	89,917	16,377	56,990	11,372	7,814	18.2	63.4	12.6	8.7
18–19	3,738	3,240	494	2	28	86.7	13.2	.1	.7
20–24	10,411	6,091	4,223	20	347	58.5	40.6	.2	3.3
25–29	10,686	2,824	7,404	57	843	26.4	69.3	.5	7.9
30–34	9,987	1,351	7,716	104	1,234	13.5	77.3	1.0	12.4
35–44	15,966	1,091	12,997	323	2,242	6.8	81.4	2.0	14.0
45–54	11,550	529	9,192	809	1,401	4.6	79.6	7.0	12.1
55–64	11,774	440	8,519	2,047	1,047	3.7	72.4	17.4	8.9
65–74	9,317	412	4,881	3,622	519	4.4	52.4	38.9	5.6
75+	6,487	400	1,565	4,390	154	6.2	24.1	67.7	2.4
1980									
MALE	74,101	17,434	50,825	1,972	3,871	23.5	68.6	2.7	5.2
18–24	13,843	10,529	3,156	2	156	76.1	22.8	0.0	1.1
25–44	29,643	5,142	22,318	64	2,119	17.3	75.3	.2	7.1
45–64	20,832	1,264	17,761	573	1,235	6.1	85.3	2.8	5.9
65+	9,783	499	7,590	1,333	361	5.1	77.6	13.6	3.7
FEMALE	82,054	13,977	51,767	10,479	5,831	17.0	63.1	12.8	7.1
18–24	14,430	8,613	5,394	26	397	59.7	37.4	.2	2.8
25–44	30,960	3,485	23,891	427	3,157	11.3	77.2	1.4	10.2
45–64	22,704	1,056	16,935	2,903	1,809	4.7	74.6	12.8	8.0
65+	13,960	824	5,546	7,121	468	5.9	39.7	51.0	3.4
1970									
MALE	62,329	11,903	46,747	2,110	1,577	19.1	75.0	3.4	2.5
18–24	10,546	7,071	3,393	1	81	67.0	32.2	0.0	.8
25–44	23,475	2,658	19,856	79	639	11.3	84.6	.3	2.7
45–64	19,946	1,514	17,253	519	660	7.6	86.5	2.6	3.3
65+	8,364	653	6,002	1,510	199	7.8	71.8	18.1	2.4

(continued)

Appendix Table 1: *Continued*

Year, Sex, & Age	Total	NUMBER (1,000)				PERCENT			
		Single	Married	Widowed	Divorced	Single	Married	Widowed	Divorced
FEMALE	69,474	9,536	47,607	9,639	2,693	13.7	68.5	13.9	3.9
18–24	11,947	5,700	6,015	27	204	47.7	50.3	.2	1.7
25–44	24,411	1,713	21,141	361	1,197	7.0	86.6	1.5	4.9
45–64	21,766	1,253	16,428	3,054	1,031	5.8	75.5	14.0	4.7
65+	11,349	871	4,024	6,196	259	7.7	35.5	54.6	2.3
1960									
MALE	52,474	7,701	41,558	2,112	1,103	14.7	79.2	4.0	2.1
20–24	4,961	2,713	2,226	0	22	54.7	44.9	0.0	.4
25–44	22,805	3,020	19,263	99	423	13.2	84.5	.4	1.9
45–64	17,650	1,470	14,952	683	545	8.3	84.7	3.9	3.1
65+	7,058	498	5,117	1,330	113	7.1	72.5	18.8	1.6
FEMALE	56,704	5,301	41,659	8,060	1,684	9.3	73.5	14.2	3.0
20–24	5,591	1,615	3,870	15	91	28.9	69.2	.3	1.6
25–44	23,835	1,664	20,905	495	771	7.0	87.7	2.1	3.2
45–64	18,695	1,296	13,697	3,011	691	6.9	73.3	16.1	3.7
65+	8,583	726	3,187	4,539	131	8.5	37.1	52.9	1.5
1950									
MALE	48,057	8,143	36,866	2,176	872	16.9	76.7	4.5	1.8
20–24	5,544	3,095	2,419	4	27	55.8	43.6	.1	.5
25–44	30,319	4,009	25,322	404	584	13.2	83.5	1.3	1.9
45–64	15,341	1,480	12,761	739	362	9.6	83.2	4.8	2.4
65+	5,449	437	3,606	1,286	120	8.0	66.2	23.6	2.2
FEMALE	50,285	5,739	36,512	6,830	1,203	11.4	72.6	13.6	2.4
20–24	5,863	1,854	3,878	25	106	31.6	66.1	.4	1.8
25–44	22,741	2,218	19,226	636	661	9.8	84.5	2.8	2.9
45–64	15,614	1,180	11,226	2,815	393	7.6	71.9	18.0	2.5
65+	6,067	488	2,183	3,354	42	8.0	36.0	55.3	.7
1940									
MALE	43,156	10,303	30,086	2,143	623	23.9	69.7	5.0	1.4
20–24	5,692	4,109	1,557	8	18	72.2	27.4	.1	.3
25–44	19,686	4,298	14,882	213	293	21.8	75.6	1.1	1.5
45–64	13,371	1,462	10,836	817	256	10.9	81.0	6.1	1.9
65+	4,406	434	2,811	1,104	57	9.9	63.8	25.1	1.3

Appendix Table 1: *Continued*

Year, Sex, & Age	Total	NUMBER (1,000)				PERCENT			
		Single	Married	Widowed	Divorced	Single	Married	Widowed	Divorced
FEMALE	43,208	7,328	29,373	5,693	823	17.0	68.0	13.2	1.9
20–24	5,895	2,781	3,026	33	56	47.2	51.3	.6	.9
25–44	19,986	3,001	15,772	738	476	15.0	78.9	3.7	2.4
45–64	12,713	1,116	8,992	2,356	249	8.8	70.7	18.5	2.0
65+	4,613	429	1,584	2,567	33	9.3	34.3	55.6	.7
1930									
MALE	38,123	9,309	26,227	2,023	488	24.4	68.8	5.3	1.3
20–24	5,336	3,779	1,500	18	22	70.8	28.1	.3	.4
25–44	18,238	4,012	13,635	317	250	22.0	74.8	1.7	1.4
45–64	11,172	1,219	8,960	803	178	10.9	80.2	7.2	1.6
65+	3,326	280	2,117	884	37	8.4	63.7	26.6	1.1
FEMALE	37,043	6,275	25,439	4,722	561	16.9	68.7	12.7	1.5
20–24	5,534	2,547	2,858	56	62	46.0	51.6	1.0	1.1
25–44	17,915	2,522	14,247	799	335	14.1	79.5	4.5	1.9
45–64	10,244	926	7,172	1,992	144	9.0	70.0	19.4	1.4
65+	3,308	268	1,147	1,869	18	8.1	34.7	56.5	.5
1920									
MALE	32,247	8,400	21,753	1,756	234	26.0	67.5	5.4	.7
20–24	4,527	3,201	1,280	21	10	70.7	28.3	.5	.2
25–44	16,029	3,975	11,558	346	115	24.8	72.1	2.2	.7
45–64	9,115	1,015	7,277	717	90	11.1	79.8	7.9	1.0
65+	2,483	182	1,607	669	19	7.3	64.7	26.9	.8
FEMALE	25,607	1,325	20,102	2,884	261	5.2	78.5	11.3	1.0
20–24	4,750	2,164	2,484	65	29	45.6	52.3	1.4	.6
25–44	15,249	2,404	11,919	755	156	15.8	78.2	5.0	1.0
45–64	7,915	722	5,466	1,645	72	9.1	69.1	20.8	.9
65+	2,450	173	830	1,431	10	7.1	33.9	58.4	.4

Source: U.S. Bureau of the Census, 1985b, Table 4; 1981, Table 49; 1971, Table 38; 1961, Table 27; 1951, Table, 30; 1933, Table 5; 1922, Table 2.

Appendix Table 2: Divorces and Annulments, United States, 1940–85.

		RATE PER 1,000	
YEAR	DIVORCES & ANNUL.	TOTAL POPULATION	MARRIED WOMEN, 15 +
1985	1,187,000	5.0	21.8*
1984	1,155,000	4.9	21.3*
1983	1,179,000	5.0	21.3
1982	1,170,000	5.0	21.7
1981	1,213,000	5.3	22.6
1980	1,189,000	5.2	22.6
1979	1,181,000	5.3	22.8
1978	1,130,000	5.1	21.9
1977	1,091,000	5.0	21.1
1976	1,083,000	5.0	21.1
1975	1,036,000	4.8	20.3
1970	708,000	3.5	14.9
1965	479,000	2.5	10.6
1960	393,000	2.2	9.2
1955	377,000	2.3	9.3
1950	385,000	2.6	10.3
1949	397,000	2.7	10.6
1948	408,000	2.8	11.2
1947	483,000	3.4	13.6
1946	610,000	4.3	17.9
1945	485,000	3.5	14.4
1943	359,000	2.6	11.0
1942	321,000	2.4	10.1
1941	293,000	2.2	9.4
1940	264,000	2.0	8.8
1930	196,000	1.6	7.5
1920	171,000	1.6	8.0

*At the time of publication these rates were not yet available from NCHS. The rates shown are provisional and were calculated from the population of married women 15 years and over in 1984 and 1985 reported verbally by the U.S. Census Bureau.

Source: National Center for Health Statistics, 1985a; 1986a; 1986b.

Appendix Table 3: Remarriages, 1965-1981.

AGE	1965	1970	1975	1976	1977	1978	1979	1980	1981
Remarriage of bride (1,000)	305	343	510	518	532	548	582	591	616
rate/1,000 widowed and divorced 14 years									
& over	33.7	36.6	40.1	39.7	40.0	40.0	40.8	38.3	39.9
14-24	471.0	317.6	319.9	324.4	323.5	321.5	312.6	231.0	280.0
25-44	139.6	142.3	144.5	133.2	129.0	126.8	127.5	117.3	119.7
45-64	24.5	24.8	23.5	23.5	22.1	21.9	21.7	19.7	19.9
65+	2.4	2.5	2.5	2.3	2.4	2.1	3.0	2.3	2.3
Remarriage of widows (1,000)	67	75	68	64	61	59	65	59	57
rate/1,000 widows 14 years									
& over	10.2	10.2	8.3	7.9	7.6	7.1	7.7	6.7	6.5
14-44	69.6	54.1	61.7	56.0	57.3	55.3	52.6	51.0	48.4
45-64	16.5	17.7	14.9	15.2	14.0	13.6	13.6	12.2	12.0
65+	2.0	2.3	2.1	2.1	2.1	1.8	2.6	2.1	2.0
Remarriage of Div. women (1,000)	195	270	365	377	391	406	432	447	475
Rate/1,000 div. women 14 & over	127.8	123.3	117.2	111.3	107.3	105.0	104.0	91.3	96.3
14-24	512.3	413.4	319.6	339.4	347.3	313.7	309.1	236.4	282.2
25-44	176.3	179.6	158.6	144.0	137.3	134.4	135.2	122.8	129.1
45-64	45.8	42.6	40.1	37.5	35.6	35.6	35.1	30.3	30.2
65+	9.6	6.1	9.1	6.9	6.4	6.4	7.4	5.3	5.7

Source: U. S. Bureau of the Census, 1984b, Table 120.

Appendix Table 4: Percent Distribution of Divorces and Annulments by Age of Husband and Wife at Time of Decree: 1970–81

AGE	1981	1980	1979	1978	1977	1976	1975	1974	1973	1972	1971	1970
HUSBAND												
– 20	.7	.8	.8	1.0	.9	1.0	1.0	1.1	1.1	1.0	1.0	.8
20–24	12.5	13.5	13.9	14.8	14.7	15.1	15.2	15.7	15.7	15.9	16.8	16.3
25–29	22.8	23.4	23.8	24.3	24.0	24.8	25.1	24.2	23.4	23.5	22.1	22.8
30–34	22.1	21.4	20.8	20.2	19.8	18.6	18.6	18.2	17.9	17.2	16.3	16.2
35–39	15.1	14.6	14.2	13.8	13.4	12.9	12.5	12.4	12.4	12.3	12.8	12.8
40–44	10.0	9.8	9.7	9.3	9.4	9.5	9.3	9.6	9.9	10.2	10.6	10.7
45–49	6.7	6.5	6.7	6.6	6.9	7.2	7.3	7.5	8.0	8.0	8.4	8.3
50–54	4.6	4.4	4.5	4.5	4.8	4.9	5.1	5.2	5.3	5.5	5.5	5.4
55–59	2.7	2.7	2.6	2.7	2.9	2.9	2.8	2.8	3.0	3.0	3.2	3.2
60–64	1.5	1.4	1.5	1.4	1.5	1.5	1.6	1.7	1.7	1.7	1.7	1.8
65 +	1.4	1.4	1.4	1.4	1.6	1.5	1.5	1.6	1.6	1.6	1.6	1.7
MEDIAN AGE	33.1	32.7	32.5	32.0	32.4	32.3	32.2	32.2	32.4	32.6	32.9	32.9
WIFE												
– 20	2.9	3.4	3.6	4.0	3.8	4.1	4.4	4.6	4.4	4.3	4.4	4.1
20–24	19.5	20.8	21.2	22.7	22.3	22.4	22.5	23.0	23.1	23.7	24.9	24.9
25–29	24.8	24.6	24.8	24.6	24.5	25.1	25.2	24.3	23.7	23.0	21.3	21.8
30–34	20.2	19.4	18.7	17.9	17.9	16.7	16.3	16.1	15.6	15.0	14.8	14.4
35–39	13.1	12.8	12.3	11.8	11.3	11.2	10.9	10.7	10.9	11.0	11.1	11.0
40–44	8.2	7.7	7.9	7.5	7.7	7.9	7.6	7.9	8.4	8.8	8.9	9.4
45–49	4.9	4.8	5.0	5.0	5.3	5.6	5.7	5.9	6.3	6.6	6.8	6.8
50–54	3.1	3.1	3.1	3.3	3.4	3.5	3.6	3.6	3.9	3.9	4.0	3.8
55–59	1.8	1.7	1.8	1.7	2.0	1.9	2.0	2.0	2.0	2.0	2.0	2.0
60–64	.9	.9	.9	.9	1.0	.9	.9	1.0	1.0	1.0	.9	1.0
65 +	.8	.8	.7	.7	.8	.8	.8	.8	.7	.8	.8	.8
MEDIAN AGE	30.6	30.3	30.1	29.7	29.9	29.7	29.5	29.5	29.7	29.8	29.8	29.8

Source: National Center for Health Statistics, 1985B: Table 2-11.

Appendix Table 5: Time Between Divorce and Second Marriage by Age and Sex, June 1980. (Numbers in Thousands)

SEX & TIME	TOTAL	AGE					
		15–19	20–24	25–29	30–34	35–39	40–44
WOMEN							
TOTAL	8739	18	328	820	1238	1186	1001
– 5 YEARS	6741	18	323	769	1069	990	795
– 1 YEAR	2408	15	172	300	376	346	311
1 YEAR	1711	2	86	220	272	240	205
2 YEARS	1216	0	42	139	205	196	125
3 YEARS	792	0	14	75	130	110	79
4 YEARS	613	0	8	33	86	97	75
5-9 YEARS	1261	0	5	49	155	159	127
5 YEARS	429	0	5	19	73	65	45
6 YEARS	285	0	0	16	38	41	22
7 YEARS	198	0	0	5	20	19	25
8 YEARS	206	0	0	3	14	24	17
9 YEARS	143	0	0	6	10	11	18
10-14 YEARS	480	0	0	2	13	35	70
10 YEARS	135	0	0	2	7	10	19
11 YEARS	114	0	0	0	3	9	17
12 YEARS	95	0	0	0	0	6	20
13 YEARS	77	0	0	0	4	5	7
14 YEARS	59	0	0	0	0	5	6
15-19 YEARS	159	0	0	0	0	2	9
20-24 YEARS	61	0	0	0	0	0	1
25-29 YEARS	24	0	0	0	0	0	0
30 & OVER	13	0	0	0	0	0	0
MEDIAN YEARS	2.2	.6	1.0	1.5	1.9	2.0	1.9
MEAN YEARS	3.2	.2	.8	1.4	2.0	2.3	2.8

SEX & TIME	TOTAL	AGE					
		45–49	50–54	55–59	60–64	65–69	70–74
WOMEN, CONTINUED							
TOTAL	8739	864	899	797	669	551	368
– 5 YEARS	6741	660	626	538	424	333	195
– 1 YEAR	2408	226	213	173	122	96	57
1 YEAR	1711	159	158	131	100	94	42
2 YEARS	1216	126	105	110	86	49	34
3 YEARS	792	80	95	66	70	43	29
4 YEARS	613	68	55	59	47	51	34
5-9 YEARS	1261	132	142	151	134	122	84
5 YEARS	429	55	38	50	38	29	13
6 YEARS	285	26	41	22	34	24	21
7 YEARS	198	18	32	27	28	18	5
8 YEARS	206	26	16	34	18	28	27
9 YEARS	143	7	15	19	17	24	17
10-14 YEARS	480	46	88	65	67	47	48
10 YEARS	135	15	30	16	12	13	12
11 YEARS	114	12	23	13	17	11	9
12 YEARS	95	5	16	12	19	7	10
13 YEARS	77	8	14	16	12	5	6
14 YEARS	59	6	5	8	6	11	10
15-19 YEARS	159	24	31	14	24	28	27
20-24 YEARS	61	2	10	18	12	8	10
25-29 YEARS	24	0	2	8	7	7	0
30 & OVER	13	0	0	1	2	6	4
MEDIAN YEARS	2.2	2.4	2.8	2.9	3.4	3.8	4.7
MEAN YEARS	3.2	3.2	4.0	4.3	4.8	5.4	6.3

(continued)

Appendix Table 5: *Continued*

SEX & TIME	TOTAL	AGE					
		15–19	20–24	25–29	30–34	35–39	40–44
MEN							
TOTAL	7894	2	93	565	1074	1142	983
– 5 YEARS	6286	2	93	530	964	995	772
– 1 YEAR	2155	2	42	184	372	358	233
1 YEAR	1654	0	20	134	241	234	247
2 YEARS	1124	0	16	105	184	184	148
3 YEARS	801	0	10	73	77	145	76
4 YEARS	552	0	5	35	90	74	68
5–9 YEARS	1114	0	0	34	97	117	172
5 YEARS	365	0	0	19	42	49	65
6 YEARS	255	0	0	12	24	33	43
7 YEARS	199	0	0	1	13	18	27
8 YEARS	182	0	0	1	11	10	16
9 YEARS	113	0	0	1	6	6	21
10–14 YEARS	324	0	0	0	13	27	30
10 YEARS	81	0	0	0	6	13	6
11 YEARS	81	0	0	0	2	6	8
12 YEARS	61	0	0	0	2	2	6
13 YEARS	61	0	0	0	0	7	8
14 YEARS	40	0	0	0	4	0	2
15–19 YEARS	109	0	0	0	0	2	9
20–24 YEARS	38	0	0	0	0	0	0
25–29 YEARS	21	0	0	0	0	0	0
30 & OVER	2	0	0	0	0	0	0
MEDIAN YEARS	2.1	.5	1.2	1.7	1.7	1.9	2.1
MEAN YEARS	2.9	.0	1.1	1.6	1.8	2.1	2.7

Appendix Table 5: *Continued*

SEX & TIME	TOTAL	AGE					
		45–49	50–54	55–59	60–64	65–69	70–74
MEN, CONTINUED							
TOTAL	7894	899	888	809	657	482	301
− 5 YEARS	6286	718	673	587	477	304	171
− 1 YEAR	2155	285	192	180	148	97	61
1 YEAR	1654	144	224	155	146	71	39
2 YEARS	1124	136	112	83	63	59	34
3 YEARS	801	100	87	104	65	38	25
4 YEARS	552	54	58	65	54	38	12
5–9 YEARS	1114	139	155	148	103	87	62
5 YEARS	365	44	38	44	22	16	25
6 YEARS	255	26	36	35	16	21	9
7 YEARS	199	29	33	23	28	13	12
8 YEARS	182	28	34	28	18	26	9
9 YEARS	113	12	13	18	19	11	6
10–14 YEARS	324	30	34	47	52	54	36
10 YEARS	81	6	12	11	9	10	8
11 YEARS	81	9	7	15	18	10	7
12 YEARS	61	8	3	10	15	13	3
13 YEARS	61	0	7	10	5	16	7
14 YEARS	40	7	5	0	5	6	11
15–19 YEARS	109	12	22	12	13	19	21
20–24 YEARS	38	0	4	14	10	6	4
25–29 YEARS	21	0	1	0	3	12	5
30 & OVER	2	0	0	0	0	0	2
MEDIAN YEARS	2.1	2.1	2.2	2.8	2.5	3.3	3.7
MEAN YEARS	2.9	2.7	3.2	3.6	3.8	5.1	5.7

Source: U.S. Bureau of the Census, 1986a.

Appendix Table 6: Time Between Divorce and Second Marriage for Women by Age, June 1980. (Numbers in Thousands)

TIME	TOTAL	AGE					
		15–19	20–24	25–29	30–34	35–39	40–44
TOTAL	11117	2	277	923	1555	1635	1419
−5 YEARS	8319	2	273	836	1284	1273	1025
−1 YEAR	2590	0	127	308	410	410	303
1 YEAR	2338	0	65	231	350	352	301
2 YEARS	1593	2	43	140	250	225	176
3 YEARS	1067	0	27	105	156	159	148
4 YEARS	731	0	11	52	117	128	97
5–9 YEARS	1907	0	4	86	251	297	306
5 YEARS	601	0	1	47	77	93	120
6 YEARS	467	0	3	14	69	83	67
7 YEARS	360	0	0	21	47	53	52
8 YEARS	291	0	0	5	38	34	52
9 YEARS	189	0	0	0	21	34	15
10–14 YEARS	510	0	0	1	20	65	73
10 YEARS	155	0	0	0	14	27	21
11 YEARS	100	0	0	1	4	9	10
12 YEARS	112	0	0	0	2	15	17
13 YEARS	82	0	0	0	0	7	18
14 YEARS	61	0	0	0	0	7	7
15–19 YEARS	239	0	0	0	0	0	16
20–24 YEARS	75	0	0	0	0	0	0
25–29 YEARS	49	0	0	0	0	0	0
30 & OVER	18	0	0	0	0	0	0
MEDIAN YEARS	2.4	2.5	1.2	1.7	2.1	2.2	2.6
MEAN YEARS	3.4	2.0	1.1	1.7	2.3	2.7	3.2

TIME	TOTAL	AGE					
		45–49	50–54	55–59	60–64	65–69	70–74	75 & Over
TOTAL	11117	1102	938	843	806	586	447	583
−5 YEARS	8319	825	671	598	582	351	276	324
−1 YEAR	2590	297	182	131	162	108	67	85
1 YEAR	2338	221	213	208	136	107	62	92
2 YEARS	1593	153	135	126	123	56	87	76
3 YEARS	1067	89	81	80	110	50	30	32
4 YEARS	731	65	60	53	51	29	29	38
5–9 YEARS	1907	155	172	141	130	140	104	121
5 YEARS	601	44	44	39	52	32	32	19
6 YEARS	467	33	43	22	35	37	35	27
7 YEARS	360	19	41	33	21	31	13	29
8 YEARS	291	33	27	30	14	20	13	26
9 YEARS	189	26	17	16	8	19	12	20
10–14 YEARS	510	73	48	64	41	49	28	47
10 YEARS	155	19	11	15	5	16	9	17
11 YEARS	100	17	12	11	14	9	7	8
12 YEARS	112	12	11	10	12	15	5	13
13 YEARS	82	13	10	14	4	5	4	6
14 YEARS	61	13	4	13	6	5	3	4
15–19 YEARS	239	43	36	30	27	14	19	55
20–24 YEARS	75	6	8	9	11	14	9	17
25–29 YEARS	49	0	2	2	10	15	8	12
30 & OVER	18	0	0	0	5	3	2	7
MEDIAN YEARS	2.4	2.2	2.5	2.7	2.9	3.4	3.2	4.1
MEAN YEARS	3.4	3.4	3.8	4.0	4.1	5.1	5.0	6.5

Note: The 1985 Current Population Survey did not ask questions concerning divorce and remarriage of male respondents.
Source: U.S. Bureau of the Census, 1986b.

Appendix Table 7: Mean Interval between Divorce and Remarriage
by Age and Sex for Persons Remarrying in 1970 and 1983.

| | INTERVAL | | | | | |
| | WOMEN | | | MEN | | |
AGE	1970	1983	CHANGE	1970	1983	CHANGE
ALL AGES	2.5	3.3	+0.8	2.2	3.0	+0.8
12–17	0.5	1.0	+0.5	0.5	1.9	+1.4
18–19	0.6	0.8	+0.2	1.0	1.2	+0.2
20–24	1.1	1.5	+0.4	0.9	1.3	+0.4
25–29	1.6	2.5	+0.9	1.4	2.1	+0.7
30–34	2.4	3.2	+0.8	1.9	2.9	+1.0
35–44	3.2	4.0	+0.8	2.4	3.2	+0.8
45–54	5.1	5.5	+0.4	3.3	3.7	+0.4
55–64	8.6	7.6	−1.0	4.1	4.9	+0.8
65 & Over	11.7	10.4	−1.3	7.1	6.3	−0.8

Source: National Center for Health Statistics, 1986c.

Notes

CHAPTER ONE

1. It is not insignificant that this was the period when studies of marital success and satisfaction began to burgeon in family research. Ernest Burgess was the co-investigator in one of the first such studies, which remains a classic (Burgess & Cottrell, 1939).

2. Some have tried to defend Parsons and Bales from criticism for their having asserted this biologically based role stereotyping in the family system. It is true that they saw the mother's role as instrumental in the mother-child subsystem. Nevertheless, while these two citations are the first explicit mention of their view, it occurs repeatedly throughout the book. Indeed, in a chapter devoted to a comparative analysis of role differentiation in the nuclear family systems of several other cultures, Morris Zelditch comes to the unequivocal conclusion that the male is the instrumental leader and the female the expressive leader in the family system (Parsons & Bales, 1955, Chapter VI). Unfortunately, this view was adopted uncritically by many family analysts in the following years.

3. Cf. Scanzoni (1972).

4. See Lenore Weitzman (1985) for an analysis of no-fault legislation and the social and economic consequences for women and children.

5. See Longfellow (1979) and Levitan (1979) for reviews of this literature.

6. In interpreting these tables it is important to make a distinction between *marital status* and the *rates* of marriage, divorce, and remarriage. The first term refers to the marital situation of the population at any given time. The second refers to the activity in the selected area in a given period. The first is a measure of the *prevalence* of marriage, divorce, and remarriage, while the second is a measure of the *incidence* of these phenomena. (It may be helpful to think of these two measures in a different context. It is possible to measure what proportion of the population owns Chevrolet or Ford automobiles at any given time—the *prevalence* of automobile ownership of given brands in the population. It is also possible to measure who obtained Chevrolet and Ford automobiles in a given year—the *incidence* of purchase of those brands of automobiles in that period. These are clearly different aspects of automobile ownership.)

   Also, a word about rates—the basis upon which a rate is computed is the most important aspect of the rate. The base of a rate ought to be one which includes most of the individuals who might be subject to a given phenomenon, but does not include those who are not subject to it. Thus, for example, using the general population as the base for rates of pregnancy is not very satisfactory, since it includes men and children who are not subject to pregnancy. In general, using the total population as the base for marriage, divorce, and remarriage rates is the least satisfactory. For marriage, it is better to use a rate such as the population 15 years of age and older or, even better, the number of single women 15 years and older. For divorce, a base which reflects the marriage population, such as the rate per 1,000 married women is more useful. For remarriage, a base which includes these who have been previously married, such as the rate per 1,000 widowed and/or divorced persons of the relevant sex is a better method. The common journalistic practice of reporting the "divorce rate" as the number of divorces granted in a given year divided by the number of marriages occurring in that year results in a totally misleading statistic. The base used, marriages in a given year, has little in common with the number of divorces which occurred in that year.

Many students and professionals require the latest information on these rates. They are readily available in any library which receives U.S. Government Printing Office documents or may be ordered directly from the GPO. Data on marital status are regularly supplied by the U.S. Census Bureau in the decennial censuses and from special reports based on sampling surveys carried out between the censuses. These special reports are usually issued in the Series P-20 and P-23 publications of the Census Bureau. Data on marriage, divorce, and remarriage rates come from the Office of Vital Statistics of the Public Health Service. These may be found in the annual reports on *Vital Statistics of the United States* in the volume on marriage and divorce, in the *Monthly Vital Statistics Reports*, and in special supplements to these reports issued annually which provide advanced analyses of marriage and divorce rates. Finally, there is the *Statistical Abstract of the United States* issued annually by the Census Bureau, which always contains a section on marriage and divorce. This latter publication is especially useful as a quick resource for more general statistics. It is less helpful for detailed statistical analyses.

7. There is no way to determine how many individuals report themselves as being "widowed" rather than "divorced" after their former spouses die — or even while they are still living. Given that being a widow or widower is more socially acceptable, we would suspect that this is the case for a substantial group of census respondents.

8. In 1981, for example, marriages among previously married individuals showed a rate per thousand population of 39.9 for women and 112.5 for men. Men exceeded women at every age category. However, in the 45–64 age group the rates were: formerly widowed, women 19.9 and men 74.2; formerly divorced, women 30.2 and men 82.6. In the over-65 age group they were: formerly widowed, women 2.0 and men 16.9; formerly divorced, women 5.7 and men 23.0 (National Center for Health Statistics, 1985b, Table 1-7).

9. In 1981 the difference in median age at marriage of various categories of brides and grooms varied widely, but only in the case of widowed brides marrying single grooms is the bride likely to be older. The greatest difference exists between widowed grooms marrying single brides, where the difference is 13.8 years, and

widowed grooms marrying divorced brides, where the difference is 9.9 years (National Center for Health Statistics, 1985b, Table 1-8).

10. Cf. U.S. Bureau of the Census, 1985a, 1985b.

CHAPTER TWO

1. There is some confusion in scholarship about the field of social psychology. Some social psychologists begin from the perspective of the individual and draw their insights primarily from a psychological perspective. Others, emphasizing the group interpersonal dynamics and its effect on individuals, have contributed on the more sociological side. This group concentrates heavily on the development and use of role theory. The social psychological literature used in this discussion draws from this latter perspective.

2. For the other examples of the use of the idea of functional prerequisites see Bell and Vogel, 1968, and Reiss, 1965.

3. In her book *From the Inside Out and Other Metaphors* Bunny Duhl traces the history of the development of the family systems approach in family therapy. Readers interested in this earlier work should consult Duhl, 1983.

4. Data of five different types were collected on these families: participant observation; audiotape recordings (some videotapes were also obtained); interviews; projective tests; and self-reports.

5. In some theories, constancy feedback loops are identified as "negative" feedback loops—a term rejected by Kantor and Lehr as confusing, since often positive messages are used to maintain constancy. Variety feedback loops are often labeled "positive" feedback. For more on feedback in systems theory consult Buckley, 1967.

6. Readers interested in the history of the family development perspective may consult Hill and Rodgers, 1964; Duvall, 1971; and Rodgers, 1977.

7. Gathering data from 98 ex-spouse pairs at approximately one year, three years, and five years after divorce, this study has a number of unique aspects to it. Unlike most of the studies of divorce, the sample is representative of a typical population of divorcing couples. The sample was drawn from the divorce court records of the county. The major restrictions on the sample were related to residency within the county on the part of both spouses, the presence of minor children, and visitation by the nonresident parent at least once in two months. Data were collected from both former spouses and from new partners acquired postdivorce. This project has completed the third phase of data collection at five years postdivorce, but is still in the data analysis stage. New partners of the divorced spouses were interviewed during both the second and third rounds of data collection. This promises some interesting analyses involving the complex interrelationships of the former spouse with the new partner, the new partner with the children of the divorced spouse, the divorced spouses' relationship with the children of the new partner, as well as the potential for analyses of the former spouse's relationships with the new partner's children and, even more complex, the former spouse's relationships with the children of the divorced spouse and the new partner. Some of these findings will be reported in later chapters.

8. Pauline Boss (1987, Chapter 4) has made an important contribution to stress theory in her clarification of the meaning of the concept of *coping*. She points out: "Technically, the term 'coping' does not allow for the possibility of change, either through evolution or revolution. . . . Coping in families has . . . implied bending and shoring-up pressure points rather than challenging the cause of the pressure. Family coping has referred to making things work in the face of difficulty, to stoicism, not to rebellion or change. We are therefore cautious about the value of the concept of coping. It may not always be good to cope." Her discussion continues by pointing out that the use of the concept of coping appears to lie in the bias for calm and serenity, orderliness and balance. But, she asserts, what may be called for is real change brought about by the crisis of *failing* to cope. This is a caution which we need to keep in mind in analyzing the family reorganization process in separation, divorce, and remarriage.

CHAPTER FOUR

1. In 1981, of those receiving divorces who had no children under 18, 33 percent of the men and 42 percent of the women were under 30. Another 16 percent of the men and 14 percent of the women were between 30 and 34 years old. It would be safe to assume that many of those at the older ages in this category actually had children over 18. Thus, this is clearly an underestimate of the proportion of young childless couples receiving divorces. (National Center for Health Statistics, 1985b, Table 2–28.)
2. Appendix Tables 5, 6, and 7 generally show median and mean intervals of under two years between divorce and remarriage for the age groups under 35 years. Even though figures on these rates for childless couples are not available, we think it is safe to assume that remarriage for the great majority of the single childless occurs within three years. At the same time, it is of interest to note that Appendix Table 7 shows that the time is lengthening, not only for these ages, but for all except the oldest age groups.
3. In 1981, 36 percent of childless couples divorced within two years of marriage. Another 19 percent of divorces occurred in childless marriages of three to four years' duration. (National Center for Health Statistics, 1985b, Table 2–21.)
4. In 1981, 60 percent of the divorcing women aged 45–49 had no children under 18, while another 22 percent had only one child under 18. Of divorcing women 50 and over, 83 percent had no children under 18 and 9 percent had one such child. Similar figures appear in the 1980 census (National Center for Health Statistics, 1985b, Table 2–28; U.S. Bureau of the Census, 1984a, Table 268).
5. The proportion of the population divorced in the 45–64 age group has more than doubled since 1970 (Appendix Table 1). At the same time, the proportion of divorces granted to men and women in this age group in 1981 as compared with 1970 dropped in each sex by about 3 percent (National Center for Health Statistics, 1985b, Table 2–11). This apparent paradox is explained, at least in part, by the fact that a higher proportion of the population reaches the 45–64 age range already divorced, thus reducing the available pool of married individuals who are eligible for divorce in this age period.

6. The research of Hagestad on midlife divorce, which we will discuss in a later chapter, is the major exception. Her findings do not provide a clear answer to this question.

7. The 1984 labor force participation rate for married women with no children under 18 was 12.3 percent, for separated .9 percent, and for divorced 3.0 percent (U.S. Bureau of the Census, 1984b, Table 671). It is probable that these low rates are accounted for by the high proportion of women in the midlife and aging cohorts. This, however, is another factor in which we should expect some change in the not too distant future as the children of the marriage cohorts of the sixties and seventies reach maturity.

CHAPTER FIVE

1. While it is possible to find greeting cards which send congratulations to divorcing individuals, casual perusal of most greeting card racks will reveal the low market potential for these. On the other hand, loss through death is clearly of high market value, judging from the large selection of sympathy cards available.

2. See Roman and Haddad (1978) and Nehls and Morgenbesser (1980) for good reviews of the history of custody.

3. The legal terminology in divorce is changing. There are two types of support payments often ordered in a divorce settlement. There are payments made to the former spouse for his/her personal use. In many jurisdictions the term "alimony" for these payments has been replaced by the term "spousal support." "Child support," of course, refers to payments ordered by the court to be paid to a spouse specifically for the expenses associated with care of the children.

4. If an out-of-home parent had not seen his or her child in the two months prior to interviewing (one year postdivorce), then the couple was not included in the study.

5. Ahrons found that the only differences reported by both parents between the cooperative colleagues and the angry associates was in the amount of positive feelings. Former spouses who were angry associates had fewer positive feelings for their ex-spouse. However, male angry associates reported consistently more anger, while women reported less interaction and satisfaction with the coparental relationship. Thus, what seems to be the critical factor between these two types is the management and resolution of the anger, with cooperative colleagues being more successful in compartmentalizing their feelings towards one another.

6. McLanahan and her colleagues (1981) have given us a bit of information on the kin and social networks of single mothers based on a small unsystematic sample. Her evidence is interesting because it shows important influences from kin and non-kin social networks as differentiating single mothers who are pursuing familistic vs. non-familistic life patterns. Unfortunately, it only whets the appetite for more detailed and extensive information. Nevertheless, it identifies as one key factor the kind of meaning for postdivorce life that these women have selected. See also Weiss (1979) and Tietjen (1985) for other discussions of the network experiences of separated and and divorced women.

7. This speculation certainly fits with Bowen's idea about "emotional cutoff" discussed in Chapter 2.

CHAPTER SIX

1. Hagestad and Smyer (1982) reported finding only two studies, not including their own—Deckert and Langlier (1978) and Chiriboga (1979). The situation has not changed appreciably at this writing.
2. We are aware of two pieces of research which are still in the data analysis stage but from which we have some preliminary and informal reports of findings. These studies are being done at the University of Minnesota under the supervision of P. Boss and at the University of Southern California under the supervision of C. R. Ahrons.

CHAPTER SEVEN

1. Glick and Spanier (1980) and Spanier (1983) provide some analysis of unmarried cohabitation. The figures in 1981 show 28 percent (502,000) unmarried couple households with children present. This is actually a drop of about 10 percent from 1970.
2. For a more thorough discussion of the differences between first marriages and remarriages see Visher and Visher (1979), Messinger (1982, 1984), Einstein (1979), and Sager et al. (1983).
3. See Table 3 in Chapter 1.
4. See Clingempeel and Brand (1985), Furstenberg and Nord (1985), Ihinger-Tallman and Pasley (1986), Jacobson (in press), Messinger (1982), and Sager et al. (1983) for elaboration of the different typologies of remarried families.
5. See Ahrons and Wallisch (in press) for a more thorough discussion of the impact of remarriage on the former spouse relationship in the Binuclear Family Study.
6. For an interesting example of this, cf. Roman and Dichter (1985). These two professional therapists, who had earlier written with great enthusiasm about the desirability of joint custody, report on their personal experiences as remarried joint-custody parents. Their enthusiasm has been dampened to a considerable extent by the experience.
7. For a fuller discussion of the differences between first marriages and remarriages see Bernard (1956), Crosbie-Burnett and Ahrons (1985), Einstein (1979), Mayleas (1977), Messinger (1982), Paris (1984), Rodgers and Conrad (1986), Sager et al. (1983), Stuart and Jacobson (1985), Visher and Visher (1979, 1982), Wald (1981), and Westoff (1977).
8. See Kelly and Wallerstein (1977) for more discussion of the relationship between the out-of-home parent and his child.
9. See Ganong and Coleman (1984) for a thorough review of the empirical research. They found little evidence that children in different family structures (nuclear, single parent, and remarried) differ on a number of usual outcome variables. They note, however, that " . . . the empirical literature does not support the dire conclusions regarding stepchildren emanating from the clinical literature, though clinicians and empiricists tend to investigate quite different variables" (p. 402). This conclusion, however, is mediated by their recognition of the severe limitations of

the research, i.e., small or non-random samples, limited conceptualizations of family structure variables, a failure to account for the complexity of stepfamilies, and the use of a "deficit-comparison" model. Such a model assumes "that variations in the nuclear family will produce undesirable deviations in children's personality, social behavior, and school success" (Marotz-Baden et al., 1979).

10. We know of only one empirical study which includes both stepfamily households of one binuclear family. Jacobson (in press) calls these families "linked family systems" and concludes that the "child is the link, influencing and being influenced by those in both households."

CHAPTER EIGHT

1. See Appendix Table 3. Furstenberg and Spanier report that the remarriage rate for divorced men is about 60 percent greater than that for divorced women (1984, p. 38). Even when midlife divorced women do remarry, they are likely to have waited an average of about two years longer to do so (Appendix Table 7).

2. Other types were conflict-habituated, passive-congenial, vital, and total.

CHAPTER NINE

1. For fuller descriptions and assessments of the divorce mediation movement, see Kressel, 1985; Haynes 1981; Folberg & Taylor, 1984; Milne, 1983.

2. See Kaslow, 1981, 1984; Kelly, 1983; Sprenkle & Storm, 1983; Storm et al., 1986.

3. Steinberg, 1980; Mosten & Biggs, 1985/86.

Bibliography

Adams, B. (1985). The family: Problems and solutions. *Journal of Marriage and the Family, 47,* 525-529.

Ahrons, C. (1979). The binuclear family: Two households, one family. *Alternative Lifestyles, 2,* 499-515.

Ahrons, C. (1980a). Divorce: A crisis of family transition and change. *Family Relations, 29,* 533-540.

Ahrons, C. (1980b). Redefining the divorced family: A conceptual framework for postdivorce family systems reorganization. *Social Work, 25,* 437-441.

Ahrons, C. (1980c). Joint custody arrangements in the postdivorce family. *Journal of Divorce, 3,* 189-205.

Ahrons, C. (1981a). The binuclear family: An emerging lifestyle for postdivorce families. In W. Dumon & C. DePaepe, (Eds.), *Free papers: The XIXth international CFR seminar on divorce and remarriage* (pp. 1-12). Leuven, Belgium: Committee on Family Research, International Sociological Association.

Ahrons, C., (1981b). The continuing coparental relationship between divorced spouses. *American Journal of Orthopsychiatry, 51,* 315-328.

Ahrons, C., & Bowman, M. (1982). Changes in family relationships following divorce of adult child: Grandmothers' perceptions. *Journal of Divorce, 5,* 49-68.

Ahrons, C., & Perlmutter, M. (1982). The relationship between former spouses: A fundamental subsystem in the remarriage family. In L. Messinger (Ed.), *Therapy with remarriage families* (pp. 31-46). Rockville, MD: Aspen Systems Corporation.

Ahrons, C., & Sorensen, A. (1985). Father-child involvement. In J. Trost, C. Szombarthy, & I. Weede (Eds.), *The aftermath of divorce: Coping with change.* Budapest, Hungary: Akademiai Kiado.

Ahrons, C., & Wallisch, L. (1986). The relationship between former spouses. In S. Duck & D. Perlman (Eds.), *Close relationships: Development, dynamics, and deterioration* (pp. 269-296). Beverly Hills, CA: Sage.

Ahrons, C., & Wallisch, L. (In press). Parenting in the binuclear family: relationships between biological and stepparents. In K. Pasley and M. Ihinger-Tallman (Eds.), *Remarriage and stepfamilies: Research and theory.* New York: Guilford Press.

Ambert, A. (1983). Separated women and remarriage behavior: A comparison of financially secure women and financially insecure women. *Journal of Divorce, 6,* 43-54.

Anspach, D. (1976). Kinship and divorce. *Journal of Marriage and the Family, 38,* 323-330.

241

Bates, F. (1956). Position, role and status: A reformulation of concepts. *Social Forces, 34*, 313–321.

Beal, E. (1985). A systems view of divorce intervention strategies. In S. Grebe (Ed.), *Divorce and family mediation* (pp. 16–33). Rockville, MD: Aspen Systems Corporation.

Bell, N., & Vogel, E. (1968). *A modern introduction to the family* (rev. ed.). New York: The Free Press.

Bennett, J., & Tumin, M. (1948). *Social life.* New York: Alfred A. Knopf, Inc.

Berman, W. (1985). Continued attachment after legal divorce. *Journal of Family Issues, 6*, 375–392.

Bernard, J. (1956). *Remarriage: A study of marriage.* New York: Dryden Press.

Bernard, J. (1972). *The future of marriage.* New York: World.

Bierstedt, R. (1963). *The social order.* New York: McGraw-Hill Book Co.

Birdwhistell, R. (1968). The American family: Some perspectives. *Psychiatry, 29*, 203–212.

Bloom, B., Niles, R., & Tatcher, A. (1985). Sources of marital dissatisfaction among newly separated persons. *Journal of Family Issues, 6*, 331–346.

Bohannan, P. (1971). *Divorce and after.* New York: Anchor Books.

Bohannan, P. (1984). *All the happy families: Exploring the varieties of family life.* New York: McGraw-Hill Book Company.

Boss, P. (1977). A clarification of the concept of psychological father presence in families experiencing ambiguity of boundaries. *Journal of Marriage and the Family, 39*, 141–151.

Boss, P. (1980a). The relationship of wife's sex role perceptions, psychological father presence, wife's personal qualities, and wife/family dysfunction in families of missing fathers. *Journal of Marriage and the Family, 42*, 541–549.

Boss, P. (1980b). Normative family stress: Family boundary changes across the life-span. *Family Relations, 29*, 445–450.

Boss, P. (1983). Family separation and boundary ambiguity. *The International Journal of Mass Emergencies and Disasters, 1*, 63–72.

Boss, P. (1986). Family stress. In M. B. Sussman & S. Steinmetz (Eds.), *Handbook on marriage and the family* (pp. 695–723). New York: Plenum Press.

Boss, P. (1987). *Family stress.* Beverly Hills, CA: Sage.

Boss, P., & Greenberg, J. (1984). Family boundary ambiguity: A new variable in family stress theory. *Family Process, 24*, 535–546.

Boss, P., McCubbin, H., & Lester, G. (1979). The corporate executive wife's coping patterns in response to routine husband-father absence. *Family Process, 18*, 79–86.

Bowen, M. (1976). Theory and practice in psychotherapy. In P. J. Guerin (Ed.), *Family Therapy.* New York: Gardner Press.

Bowen, M. (1978). *Family therapy and clinical practice: Collected papers of Murray Bowen.* New York: Aronson.

Bowman, M., & Ahrons, C. (1985). Impact of legal custody status on fathers' parenting postdivorce. *Journal of Marriage and the Family, 47*, 481–488.

Brandwein, R., Brown, C., & Fox, E. (1974). Women and children last: The social situation of divorced mothers and their families. *Journal of Marriage and the Family, 36*, 498–514.

Brown, E. (1976). Divorce counseling. In D. Olson (Ed.), *Treating relationships* (pp. 399–429). Lake Mills, IA: Graphic Publishing Co.

Brown, E. (1982). Divorce and the extended family: A consideration of services. In E. Fisher (Ed.), *Impact of divorce on the extended family* (pp. 159–171). New York: Haworth Press.

Brown, E. (1985). The comprehensive divorce treatment center: The divorce and marital stress model clinic. In D. Sprenkle (Ed.), *Divorce therapy* (pp. 159–169). New York: Haworth Press

Buckley, W. (1967). *Sociology and modern systems theory.* Englewood Cliffs, NJ: Prentice-Hall.

Burgess, E. (1926). The family as a unity of interacting personalities. *The Family, 7,* 3–9.

Burgess, E., & Cottrell, L., Jr. (1939). *Predicting success or failure in marriage.* New York: Prentice-Hall.

Burgess, E., & Locke, H. (1945). *The family: From institution to companionship.* New York: American Book Company.

Burr, W. (1973). *Theory construction and the sociology of the family.* New York: John Wiley & Sons.

Burr, W., Hill, R., Nye, F. I., & Reiss, I. (Eds.). (1979). *Contemporary theories about the family* (Vol. I). New York: The Free Press.

Carter, E., & McGoldrick, M. (1980). The family life cycle and family therapy: An overview. In E. Carter and M. McGoldrick (Eds.), *The family life cycle* (pp. 3–20). New York: Gardner Press.

Cherlin, A. (1977). The effects of children on marital dissolution. *Demography, 14,* 266–272.

Cherlin, A. (1978). Remarriage as an incomplete institution. *American Journal of Sociology, 84,* 636–640.

Cherlin, A., & McCarthy, J. (1985). Remarried couple households: Data from the June 1980 Current Population Survey. *Journal of Marriage and the Family, 47,* 23–30.

Chiriboga, D. (1979). Marital separation and stress: A life-course perspective. *Alternative Lifestyles, 2,* 461–470.

Clingempeel, W., & Brand, E. (1985). Quasi-kin relationships, structural complexity, and marital quality in stepfamilies: A replication, extension, and clinical implications. *Family Relations, 34,* 401–409.

Combrinck-Graham, L. (1985). A developmental model for family systems. *Family Process, 24,* 139–150.

Coogler, O. (1978). *Structured mediation in divorce settlements.* Lexington, Mass.: D. C. Heath.

Coogler, O., Weber, R., & McKenney, P. (1979). Divorce mediation: A means of facilitating divorce and adjustment. *The Family Coordinator, 28,* 255–259.

Cooley, C. (1902). *Human nature and the social order.* New York: Charles Scribner's Sons.

Crosbie-Burnett, M. (In press). Gender roles of remarried couples in mother-stepfather families. *Journal of Family Issues.*

Crosbie-Burnett, M. (1984). The centrality of the step relationship: A challenge to family theory and practice. *Family Relations, 33,* 459–464.

Crosbie-Burnett, M., & Ahrons, C. (1985). From divorce to remarriage: Implications for therapy with families in transition. *Psychotherapy and the family, 1,* 121–137.

Cseh-Szombathy, L., Koch-Nielsen, I., Trost, J., & Weeda, I. (1985). *The aftermath of divorce — coping with family change.* Budapest: Akademiai Kiado.

Cuber, J., & Harroff, P. (1965). *The significant Americans: A study of sexual behavior among the affluent.* New York: Appleton-Century.

Deckert, P., & Langlier, R. (1978). The late divorce phenomenon: The causes and impact of ending a 20-year-old or longer marriage. *Journal of Divorce, 1,* 381–390.

Deutscher, I. (1959). *Married life in the middle years.* Kansas City, MO: Community Studies, Inc.

Duberman, L. (1975). *The reconstituted family: A study of remarried couples and their children.* Chicago: Nelson-Hall Publishers.

Duck, S. (1982). A topography of relationship disengagement and dissolution. In S. Duck (Ed.), *Personal relationships. 4: Dissolving personal relationships* (pp. 1–30). London: Academic Press.

Duhl, B. (1983). *From the inside out and other metaphors.* New York: Brunner/Mazel.

Duvall, E. (1971). *Family development* (4th edition). Philadelphia: J. B. Lippincott Co.

Einstein, E. (1979). Stepfamily lives. *Human Behavior, 8,* 63–68.

Eno, M. (1985). Sibling relationships in families of divorce. In D. Sprenkle (Ed.), *Divorce therapy* (pp. 139–156). New York: Haworth Press.

Erikson, E. (1968). *Identity, youth and crisis.* New York: Norton.

Farber, B. (1961). The family as a set of mutually contingent careers. In N. Foote (Ed.), *Consumer behavior: Models of household decision-making* (pp. 276–297). New York: New York University Press.

Farber, B. (1964). *Family organization and interaction.* San Francisco: Chandler.

Fisher, E., (Ed.) (1982). *Impact of divorce on the extended family.* New York: The Haworth Press.

Folberg, J. (1981). The changing family: Implications for the law. *Conciliation Courts Review, 19,* 1–6.

Folberg, J. (1984). Child custody law: The American perspective. In I. Koch-Nielsen (Ed.), *Parent-child relationship, post-divorce: A seminar report* (pp. 252–301). Copenhagen, Denmark: The Danish National Institute for Social Research.

Folberg, J., & Graham, M. (1979). Joint custody of children following divorce. *University of California at Davis Law Review, 12,* 523–581.

Folberg, J. and Taylor, A. (1984). *Mediation: A comprehensive guide to resolving conflicts without litigation.* San Francisco, CA: Jossey-Bass Publishers.

Foster, H., & Freed, D. (1982). Grandparent visitation: Vagaries and vicissitudes. In E. Fisher (Ed.), *Impact of divorce on the extended family* (pp. 79–100). New York: Haworth Press.

Friedan, B. (1963). *The feminine mystique.* New York: W. W. Norton.

Furstenberg, F., Jr., & Nord, C. (1985). Parenting apart: Patterns of childrearing after marital disruption. *Journal of Marriage and the Family, 47,* 893–912.

Furstenberg, F., Jr., & Spanier, G. (1984). *Recycling the family: Remarriage after divorce.* Beverly Hills, CA: Sage.

Ganong, L., & Coleman, M. (1984). The effects of remarriage on children: A review of the empirical literature. *The Family Coordinator, 33,* 389–406.

Gilligan, C. (1982). *In a different voice: Psychological theory and women's development.* Cambridge, MA: Harvard University Press.

Glenn, N., & McLanahan, S. (1982). Children and marital happiness: A further specification of the relationship. *Journal of Marriage and the Family, 44,* 63–72.

Glick, P. (1980). Remarriage: Some recent changes and variations. *Journal of Family Issues, 1,* 455–478.

Glick, P. (1984). Marriage, divorce, and living arrangements: Prospective changes. *Journal of Family Issues, 5,* 7–26.

Glick, P., & Spanier, G. (1980). Married and unmarried cohabitation in the United States. *Journal of Marriage and the Family, 42,* 19–30.

Golan, N. (1978). *Treatment in crisis situations.* New York: The Free Press.

Golan, N. (1983). *Passing through transitions: A guide for practitioners.* New York: Free Press.

Goldner, V. (1982). Remarriage family: Structure, system, future. In J. Hansen and L. Messenger (Eds.), *Therapy with remarried families* (pp. 187–206). Rockville, MD: Aspen.

Goldsmith, J. (1980). Relationships between former spouses: Descriptive findings. *Journal of Divorce, 2,* 1–20.

Goode, W. (1956). *World revolution and the family.* New York: The Free Press.

Greif, J. (1979). Fathers, children and joint custody. *American Journal of Orthopsychiatry, 49,* 311–319.

Hagestad, G. (1981). Problems and promises in the social psychology of intergenerational relations. In R. Fogel, E. Hatfield, S. Kiesler, & J. March (Eds.), *Stability and change in the family* (pp. 11–46). New York: Academic Press.

Hagestad, G., & Smyer, M. (1982). Dissolving long-term relationships: Patterns of divorcing in middle age. In S. Duck (Ed.), *Personal relationships, 4: Dissolving personal relationships* (pp. 155–188). London: Academic Press.

Hagestad, G., Smyer, M., & Stierman, K. (1984). The impact of divorce in middle age. In R. Cohen, B. Cohler, & S. Weissmann (Eds.), *Parenthood: Psychodynamic perspectives* (pp. 247–262). New York: Guilford Press.

Halem, L. (1980). *Divorce reform.* New York: Free Press.

Hall, C. (1981). *The Bowen family theory and its uses.* New York: Jason Aronson.

Haynes, J. (1981). *Divorce mediation: A practical guide for therapists and counselors.* New York: Springer.

Hess, R., & Camara, K. (1979). Post-divorce family relationships as mediating factors in the consequences of divorce for children. *Journal of Social Issues, 35,* 79–96.

Hetherington, E. (1979). Divorce: A child's perspective. *American Psychologist, 34,* 851–858.

Hetherington, E., & Deur, J. (1971). The effects of father absence on child development. *Young Children, 26,* 233–248.

Hetherington, E., Cox, H., & Cox, R. (1976). Divorced fathers. *The Family Coordinator, 25,* 417–428.

Hetherington, E., Cox, H., & Cox, R. (1978). The aftermath of divorce. In J. Stevens,

Jr. & M. Matthews (Eds.), *Mother/child, father/child relationships.* Washington, DC: NAEYC.

Hetherington, E., Cox, H., & Cox, R. (1979). Stress and coping in divorce: Focus on women. In J. Gullahorn (Ed.), *Psychology and women in transition.* New York: B. H. Winston and Sons.

Hill, R. (1949). *Families under stress.* New York: Harper and Brothers.

Hill, R. (1971). *Family development in three generations.* Cambridge, MA: Schenkman.

Hill, R., & Rodgers, R. (1964). The developmental approach. In H. Christensen (Ed.), *Handbook of marriage and the family* (pp. 171–211). Chicago: Rand McNally & Company.

Hoffman, L. (1980). The family life cycle and discontinuous change. In E. Carter and M. McGoldrick (Eds.), *The family life cycle* (pp. 53–68). New York: Gardner Press.

Ihinger-Tallman, M., & Pasley, K. (1986). Remarriage and integration within the community. *Journal of Marriage and the Family, 48,* 395–405.

Isaacs, M., & Leon, G. (1986). *Friends and foes: The exspousal relationship and child outcome.* Unpublished manuscript. Philadelphia: Families of Divorce Project, Philadelphia Child Guidance Clinic.

Jacobsen, N., Waldron, H., & Moore, D. (1980). Toward a behavioral profile of marital distress. *Journal of Counseling and Clinical Psychology, 48,* 696–703.

Jacobson, D. (1978a). The impact of marital separation/divorce on children: I. Parent-child separation and child adjustment. *Journal of Divorce, 1,* 341–360.

Jacobson, D. (1978b). The impact of marital separation/divorce on children: II. Interparent hostility and child adjustment. *Journal of Divorce, 2,* 3–19.

Jacobson, D. (1978c). The impact of marital separation/divorce on children: III. Parent-child communication and child adjustment, and regression analysis of findings from overall study. *Journal of Divorce, 2,* 175–194.

Jacobson, D. (In press). Family structure, visiting, and child adjustment in the stepfamily, a linked family system. In K. Pasley and M. Ihinger-Tallman (Eds.), *Remarriage and stepfamilies: Research and theory.* New York: Guilford Press.

Jacobson, G. *The multiple crises of marital separation and divorce.* New York: Grune & Stratton.

Kantor, D., & Lehr, W. (1975). *Inside the family.* San Francisco: Jossey-Bass.

Kaslow, F. (1981). Divorce and divorce therapy. In A. Gurman & D. Kniskern (Eds.), *Handbook of family therapy* (pp. 662–696). New York: Brunner/Mazel.

Kaslow, F. (1984). Divorce: An evolutionary process of change in the family system. *Journal of Divorce, 7,* 21–39.

Kaslow, F., & Hyatt, R. (1982). Divorce: A potential growth experience for the extended family. In E. Fisher (Ed.), *Impact of divorce on the extended family* (pp. 115–126). New York: Haworth Press.

Kelly, J. (1983). Mediation and psychotherapy: Distinguishing the differences. *Mediation Quarterly, 1,* 33–44.

Kelly, J., & Wallerstein, J. (1977). Part-time parent, part-time child: Visiting after divorce. *Journal of Clinical Child Psychology, 6,* 51–54.

Keshet, H., & Rosenthal, K. (1978). Fathering after marital separation. *Social Work, 23*, 11-18.

Kitson, G. (1982). Attachment to spouse in divorce: A scale and its application. *Journal of Marriage and the Family, 44*, 379-393.

Kitson, G., & Raschke, H. (1981). Divorce research: What we know; what we need to know. *Journal of Divorce, 4*, 1-37.

Kitson, G., Barri, K., & Roach, M. (1985). Who divorces and why: A review. *Journal of Family Issues, 6*, 255-293.

Klein, D., & Hill, R. (1979). Determinants of family problem-solving effectiveness. In W. Burr, R. Hill, F. Nye, & I. Reiss (Eds.), *Contemporary theories about the family* (Vol. I) (pp. 493-548). New York: The Free Press.

Kressel, K. (1985). *The process of divorce.* New York: Basic Books.

Kressel, K., & Deutsch, M. (1977). Divorce therapy: An in-depth survey of therapists. *Family Process, 16*, 413-443.

Kressel, K., Lopez-Morillas, M., Weinglass, J., & Deutsch, M. (1978). Professional interventions in divorce: A summary of the views of lawyers, psychotherapists, and clergy. *Journal of Divorce, 2*, 119-155.

Levinger, G. (1979). A social psychological perspective on marital dissolution. In G. Levinger & O. Moles (Eds.), *Divorce and separation: Context, causes, and consequences* (pp. 37-60). New York: Basic Books.

Levinger, G., & Moles, O. (1979). *Divorce and separation: Context, causes, and consequences.* New York: Basic Books.

Levitan, T. (1979). Children of divorce. *The Journal of Social Issues, 35*, 1-25.

Litwak, E. (1960a). Occupational mobility and extended family cohesion. *American Sociological Review, 25*, 9-21.

Litwak, E. (1960b). Geographical mobility and extended family cohesion. *American Sociological Review, 25*, 385-394.

Litwak, E., & Szelenyi, I. (1969). Primary group structure and their functions: Kin, neighbors, and friends. *American Sociological Review, 34*, 465-481.

Longfellow, C. (1979). Divorce in context: Its impact on children. In G. Levinger & O. Moles (Eds.), *Divorce and separation: Context, causes, and consequences.* New York Basic Books.

Marotz-Baden, R., Adams, G., Bueche, N., Munro, B., & Munro, G. (1979). Family form or family process? Reconsidering the deficit family model approach. *The Family Coordinator, 28*, 5-14.

Mayleas, D. (1977). *Rewedded bliss: Love, alimony, incest, ex-spouses and other domestic blessings.* New York: Basic Books.

McCubbin, H., & Patterson, J. (1983). The family stress process: The double ABCX model of adjustment and adaptation. In H. McCubbin, M. Sussman, & J. Patterson (Eds.), *Social stress and the family: Advances and developments in family stress theory and research* (pp. 7-37). New York: Haworth Press.

McLanahan, S., Wedemeyer, N., & Adelberg, T. (1981). Network structure, social support, and psychological well-being in the single-parent family. *Journal of Marriage and the Family, 43*, 601-612.

Mead, G. (1936). *Mind, self, and society.* Chicago: University of Chicago Press.

Mead, M. (1971). Anomalies in American postdivorce relationships. In P. Bohannan (Ed.), *Divorce and after* (pp. 97-112). New York: Anchor Books.

Mendes, H. (1976). Single fatherhood. *Social Work, 21*, 308-313.

Messinger, L. (Ed.). (1982). *Therapy with remarried families.* Rockville, MD: Aspen Systems Corporation.

Messinger, L. (1984). *Remarriage: A family affair.* New York: Plenum.

Mills, D. (1984). A model for stepfamily development. *Family Relations, 33*, 365-372.

Milne, A. (1983). Divorce mediation: The state of the art. *Mediation Quarterly, 1*, 15-31.

Minuchin, S. (1974). *Families and family therapy.* Cambridge, MA: Harvard University Press.

Mosten, F., & Biggs, B. (1985/86). The role of the therapist in the co-mediation of divorce: An exploration by a lawyer-mediator team. *Journal of Divorce, 9*, 27-39.

National Center for Health Statistics. (1985a). Advance report of final divorce statistics, 1982. *Monthly Vital Statistics Report*, Volume 34, NO. 9. Supp. DHHS Pub. No. (PHS) 85-1120. Washington, DC: U.S. Government Printing Office.

National Center for Health Statistics. (1985b). *Vital Statistics of the United States, 1981, Vol. III, Marriage and Divorce.* DHHS Pub. No. (PHS) 85-1121. Washington, DC: U.S. Government Printing Office.

National Center for Health Statistics. (1986a). Advance report of final divorce statistics, 1983. *Monthly Vital Statistics Report*, Volume 34, No. 11. Supp. DHHS Pub. No. (PHS) 86-1120. Washington, DC: U.S. Government Printing Office.

National Center for Health Statistics. (1986b). Births, marriages, divorces, and deaths for 1985. *Monthly Vital Statistics Report*, Volume 34, No. 12. DHHS Pub. No. (PHS) 86-1120. Washington, DC: U.S. Government Printing Office.

National Center for Health Statistics. (1986c). Average (mean) interval to remarriage by previous marital status and age of bride and groom: Reporting states, 1970 and 1983. Unpublished data.

Nehls, N., & Morgenbesser, M. (1980). Joint custody: An exploration of the issues. *Family Process, 19*, 117-125.

Nichols, W. (1984). Therapeutic needs of children in family system reorganization. *Journal of Divorce, 7*, 23-44.

Nichols, W. (1985). Family therapy with children of divorce. In D. Sprenkle (Ed.), *Divorce therapy* (pp. 55-68). New York: Haworth Press.

Okun, B., & Rappaport, L. (1980). *Working with families: An introduction to family therapy.* North Scituate, MA: Duxbury Press.

Paris, E. (1984). *Stepfamilies: Making them work.* New York: Avon.

Parsons, T., & Bales, R. (1955). *Family, socialization and interaction process.* New York: The Free Press.

Pasley, K., & Ihinger-Tallman, M. (1982). Remarried family life: Supports and constraints. In G. Rowe (Ed.), *Building family strengths, 4* (pp. 367-384). Lincoln, NE: University of Nebraska Press.

Pogrebin, L. (1983). *Family politics.* New York: McGraw-Hill.

Price-Bonham, S., & Balswick, J. (1980). The noninstitutions: Divorce, desertion, and remarriage. *Journal of Marriage and the Family, 42*, 959-972.

Reiss, D. (1981). *The family's construction of reality*. Cambridge, MA: Harvard University Press.

Reiss, I. (1965). The universality of the family: A conceptual analysis. *Journal of Marriage and the Family, 27*, 343-353.

Rodgers, R. (1962). *Improvements in the construction and analysis of family life cycle categories*. Kalamazoo, MI: School of Graduate Studies, Western Michigan University.

Rodgers, R. (1973). *Family interaction and transaction: The developmental approach*. Englewood Cliffs, N.J.: Prentice-Hall.

Rodgers, R. (1977). The family life cycle concept — past, present, and future. In J. Cuisenier (Ed.), *The family cycle in European societies* (pp. 39-57). Paris: Mouton.

Rodgers, R. (1986). Postmarital reorganization of family relationships: A propositional theory. In S. Duck & D. Perlman (Eds.), *Close relationships: Development, dynamics, and deterioration* (pp. 239-268). Beverly Hills, CA: Sage.

Rodgers, R., & Conrad, L. (1986). Courtship for remarriage: Influences on family reorganization after divorce. *Journal of Marriage and the Family, 48*, 767-775.

Roman, M., & Dichter, S. (1985). Fathers and feminism: Backlash within the women's movement. *Conciliation Courts Review, 23*, 37-46.

Roman, M., & Haddad, W. (1978). *The disposable parent: The case for joint custody*. New York: Holt, Reinhart & Winston.

Rubin, L. (1983). *Intimate strangers*. New York: Harper and Row.

Sager, C., Brown, H., Crohn, H., Engel, T., Rodstein, E., & Walker, E. (1983). *Treating the remarried family*. New York: Brunner/Mazel.

Scanzoni, J. (1972). *Sexual bargaining*. Englewood Cliffs, NJ: Prentice-Hall.

Scanzoni, J. (1979). A historical perspective on husband-wife bargaining power and marital dissolution. In G. Levinger & O. Moles (Eds.), *Divorce and separation: Context, causes, and consequences* (pp. 20-36). New York: Basic Books.

Shields, L. (1981). *Displaced homemakers: Organizing for a new life*. New York: McGraw-Hill.

Skolnick, A. (1979). Public images, private realities: The American family in popular culture and social science. In V. Tufte & B. Myerhoff (Eds.), *Changing images of the family* (pp. 297-315). New Haven: Yale University Press.

Spanier, G. (1983). Married and unmarried cohabitation in the United States: 1980. *Journal of Marriage and the Family, 45*, 277-288.

Spanier, G., & Glick, P. (1980). Paths to remarriage. *Journal of Divorce, 3*, 283-298.

Spanier, G., & Lewis, R. (1980). Marital quality: A review of the seventies. *Journal of Marriage and the Family, 42*, 825-839.

Sprenkle, D., & Storm, C. (1981). The unit of treatment in divorce therapy. In A. Gurman (Ed.), *Questions and answers in the practice of family therapy* (pp. 284-289). New York: Brunner/Mazel.

Sprenkle, D., & Storm, C. (1983). Divorce therapy outcome research: A substantive and methodological review. *Journal of Marital and Family Therapy, 9*, 239-258.

Steinberg, J. (1980). Towards an interdisciplinary commitment: A divorce lawyer proposes attorney-therapist marriages or, at the least, an affair. *Journal of Marital and Family Therapy, 6*, 259-268.

Steinberg, J. (1985). Through an interdisciplinary mirror: Attorney-therapist similarities. *Journal of Divorce, 8*, 9–13.

Storm, C., Sprenkle, D., & Williamson, W. (1986). Innovative divorce approaches developed by counselors, conciliators, mediators, and educators. In R. Levant (Ed.), *Psycho-educational approaches to family therapy*. New York: Springer.

Stuart, R., & Jacobson, B. (1985). *Second marriage*. New York: Norton.

Sussman, M. (1953). The help pattern in the middle-class family. *American Sociological Review, 18*, 22–28.

Sussman, M. (1959). The isolated nuclear family: Fact or fiction? *Social Problems, 6*, 333–340.

Terkelson, K. (1980). Toward a theory of the family life cycle. In E. Carter and M. McGoldrick (Eds.), *The family life cycle* (pp. 21–52). New York: Gardner Press.

Tietjen, A. (1985). The social networks and social support of married and single mothers in Sweden. *Journal of Marriage and the Family, 47*, 489–496.

Tufte, V., & Myerhoff, B. (Eds.). (1979). *Changing images of the family*. New Haven: Yale University Press.

U.S. Bureau of the Census. (1922). *Fourteenth census of the United States, 1920, Vol. II*. Washington, DC: U.S. Government Printing Office.

U.S. Bureau of the Census. (1933). *Fifteenth census of the United States, 1930, Vol. II*. Washington, DC: U. S. Government Printing Office.

U.S. Bureau of the Census. (1951). *Statistical abstract of the United States: 1952 (72nd Edition)*. Washington, DC: U.S. Government Printing Office.

U.S. Bureau of the Census. (1961). *Statistical abstract of the United States: 1962 (82nd Edition)*. Washington, DC: U.S. Government Printing Office.

U.S. Bureau of the Census. (1971). *Statistical abstract of the United States: 1972 (92nd Edition)*. Washington, DC: U.S. Government Printing Office.

U.S. Bureau of the Census. (1981). *Statistical abstract of the United States: 1982 (102nd Edition)*. Washington, DC: U.S. Government Printing Office.

U.S. Bureau of the Census. (1984a). *1980 census of the population, Vol. I, characteristics of the population, Chapter D, detailed population characteristics. Part 1, U.S. summary, section A: United States*. Washington, DC: U.S. Government Printing Office.

U.S. Bureau of the Census. (1984b). *Statistical abstract of the United States: 1985 (105th Edition)*. Washington, DC: U.S. Government Printing Office.

U.S. Bureau of the Census. (1985a). Population profile of the United States: 1983–84. *Current Population Reports*, Series P-23, No. 145. Washington, DC: U.S. Government Printing Office.

U.S. Bureau of the Census. (1985b). Population characteristics: Households, families, marital status, and living arrangements: March 1985 (Advance Report), *Current Population Reports*, Series P-20, No. 402. Washington, DC: U.S. Government Printing Office.

U.S. Bureau of the Census. (1986a). Current Population Survey, June 1980, unpublished data.

U.S. Bureau of the Census. (1986b). Current Population Survey, June 1985, unpublished data.

Vinick, B. H. (n.d.). The displaced homemaker: A state-of-the-art review. Working Paper No. 52. Wellesley, MA: Wellesley College Center for Research on Women.

Vinick, B. H., & Sheldrick, G. (1979). Bibliography on the displaced homemaker. Working Paper No. 51. Wellesley, MA: Wellesley College Center for Research on Women.

Visher, E., & Visher, J. (1979). *Stepfamilies: A guide to working with steppurents and stepchildren.* New York: Brunner/Mazel.

Visher, E., & Visher, J. (1982). *How to win as a stepfamily.* New York: Dembner.

Volgy, S., & Everett, C. (1985). Joint custody reconsidered: Systemic criteria for mediation. *Journal of Divorce, 8,* 131–150.

Wald, E. (1981). *The remarried family: Challenge and promise.* New York: Family Service Association of America.

Walker, K., & Messenger, L. (1979). Remarriage after divorce: Dissolution and reconstruction of family boundaries. *Family Process, 18,* 185–192.

Waller, W., & Hill, R. (1951). *The family: A dynamic interpretation* (rev. ed.). New York: Dryden Press.

Wallerstein, J., & Kelly, J. (1980). *Surviving the breakup: How children and parents cope with divorce.* New York: Basic Books.

Walsh, F. (1982). Conceptualizations of normal family functioning. In F. Walsh (Ed.), *Normal family processes* (pp. 3–42). New York: Guilford Press.

Weiss, R. (1975). *Marital separation.* New York: Basic Books.

Weiss, R. (1979). *Going it alone.* New York: Basic Books.

Weitzman, L. (1985). *The divorce revolution.* New York: The Free Press.

Westoff, L. A. (1977). *The second time around: Remarriage in America.* New York: Viking.

Whiteside, M. (1982). Remarriage: A family developmental process. *Journal of Marital and Family Therapy, 8,* 59–68.

Whiteside, M., & Auerbach, L. (1978). Can a daughter of my father's new wife be my sister? Families of remarriage in family therapy. *Journal of Divorce, 1,* 271–283.

Wood, V., & Robertson, J. (1976). The significance of grandparenthood. In J. Gubrium (Ed.), *Time, roles, and self in old age* (pp. 278–304). New York: Human Sciences Press.

Wood, V., & Robertson, J. (1978). Friendship and kinship interaction: Differential effect on the morale of the elderly. *Journal of Marriage and the Family, 40,* 367–375.

Wooley, P. (1978). Shared custody, demanded by parents, discouraged by courts. *Family Advocate, 6–8,* 33–34.

Wooley, P. (1980). *The custody handbook.* New York: Summit.

Index

abortion, 14
Adams, B., 23
adultery, 10, 15, 16, 58, 60, 65
Ahrons, C. R., 42–45, 47, 55, 108, 110,
    113–15, 117, 137, 162, 168, 173, 174
alcoholism, 4, 16
ambivalence:
    in early separation, 64–66
    of friends, 80–81, 96
    societal, 103–4
anger:
    adversarial process and, 82, 113, 202
    over child-rearing, 77
    as defense against depression, 205
    of former spouses, 118–20, 126–29,
        132–33, 135
    joint decisions and, 65, 111
    remarriage and, 160–61
annulment statistics, 224, 226
anomie, 64, 100
Anspach, D., 174

Bales, R., 10, 11, 12, 13
Bates, F., 29
Beal, E., 217
Bennett, J., 26–27
Berman, W., 137
Bernard, J., 62
Bierstedt, R., 26
binuclear families, ix
    combinations in, 22, 108, 158
    definition of, 42
    expansion of, 156–80, 212
    functional vs. dysfunctional, 130–37,
        175–79
    normative view of, 201, 205, 207
    nuclear families vs., 22, 201
    social views of, 207–8
    transitional processes in, 42–43, 76, 103,
        104–5, 133–35
Binuclear Family Study, 117, 120, 135, 137,
    162, 168, 173
Birdwhistell, R., 11

birth control, 14
blended families:
    adjustment of, 217
    definition of, 21
    problems of, vii, 165–74, 191
    sexual taboos in, 178–79
    stepsiblings in, 196
Bloom, B., 137
Bohannan, P., 105–6, 202, 219
Bombeck, E., 200
bonds:
    accommodation of, 164
    creation of, 217–18
    maintenance of, 165, 181
    persistent, 64–65, 112–13, 137, 144–45
Boss, P., 35–36, 75, 107
boundaries:
    ambiguity of, 35, 75
    in binuclear families, 135–37
    clear, 33–34, 43, 106–7, 135, 137, 175
    definition of, 33
    intimacy, 178–79
    redefinition of, 50
Bowen, M., 36–37
Bowman, M., 174
Brandwein, R., 108
bureaucracy, 4–5, 207
Burgess, E. W., 10, 28
Burr, W., 29, 44

Carter, E., 39
Cherlin, A., 21, 165
child abuse, 4, 5, 10
child-care:
    by out-of-home fathers, 69, 71–72
    outside, 14, 72, 78, 211
    during separation, 66–72
    traditional, 12
child custody:
    former spouses' relations and, 108–10
    history of, 16–17, 109, 215
    joint, 16–17, 32, 66–67, 108–10, 122–23,
        125, 168, 214–16

child custody (*continued*)
 legislation on, 105, 109, 215–16, 219
 single-parent, 21, 108, 120–21, 128
 support payments and, 127, 128
children:
 adult, 94–95, 100, 147–49, 183–84,
  188–94, 196
 behavior rules for, 77, 178
 in binuclear families, 165–75
 birth of, 59, 89–90
 competition among, 168–70
 developmental categories of, 89
 effects of marital disruption on, 40–41,
  71, 95, 118, 126, 131, 133, 149
 emotional needs of, 71, 126, 213
 illness of, 66, 72, 124
 increased responsibility of, 67
 kidnapping of, 120
 loyalty of, 95, 168
 as pawns, 120, 127, 133, 147
 rearing of, 17, 32, 39, 77–78, 89–91,
  213–14
 rights of, 213
 sibling relationships of, 34–35, 67, 94, 99,
  168–71
 socialization of, 77, 91, 124, 211
cohabitation of, 84, 86, 139, 154
Combrinck-Graham, L., 39
community support services, 73, 78–79, 211
consumer goods, 6, 7, 68
Coogler, O. J., 203
coping patterns, 50–56
 dysfunctional, 68, 74
 phases in, 45–49, 52–53, 72
 strategies in, 53–54, 56, 58, 60, 68, 74, 139
counselors, marriage, 52, 58, 204
couples:
 aging, 98–101, 149–53, 199–200
 childless, 84–89, 106, 138–43, 181–83, 213
 midlife, 91–98, 143–49, 183–99
 rituals of, 59
 see also spouses, former
courtship, 85, 144, 187, 194
credit ratings, 87
crisis:
 characteristics of, 54–55, 132
 conditions producing, 66, 96, 103, 187
 early separation, 66–68
 intervention in, 54
 midlife, 193
 support systems in, 68, 72–73, 89
Crosbie-Burnett, M., 165, 168
Cuber, J., 193

death, 19, 20, 98, 99, 101

death benefits, 185
delinquency, 4
denial mechanisms, 53
depression, 64–65, 108, 205
desertion, 15
Deutsch, M., 107
Deutscher, I., 37
divorce:
 adversarial character of, 79, 82, 111,
  132–33, 202
 age factors in, 18–19
 of aging couples, 149–53, 210
 causes of, 13, 15, 23, 152
 of childless couples, 138–43
 constructive, 130–31, 136
 delay vs. initiation of, 41, 210
 friendly, 115–17, 122–24, 133–34
 increased rates of, 7, 11, 13, 17–19,
  91, 201
 mediation approach to, 203–4
 midlife, 40–41, 143–49, 184–96, 210
 in name only, 41, 45
 no-fault, 15–16, 82, 110, 202
 normative view of, 23–24, 50, 206
 orderly vs. disorderly, 41–42
 overlapping aspects of, 105–6
 pathology of, 15–17, 23–24, 104, 109,
  131, 201
 planning for, 206
 process of, ix, 17, 23–51, 110–12,
  135, 208–13
 "pro se," 141
 public policy on, 51, 91
 reform movement in, 15–17, 219–20
 research on, 209–10
 in second marriages, 165, 188
 social attitudes toward, 13–17, 23–25,
  116, 207–9
 statistics on, 7, 11, 13, 17–19, 90, 91,
  165, 201, 206, 224, 226–31
 stress in, 24, 25
 transition of, 103–53
 as unscheduled event, 41, 206
"divorce industry," 202
divorce therapy, 204–5
Duberman, L., 165
Duck, S., 113

economic resources:
 for child support, 111, 206
 conflict over, 78, 87, 111, 118, 196–97
 midlife consolidation of, 92
 of older women, 151, 185–87, 194
 of retired couples, 100
 of separated couples, 67–69

Erikson, E., 42–43
escape mechanisms, 58, 74
Everett, C., 130, 132
expectations:
  of adult children, 196
  of former spouses, 176–77
  midlife, 92
  of new spouses, 185–86, 196–97
  realistic, development of, 212
  about retirement, 97, 184

families:
  adaptability of, viii, 3–4, 46, 103
  adjustment of, 45, 54, 66–68
  authority in, 27, 77–78
  consolidation of, 45–46
  definitions of, 29, 37, 91, 213
  dual-worker, 13–14, 71, 165
  extensions of, 72, 73, 174
  "instant," 175, 182
  modern vs. traditional, 4–5
  new forms of, vii, 21–22
  parenting concerns of, 89, 91
  redefinition process in, 104–5, 106
  restructuring of, 45–50, 75, 101–7, 143, 153
  see also binuclear families; blended families; nuclear families; single-parent families
family careers, 37–51
  aging spouse in, 98–101, 149–53, 199–200
  bearing and rearing of children in, 17, 32, 39, 77–78, 89–91
  childless spouse in, 84–89, 138–43
  definition of, 37
  developmental theory of, 37–40, 84
  divorce transition and, 138–53
  midlife couples in, 91–98, 143–49
  remarriage transition and, 181–200
  separation transition and, 84–102
  stability vs. transition in, 39–40
  stress and crisis theory of, 44–47
family development theory, 37–40, 84
family lineages, 40–42
family problems:
  communication of, 60–62
  counseling on, 5, 202–5, 212
  recording of, 4–5
family stress theory, 44–47
family systems, 26–37
  boundaries in, 33–35, 43, 50, 75, 135–37, 175, 178–79
  developmental processes in, 50, 59
  individual dynamics in, 28–29, 33, 35
  psychological approach to, 28–29
  relationship styles in, 32–33

reorganization of, 103–5
sociological approach to, 26–28
strategies in, 32, 47, 50–51, 53–54
subsystems of, 30, 33–34, 43, 50, 106–7, 158–74
therapy based on, 30–37, 39, 205, 212
fantasies:
  relief, 64–65
  reunion, 123, 160
  sexual, 58
Farber, B., 37, 38, 107
Fathers United, 215
fears:
  of loss of image, 59
  of starting over, 88
feedback, 28–29
Folberg, J., 109
Friedan, B., 13
friends:
  ambivalence of, 80–81, 96
  former spouses as, 115–17
  loss of, 80–81, 96, 99
  new, 60, 63–64, 81–82, 97–98
  same-sex, 195
  support of, 80–82, 94, 195
Furstenberg, F., Jr., 31, 165, 174

Gilligan, C., 61
Glick, I., 121, 165
goals, longterm, 217
Goldsmith, J., 113
Golan, N., 54–55, 102
Goode, W., 8, 9
grandparents, 97, 100, 174–75, 189
Greif, J., 108
guilt:
  by association, 81
  feelings of, 62, 74–75, 148, 185, 217

Hagestad, G., 40–42, 45, 143, 206
Halem, L., 15
Haley, J., 37
Harroff, P., 193
Hetherington, E., 71, 108, 114, 135
Hill, R., xi, 29, 45, 94, 107, 145, 163
Hoffman, L., 39
home:
  "bird's nest" pattern in, 122–23
  idealization of, 12
  parental, 85
  role of women in, 10, 12
  security of, 123, 149
homemakers, displaced, 93, 97, 148, 184, 186–87, 195
household tasks, 66–67, 86–87, 94, 140, 157

Ihinger-Tallman, M., 157, 165
illness:
  of aging, 99
  of children, 66, 72, 124
incest, 4, 5, 113, 178
industrialization, 6-8
Isaacs, M., 113

Jackson, D. D., 37
jealousy, 160, 182

Kantor, D., 30-33, 36, 47, 163, 165
Kaslow, F., 130
Keshet, H., 108
Kelly, J., 108, 114, 135
kin networks, 11
  concerns of, 87, 151
  grandparents in, 97, 100, 174-75, 189
  maintenance of, 140-41, 144
  in midlife, 92-96, 151
  nuclear family and, 9
  prevalence of divorce in, 95
  problem solving in, 8
  reduced availability of, 14, 73, 99, 175, 179
  reorganization of, 80, 82, 96, 197-98
  support of, 72, 80, 94-95, 101
Kitson, G., 137
Klein, D., 163
Kressel, K., 107, 112, 130-31, 135

labor:
  agrarian division of, 6
  changing roles in, 6-7
  family division of, 27, 67, 79, 93, 125, 139-40, 177
  gender specialization of, 6-7, 94, 140, 144
lawyers, 141, 204, 212
legislation:
  child-custody, 105, 109, 215-16, 219
  divorce, 15-16, 82, 110, 141, 202
  social welfare, 208
Lehr, W., 30-33, 36, 47, 163, 165
Leon, G., 113
Lewis, R., 90
Litwak, E., 9
life meaning:
  centrality of marriage to, 96, 98, 101, 151
  importance of work to, 97
  new patterns of, 89, 97, 101, 151
  sense of, 88
lifestyles:
  attachment to, 187
  changes of, 78-81, 93
Locke, H. J., 10
loneliness, 64-65, 77

loyalty:
  of children, 95, 168, 189
  of friends, 80-81, 96, 128
  of kin, 128, 157

McCarthy, J., 21
McCubbin, H., 44-47, 52-54, 73, 103, 159, 163, 165, 211
McGoldrick, M., 39
marriage:
  business aspects of, 186
  communication in, 56-57
  decision-making patterns in, 87
  delay of, 20-21, 91
  devitalized, 193
  emotional needs and, 10-11, 15, 88-89
  fidelity in, 65
  increased rates of, 19-20
  lifelong commitment in, 17, 84, 88, 98
  longterm, "fruits" of, 188
  reasons for, 10-11, 15, 85
  religious view of, 207-8
  statistics on, 221-23
  status in, 10-11, 14
  successful, 85, 97
  see also remarriage
Mead, G. H., 29
Mead, M., 113, 207
mealtimes, 67, 77
men:
  increased parenting role of, 218-19
  occupational orientation of, 97
  as out-of-home fathers, 69, 71-72, 79, 133, 169
  rationality of, 61
  traditional responsibilities of, 6, 11-12, 67-68
  younger women and, 19, 185, 190-91
Mendes, H., 108
mental health professionals, 202-5, 212
Mills, D., 217-18
Minuchin, S., 33-35, 36, 43, 104, 106-7, 118
Myerhoff, B., 91

National Organization of Women (NOW), 215
Nord, C., 21, 174
nuclear families:
  binuclear families vs., 22, 201
  breakdown of, 3-4, 17
  causes of change in, 6-10
  effects of industrialization on, 6-8, 16
  expressive vs. instrumental values in, 10-13, 16
  idealization of, 10-12, 13, 16, 83, 84, 201

isolation of, 9, 52
myth of, 213
role playing in, 11-13
specialization of, 11
after World War II, 7, 93
Nye, F. I., 29

Okun, B., 36
"other woman," 191

parents:
  biological, 213-14, 217
  caring for, 94, 184
  coparenting relationships of, 73, 117,
    125-27, 158, 160, 162, 172-73, 175, 180
  manipulation of, 178
  noncustodial, 120, 129, 130, 176, 214
  responsibilities of, 118, 213-16
  rights of, 109
  of separated children, 87, 94-95
Parsons, T., 10, 11, 12, 13
Pasley, K , 157, 165
Patterson, J., 44-47, 52-54, 73, 103, 159,
  163, 165, 211
pension plans, 100
Pogrebin, L., 91
prenuptial agreements, 186
privacy:
  lack of, 164
  masculine norms of, 61
  protection of, 60, 123
property, division of, 25, 68, 100, 110-11, 203
psychopolitics, 33

Rappaport, L., 36
reconciliation, 67
  as coping strategy, 73-74
  repetitive patterns of, 75
  temporary, 69-70, 74-75
recreation, 97, 145
redivorce, 165, 188
Reiss, D., 47-50
Reiss, I., 29
relationships:
  comparison of, 164-65
  coparenting, 73, 117, 125-27, 158, 160,
    162, 172-73, 175, 180
  of current and former spouses, 171-74,
    182
  declined, 113-14
  dissolved, 120-21, 129, 136, 142-43,
    148-49, 152, 183
  extramarital, 10, 15, 16, 58, 60, 65
  father-daughter, 167, 169, 190, 191
  father-son, 191-92

in-law, 82, 95-96, 125, 127-28, 183
  negotiation and compromise in, 104,
    126-27, 178, 202-3
  new terms for, 168, 171, 207
  parent-child, 43, 64, 126, 165-68, 190-93
  platonic, 65
  role revisions in, 157
  sibling, 34-35, 67, 94, 99, 168-71
  spousal, 41-43
  stepparent-stepchild, 165-68, 177, 191,
    217-18
  stepparent-stepparent, 174
  transactional social, 78-79, 80-82
  see also friends; kin networks; spouses,
    former
religious groups, 207-8, 211
remarriage, ix, 46
  age factors in, 19-20, 194, 225-29
  of aging couples, 199-200
  of childless couples, 181-83
  complexities of, 163, 179-80, 200
  delay of, 159
  dependent children in, 84, 157, 196
  financial issues in, 185-86
  functional vs. dysfunctional relationships
    in, 175-79
  of midlife couples, 183-99
  old vs. new relationships in, 198-99
  potential for, 19-20, 87-88, 98, 194
  as serial monogamy, 21
  statistics on, 20-21, 88, 121, 154, 159,
    230-31
  transition of, 154-200
reproduction, 86-87
  control of, 14-15, 27
retirement:
  community living in, 99
  economic realities of, 100
  planning for, 97
rituals:
  celebratory, 95, 103, 128-29, 130, 146,
    147-48, 188
  of couples, 59
  family, 67, 95, 122, 149, 197-98
  importance of, 103
  new, development of, 95
Robertson, J., 174
Rodgers, R. H., 26, 38, 45, 47, 84
roles:
  breadwinner, 6, 11-12, 67-68, 148
  combined, 85-86, 90, 96-97
  in family systems, 28-29, 35, 37-38
  grandparent, 97, 100, 174-75, 182
  habituation of, 70, 93-94
  husband and father, 12, 61, 67-68, 96

roles (*continued*)
  in marriage, 6, 10–11, 13, 61–62
  of newly separated, 65–68
  of outsiders, 49, 80–82
  overload of, 71
  parental, 89–91, 96, 105, 106–7
  redefinition of, 16, 43, 106, 164
  sex specialization of, 86, 87, 214–15
  social and public, 59–60, 62
  stepparent, 165–68, 171–74
  transitional, 50, 65, 166–68
  wife and mother, 59, 96
Rosenthal, K., 108
Rubin, L., 195

Satir, V., 37
schools, 207, 209, 211
self-image:
  enhanced, 102, 187, 194
  loss of, 160
  maintenance of, 59, 73
separation, marital, ix
  aging couples and, 98–101
  early phase of, 62–68
  effects of legal system on, 82–83
  emotional, 56, 58, 61, 111
  impact of, 62–66, 68–72
  lack of guidelines in, 64–65, 101, 103
  late phase of, 75–83, 88
  mechanics of, 64–68
  midlife, 91–98
  mid-separation phase of, 68–75
  one-sided decisions in, 57–58, 61, 62, 132
  pregnancy during, 86
  preseparation phase of, 56–62
  social elements of, 55–56, 59–62, 79
  systemic, 47, 76–77
  transitional processes of, 52–102, 211–13
  trial, 52, 63, 65–66
sexual relations:
  extramarital, 10, 15, 16, 58, 60, 65
  recreational, 14–15
  of separated couples, 86
sexual revolution, 13, 14–15
Sheldrick, G., 93
Shields, L., 93
sibling rivalry, 168–70
single-parent families:
  definitions of, 21, 107–8, 121, 205
  noncustodial parent in, 121, 129
  problems of, vii, 108
Skolnick, A., 11–12
Smyer, M., 40–42, 143, 206
society:
  couple orientation of, 80
  divorce ambivalence of, 103–4

gender appropriate behavior in, 195
  importance of parenting in, 89, 90
  value of nuclear family in, 10, 83–84, 201
Spanier, G., 90, 121, 165
spouses, former:
  angry, 118–20, 126–29, 132–33, 135,
    141–42, 146–48, 149–51, 182–83
  assigning blame to, 141
  child custody and, 108–10
  as confidants, 144
  cooperative, 117–18, 124–26, 133–34,
    140–41, 145–46, 151–52
  dependent, 87, 93
  friendly, 115–17, 122–24, 133–34, 138–40,
    144–45, 152–53, 183
  impact of legal divorce on, 110–12
  perceived presence of, 171
  persisting bonds of, 64–65, 112–13,
    137, 144–45
  power struggles of, 77–78, 120, 127–28
  relationship styles of, 114–15, 157, 182
  remarriage of, 159–74
  task sharing of, 79, 117, 122, 144
standard of living:
  lowered, 68
  midlife, 93
status:
  of displaced homemakers, 93, 97, 148,
    184, 186–87
  family, 66, 206
  marriage as source of, 10–11, 14
  midlife consolidation of, 92
stereotypes, 145
  of aging, 150
  of former spouses, 112–13, 139, 171, 183
  gender, 61, 94, 194–95
  of midlife men, 193–94
Stierman, K., 40–41, 143, 206
stress:
  coping with, 45–47, 50–56, 72–75
  of divorce, 24, 25
  in early marriage, 85–86
  in families, 27–28, 35, 44–51, 75
  financial, 67–69, 78, 87
  of midlife separation, 98
  pileup of, 73, 159
  in remarriage, 46, 157, 159, 177–79
  of reorganization, 78–80, 103, 157, 159
stressors, definition of, 45
suburban developments, 7, 9
Sussman, M., 9
Szelenyi, I., 9

Terkelson, K., 39
textbooks, 207
therapists, 24, 62, 89, 204–5, 211–12, 216–19

Tufte, V., 91
Tumin, M., 26-27
"Twice in a Lifetime," 191-92, 195-96

urbanization, 8-10
urban life, anonymity of, 9

values:
    family, 9, 27, 83
    redefinition of, 77, 83
    traditional, 3, 5, 9-13, 152, 208
Vinick, B. H., 93
Volgy, S., 130, 132

Waller, W., 29
Wallisch, L., 113, 162, 168, 173, 174
Wallerstein, J., 108, 114, 135
Walsh, F., vii

Weiss, R., 64, 137
Weitzman, L., 16
women:
    cliches about, 61
    demographic disadvantages of, 19, 98,
        184, 206
    inequality of, 13, 19, 20
    as kin-keepers, 197-98
    in labor market, 6-7, 13-14, 68, 186-87
    life expectancy of, 19, 20
    reproductive control by, 14-15, 27
    support groups of, 195
    widowhood of, 19, 20, 98, 101, 221-23
    younger men and, 194, 195
women's movement, 7, 13-14
Wood, V., 174
Wooley, P., 122-23